Praise for *Discovering Good News in John*

"Don't let the beauty of the cover and cleverness of the page layouts make you think this book is not a serious study of God's Word. It's filled with life, knowledge, and joy. The learning available through this study reminds me of the apostle Peter's conclusion about Jesus in John 6:68, 'You have the words of eternal life.' This lovely book puts the life-giving messages and deeds of Jesus on brilliant display. Read, study, decorate, and be prepared to grow."

—**Craig J. Hazen, PhD.,** Biola University apologetics program founder and director, author of *Five Sacred Crossings* and *Fearless Prayer*

"Oh, my gospel-loving heart! What could be better than deep diving into the book of John? Package the amazing study with creative activities, beautiful art, and coloring features, and you have about the best devotional day ever. Possibly my fave of all time!"

—**Rhonda Rhea,** TV personality, award-winning humor columnist, author of 19 books

"The *Discovering* Bible studies by Pam Farrel, Jean E. Jones, and Karla Dornacher are gold. As a Bible study teacher who has led women through *Discovering Hope in the Psalms,* I enthusiastically recommend *Discovering Good News in John.* Each study is well-researched, is designed for multiple learning styles, and offers personal applications that are immediately transferrable. Personally, I grow with each new book."

—**Janet Holm McHenry,** speaker and author of 24 books, including *PrayerWalk*

"*Discovering Good News in John* takes participants deep into the Word and leads them to a rich understanding of who Jesus is. Special features such as 'The Little Details' sidebars, instructions for artwork relevant to the lessons, and creative suggestions to share Jesus's love with others make this a Bible study like no other."

—**Grace Fox,** author of *Finding Hope in Crisis* and cohost for *Your Daily Bible Verse* podcast

"*Discovering Good News in John* is a hope-filled collection of daily devotionals interwoven with moments of creativity to cultivate a greater connection to the lessons. This book invites us to experience Jesus anew through the book of John. It's an excellent addition to morning prayer time."

—**Saundra Dalton-Smith, MD,** physician, author, and host of *I Choose My Best Life* podcast

"God, the Author of all creation, fashioned us as creative people—His 'masterpiece.' I was thrilled to delve into this latest Bible study in a great series that engages through art and all the senses. *Discovering Good News in John* includes wonderful stories, biblical exposition, and creative projects to help readers not just *study* the Gospel of John, but also creatively incorporate the teachings of Jesus into their lives. I highly recommend gathering a group to go through this study. The great research, sidebars, illustrations, and creative touches will stir the 'maker' in you to worship the original Maker. All this wisdom and beauty is a great way to learn about the life of Jesus. I'm grateful to Farrel, Jones, and Dornacher for combining their gifts as the body of Christ and showing us the way."

—**Lucinda Secrest McDowell,** award-winning author of *Soul Strong* and *Life-Giving Choices*

"If you're looking for a uniquely different way to approach Bible study, this is it. The authors combine their gifts to provide deep theology, practical applications, and a creative approach to Scripture memorization. This book is visionary, captivating, stunning, and profound. Study it on your own, or, better yet, gather a group of friends and experience a new way to study the book of John."

—**Carol Kent,** speaker and author of *He Holds My Hand*

"*Discovering Good News in John* is more than a Bible study—it's an experience! With beautiful coloring opportunities and deep biblical truths, this verse-by-verse study will expand your knowledge of John's Gospel and hone your heart."

—**Rachel Wojo,** author, entrepreneur, podcaster, and director of Speak Up Growth Groups

"This is one of the most comprehensive Bible studies of the Gospel of John I have ever read. Pam, Jean, and Karla have crafted a resource that impacts the mind and heart with life-changing truths from the Source of truth. Be prepared to know Jesus more intimately than ever before."

—**Sharon Jaynes**, bestselling author of 25 books, including *When You Don't Like Your Story*

"*Discovering the Good News in John* will help you dig deep into the story of Jesus on a personal and intellectual level, as well as an inspirational level. Pray and worship through these pages as you enjoy Jean's deep teaching, Pam's life lessons, and Karla's illustrations ready for your creative touch. A treasure designed to help you activate the Word straight into your heart."

—**Linda Evans Shepherd,** bestselling author, publisher of *Leading Hearts* magazine, and founder of the Advanced Writers & Speakers Association

"The world has seemed very weary recently, and as a professional counselor of 25 years who sits beside people who are struggling, I realize how important good news is for the soul. The authors of *Discovering Good News in John* encourage their readers to hold on to hope by using various modalities similar to those our counseling staff use in the art therapy office. As someone who has had in-depth Bible training from several seminaries, I am amazed and delighted at the depth of biblical exploration and practical application in this book."

—**Michelle Nietert, LPC-S,** clinical director of Community Counseling Associates, author of *Loved and Cherished* and *Make Up Your Mind,* podcast host of *Raising Mentally Healthy Kids*

"The *Discovering* Bible study series is my favorite recommendation for women's Bible studies. I love how these books balance teaching the basics of what Scripture says with guiding readers deeper into some rich details in the sidebar notes—I learn new things every time one of these studies comes out! *Discovering Good News in John* continues the excellence of the series with a highly accessible yet in-depth study of one of the most powerful books in the Bible. If you're looking for a Bible study that will appeal to a mix of women with different biblical backgrounds—including nonbelievers!—this is it."

—**Natasha Crain,** speaker, blogger, podcaster, and author of four books, including *Faithfully Different*

"One of my favorite books in the Bible is the Gospel of John, and the team that brought us creative Bible studies on the Psalms and Jesus in the Old Testament has come together once again to give women an accessible, engaging, and insightful study of this beautiful account of Jesus's life. Let this study help you connect your head with your heart as you discover the context, depth, and meaning of John's Gospel."

—**Alisa Childers,** author of *Another Gospel* and host of the *Alisa Childers* podcast

DISCOVERING GOOD NEWS IN JOHN

PAM FARREL & JEAN E. JONES
author &
illustrator **KARLA DORNACHER**

Pam Farrel
John 10:10b

HARVEST HOUSE PUBLISHERS
EUGENE, OREGON

Cover Design by Kyler Dougherty

Cover Illustrations by Karla Dornacher

Cover Photo © tomograf, perori 00, (RF) royalty free / Getty Images

Interior Design by Janelle Coury

For bulk, special sales, or ministry purchases, please call 1-800-547-8979. Email: Customerservice@hhpbooks.com

This logo is a federally registered trademark of the Hawkins Children's LLC. Harvest House Publishers, Inc., is the exclusive licensee of this trademark.

Discovering Good News in John

Dedication

To all those joining us in this journey to discover the good news that Jesus offers: Welcome! May your journey through John's Gospel be richly rewarded as you grasp the depth of God's love and the greatness of his plan. May you abide in the vine and bear much fruit (John 15:5).

~ All of us

To Janeen, Nora, and Jim and Sally, my mentors whom I value so much! And to Kathy, thanks for being my mom's best friend, who brought the Good News to our family! You are each in heaven, enjoying the Savior and you are hearing, "Well Done, Good and Faithful Servant." Thank you for pouring God's Word, the love of Jesus, and the desire to serve Christ into my heart.

~ Pam

To Linda Vernier, who first guided me into knowing God and who gave me the Bible in which I discovered who Jesus is: Thank you, my dear friend! To Clay, your love and help made this book possible.

~ Jean E.

To my precious husband, Michael, who is now at home with Jesus. Thank you, my love, for believing in and accepting the good news of God's love, because even though I miss you terribly, I know I'll see you again before you know it!

~ Karla

Contents

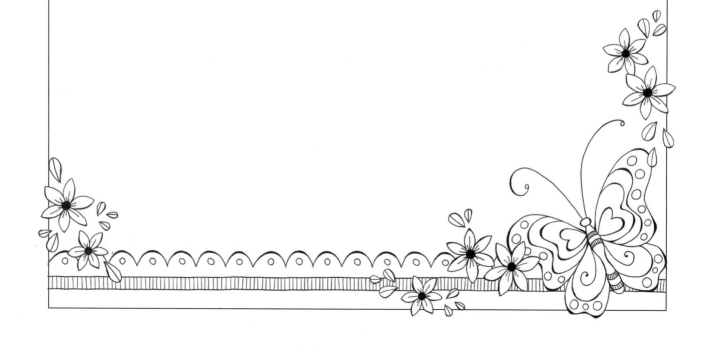

Do You Want to See Good News in John?

I (Jean) became a Christian through reading the Gospel of John. And since then I've met others who also became Christians through reading John's Gospel, including former Muslims. John's clear presentation of the good news Jesus preached amazes me, so I was eager to write an in-depth study of his Gospel, and I rejoiced when Pam and Karla wanted to join in.

When I was 14, a new friend told me the Bible says people have to pray to receive Jesus in order to go to heaven. I thought that was ridiculous. After all, wasn't Jesus just some shepherd who liked children but couldn't get along with adults—so people killed him?

I wasn't going to take this friend's word for it; I wanted to read the Bible and investigate for myself. After all, I'd been told conflicting things about him. My dad told me God didn't exist and that to think otherwise was stupid. My closest girlfriend told me the way to heaven was for my good deeds to outweigh my bad deeds at the end of my life. Now this teenage boy was telling me I was separated from God and had to pray certain words to have a relationship with him and go to heaven.

My mother was a lapsed Catholic who didn't even want to discuss God, but I believed he existed, probably because my maternal grandmother had told me he did and that he was good. Although my dad and his parents mocked the Bible, this grandmother esteemed it. I trusted her because I'd never known her to lie to anyone or to try to deceive me, and she and my grandfather were the kindest and most caring adults I knew. Additionally, the existence of the world with all its complexities suggested a creator. I reasoned that a good God would want to communicate how to reach him in a way people could discover. An all-powerful God could put how to reach him in written form—such as the Bible—and preserve that message throughout centuries.

I started reading my girlfriend's Bible when I was at her house, and then she gave me a copy—a paperback New Testament called *Good News for Modern Man*. Every day I rushed through my homework so I could open that Bible and read about how to get to heaven.

When I finished reading the first three Gospels, I was disappointed that the authors talked so much about Jesus. I thought, *Wow, that guy argued a lot. No wonder people didn't like him.* Besides, I didn't want to read about *him*; I wanted to read about God and the way to God.

Then I began reading the Gospel of John, and in those powerful pages I discovered the good news that changed my life forever.

That's why I'm so excited to share this study on discovering good news in John's Gospel. John details the message of good news Jesus preached. He explains how God, through signs and prophecies that Jesus fulfilled, gave evidence that he sent Jesus. Nonetheless, some rejected Jesus's message, and John examines why, including what was behind all those arguments. He shows God's purpose for the cross and why it was essential to bring people the hope of eternal life. And finally, John offers evidence that Jesus rose from the dead.

John's Gospel is remarkable. We're glad you're joining us for this journey in *Discovering Good News in John*.

Why We Wrote This Discovery Book for You

Pam, Karla, and I, with our different paths and gifts, have connected over our love for interacting with God's Word and encouraging others to experience the hope of his promises and faithfulness.

Jean F. Pam Karla

The Treasures in Each Chapter

We collaborated on this book to inspire *you*. Here's what you'll find in every chapter.

Daily Lessons—Jean

You'll hear from me throughout this journey. In each chapter, I share an introduction that explains the Old Testament passages John alludes to or quotes. The chapters have five daily lessons that will take 20 to 25 minutes to finish. Each Day 5 lesson concludes by guiding you in a private time of worship and prayer. The lessons use these icons:

> ♥   This personal question is designed to help you apply what you're learning to your life and to possibly spark a rich discussion with others.

> 💭   This activity guides you in prayer and worship.

> 🖥   This is an activity with further instructions on www.DiscoveringTheBibleSeries.com.

The Little Details—Jean

Along the way you'll see sidebars titled The Little Details. These are extra insights for both seasoned Christians and seekers who thrive on details.

Pam's Heart-to-Heart with the Great I Am—Pam

Pam's Heart-to-Heart with the Great I Am devotionals invite you to rest in God's strength and love. She shares some of her go-to ways for remembering and holding on to the promises of Jesus. She'll take you forward with faith and hope.

Karla's Creative Connection—Karla

You'll hear from Karla at the end of each chapter. She'll encourage you to connect creatively with God and others as you delight in God's eternal plan throughout this study.

Illustrations—Karla

The bookmarks and coloring pages will help you connect with and memorize God's Word as you color and meditate on each verse. You can also slip designs under a page in your Bible, sketchbook, or journal for tracing.

Creative Ideas—All of Us

The Creative Ideas appendix offers ways to express, experience, and meditate on Scripture passages. Discover your favorites! What a gift it is to have God's eternal plan to save us etched on our minds, hearts, and spirits.

Discover More on www.DiscoveringTheBibleSeries.com

🖥 Here are the extras you'll find on our website:

- Instructions for how to use this discovery book for both small groups and individual study
- A small group leader's guide
- Timelines
- Links to worship music to go with each chapter
- Links to Karla's art instructions
- Links to articles that go deeper into chapter topics
- More inspiring ideas

Chapter 1

John 1:1–2:25
The Word Was God

Who Is Jesus?

Day 1

There Is Good News

The Gospel of John holds a special place in my heart because I (Jean) became a Christian while reading it. That's why I'm excited that you're joining Pam, Karla, and me on this journey to discover its good news. After all, we all need good news!

Gospel means "good news." And indeed, the book of John tells of the good news Jesus proclaimed during his three years of earthly ministry. In the pages that follow, we'll discover what that good news is. And believe me, it's very good news!

The author of this Gospel—John—was one of Jesus's earliest disciples. That means he was an eyewitness to much that happened. In fact, John was one of the inner three whom Jesus often pulled aside: Peter, James, and John. Thus, he experienced firsthand some things the other Gospel writers had to learn from him and these other two men.

God's Word to Us in the Old Testament

John assumes his readers are familiar with the Old Testament, so let's look at a few OT passages that will help you understand his Gospel. Throughout this book I'll bold phrases and words to indicate where John references Old Testament terms. I'll also italicize words from the Bible passage we're exploring.

The Prophet and Leader Moses Led an Exodus from Slavery

John often mentions the prophet **Moses** and events in Moses's lifetime. God called Moses to lead the Israelites out of slavery in Egypt to the land God promised their ancestor, Abraham. The slave masters were harsh, even killing newborn boys to control the Hebrews' population growth.

When Moses told Pharaoh (Egypt's ruler) that God demanded he let his people go, Pharaoh refused. So God gave **signs** to confirm he had sent Moses. These signs included **turning water to blood**. Moses announced that the last sign would be the death of all firstborn males. This plague judged Egypt for killing Hebrew boys.

But Moses told the Israelites to sacrifice an unblemished **lamb** and paint its blood on the top and sides of their doorframes before roasting and eating the lamb that evening. Then when the destroyer came, he would **pass over** the houses displaying lambs' blood.

Just as Moses said, that night the Israelite sons did not die, but the Egyptian firstborn males did. Then Pharaoh told Moses to take the Hebrews away.

BUT TO ALL who did receive him who believed in His Name he gave THE RIGHT to become children of GOD

John 1:12

As noted in the text, David and his descendants who ruled were anointed as kings. Because of that they were called *anointed ones* or *messiahs*.

Any prophets and priests anointed for service could also be called *anointed ones*. For example, Moses anointed Aaron and his sons as priests, and the prophet Elijah anointed Elisha as prophet in his place (Exodus 28:41; 1 Kings 19:16).

The anointings of Old Testament kings, priests, and prophets foreshadowed the anointing of Jesus as King, High Priest, and the prophet like Moses. We'll see these unfold in John's Gospel.

Consequently, God told the Israelites they must celebrate **Passover** every year by sacrificing a **lamb** to eat in commemoration of his deliverance.

Moses led the people to Mount Sinai, where God spoke **Ten Words**, better known today as the Ten Commandments. There God instructed the people to build a **tabernacle** where he would place his presence so they could meet with him. The Israelites entered a covenant with the Lord wherein they would keep his **law** and he would provide the promised land for them to live as his people. Moses warned that if the people broke their covenant with God, he would send them away from the land.

To disobey God's law was sin, but the law had provisions to **take away sins** so people could fellowship with God. Namely, priests could offer sacrifices to atone for **sins.** (We'll learn more about atonement in the next chapter.)

Moses prophesied that one day God would send a prophet like him, and he said when the **prophet like Moses** appeared, the people must be sure to listen to him.

The Prophet and Messiah David Ruled Israel

Eventually, the people wanted a king to rule them. A prophet anointed David as king. He ruled over all the Israelites in the promised land, which was then called Israel. God told David that one of his descendants would build a **temple** for him and have a throne that lasted forever. When David's son built a **temple** to replace the tabernacle, people hoped he was the king whose throne would last forever.

Priests or prophets anointed David and his descendants as kings, so they were called **anointed ones**. The transliteration of the Hebrew for *anointed one* is **messiah**.

Later Prophets Promised a Future Messiah

When David's grandson took the throne, Israel split into two kingdoms: Israel and Judah. David's descendants ruled Judah, but Israel abandoned the temple and God right away. So prophets warned that God would exile them if they didn't repent.

The people, however, refused to turn back to God, so eventually he announced that exile was imminent. But he also promised to bring the exiles back later. Moreover, he said that one day he would give them another anointed king—another **messiah** descended from David—and that this king's throne would last forevermore (Isaiah 9:7). This messiah would be called **Mighty God** and **Everlasting Father** (Isaiah 9:6). Abundant **wine** would flow in his reign (Amos 9:13-14; Isaiah 25:6).

In the meantime, God comforted the exiles with a promise to one day pardon their sin (Isaiah 40:1-2). At that time, they should prepare for something special.

 Take a moment to pray for insight as you read God's Word.

1. Read Isaiah 40:3-5 below. Underline what a voice says to prepare in the wilderness. Box what it says to make straight in the desert. Circle what will then be revealed.

   A voice cries, "In the wilderness prepare the way of the Lord; make straight in the desert a highway for our God. Every valley shall be lifted up, and every mountain and hill be made low; the uneven ground shall become level, and the rough places a plain. And the glory of the Lord shall be revealed."

A *voice cries* out because **the Lord God is on his way**, and the people must prepare for his visit.

> 2. In Isaiah 40:9 (NIV) below, circle what the herald is bringing (two words mentioned twice). Underline how the herald should deliver the message. Box the message.
>
> You who bring good news to Zion, go up on a high mountain. You who bring good news to Jerusalem, lift up your voice with a shout, lift it up, do not be afraid; say to the towns of Judah, "Here is your God!"

Here, the herald should shout the **good news** that **God has arrived**.

God Promised a Future Light of the World

God also told of a future suffering servant who would be a **light**, who would die like a slaughtered **lamb**, and whose soul would make an offering for guilt, bearing people's **sin** (Isaiah 49:6; 53:7-12). He said this about his **word** (Isaiah 55:10-11):

> For as the rain and the snow come down from heaven and do not return there but water the earth, making it bring forth and sprout, giving seed to the sower and bread to the eater, so shall **my word** be that **goes out** from my mouth; it shall not return to me empty, but it shall accomplish that which I purpose, and shall succeed in the thing for which I **sent** it.

God's Word Comes to Pass

Just as God warned, Israel went into exile in Isaiah's day. A little over a century later, a foreign king burned Judah's temple and exiled its people too. Although the people returned from exile and built another temple, foreign kings continued to rule them. The people longed to have their own king again.

God's Word to Us in John

When Jesus was born, foreign kings had ruled the Jews for about 500 years. Many eagerly awaited the king (the Messiah) God promised to send. They wanted him to overthrow Rome's rule and establish their own kingdom on earth.

Now that we understand the background to John's first two chapters, let's read them. They will mention a prophet named John. Note that this is John the Baptist, not John the apostle who wrote the Gospel bearing his name.

> 3. ♥ Read John 1:1–2:25. What stands out to you from your initial reading of these passages? Why?

That's it for today. We learned a lot about what preceded Jesus's arrival on earth. Tomorrow we'll dig into the details of John's incredible prologue.

▄ Go to www.DiscoveringTheBibleSeries.com to download biblical event timelines you can keep handy as you go through this discovery book.

The Little Details
Greg D. Gilbert: The Gospel

The word "gospel" derives from the Anglo-Saxon term "godspell," meaning "good tidings" or "good news." The Greek word *euangelion* ("gospel") and its verbal cognate *euangelizomai* ("evangelize" or "speak good news") together occur more than 130 times in the NT. Whether used in a military, imperial, or religious sense, a "gospel" was always a *message* of good news. It was proclaimed with words, had a definite content, and expected a response from those who heard it.

The gospel that Jesus and his earliest followers proclaimed was no different. It was a well-defined message of good news: Jesus the Messianic King had come to establish God's kingdom on earth and forgive sinful people through his own substitutionary life, death, and resurrection, thereby qualifying them to inherit God's kingdom if they would turn from their sin and rely on him to save them.[1]

Pam's Heart-to-Heart with the Great I Am—"I Am"

"Very truly I tell you," Jesus answered, "before Abraham was born, I am!"
John 8:58 NIV

The name "I am" is the connection of Jesus, God incarnate of the New Testament, to the person of God from the Old Testament. When God called Moses to free his people from the bondage of slavery in Egypt, Moses expressed how intimidated he was to share the plan to the leaders of the Israelites:

Moses said to God, "Suppose I go to the Israelites and say to them, 'The God of your fathers has sent me to you,' and they ask me, 'What is his name?' Then what shall I tell them?" (Exodus 3:13 NIV).

God answered him then, and this answer can encourage each of us now:

God said to Moses, "I AM WHO I AM. This is what you are to say to the Israelites: 'I AM has sent me to you'" (Exodus 3:14 NIV).

This Is Good News!

There is one God, and this God is self-existent. He calls himself "I am" because no one created him! He is the Creator who set history in motion. The creation story (chapter 1 of the first book of the Bible you hold) explains that God created light and dark, the sun, the moon, vegetation, animals, and fish, and as he looked at all he created each day, he commented that it was good. When he fashioned man and woman, he said that was *very good*!

Good in Hebrew is *Tob*, which I summarize into an easy-to-remember definition: all that is beautiful, beneficial, blessed, and best. God initiated creation, and he cultivated relationship with Adam and Eve. The garden he made for them to dwell in was also beautiful, beneficial, blessed, and best. When Adam and Eve disobeyed and blew their opportunity of a forever in paradise, even then God intervened. In his mercy, he allowed death to enter so humankind would not be chained to decay and destruction forever. Then God set in motion the redemption of all humankind:

God demonstrates his own love for us in this: While we were still sinners, Christ died for us (Romans 5:8 NIV).

"Truly, truly, I say to you, whoever hears my word and believes him who sent me has eternal life. He does not come into judgment, but has passed from death to life" (John 5:24).

God's love sets prisoners free from literal slavery in the Old Testament and from bondage to sin in the New Testament—through Jesus. The "I am" came to earth as both fully human and fully God to give his life for you and for me. So the ultimate good news is that Jesus is the "great I am!" He was there at creation, so Jesus, "I am," the Creator, is the answer to everything you need in life! And this is *tob*!

In the Gospel of John, we see Jesus giving many word pictures describing who he is. You will be doing a deeper dive into these qualities of Christ in this creative devotional experience. You will gain strength by studying John and the "great I am." Years ago, while writing *Becoming a Brave New Woman: Step into God's Adventure for You*, I explored these metaphors of Christ to help me and my readers gain courage, confidence, wisdom, and peace no matter what life was sending our way. Which do you most need to hang your heart on today to gain hope for tomorrow?

- *Jesus is the Word*—When you need clarification, wisdom, or discernment, look to the ultimate guide (John 1:1).

- *Jesus is the light*—When you need guidance, look to him for your next step (John 1:4; 8:12; 9:5).
- *Jesus is the bread of life*—When you feel empty inside, look to him for fulfillment (John 6:35,41,48,51).
- *Jesus is from above*—When you need perspective, look to him and ask to see life from his vantage point (John 8:23-24; 12:32).
- *Jesus is the Son of Man*; he is truly human and sympathetic to our frailties, and yet he is perfect—When you're feeling fragile, fallible, and frail, look to your sympathetic Lord for aid (John 8:28).
- *Jesus is the gate for the sheep*—When you need a place of safety, go to him, and you'll find rest (John 10:7,14).
- *Jesus is God's Son*—When you need power beyond your own to cope with life, take your concern to him (John 10:36).
- *Jesus is the resurrection*—If you feel hopeless, despondent, or frustrated, look to the One who raised himself from the grave to raise you up and give you hope and help (John 11:25).
- *Jesus is the true vine*—We must be connected to him for nourishment (John 15:1).
- *Jesus is King*—When you need to appeal to a higher power, a greater authority, appeal to Jesus, who reigns in majesty (John 18:37).
- *Jesus is the living water*—When you're thirsty for something to quell your longings, to handle the cravings that seem to overpower you, look to Jesus, and his presence will bring refreshment (John 4:10).
- *Jesus is God*—When you need forgiveness, grace, mercy, eternal life, and a fresh start, go to the Author of life (John 13:19; 14:11,20; 18:8).[2]

Experiencing Scripture Creatively

The arts played a big part in Israel's worship of God. Experiencing Scripture through multiple means helps plant its messages in us so we can better remember its truths. It also gives us more ways to draw near to God in worship.

The Creative Ideas appendix to this book lists many ways you can engage with Scripture creatively. Peruse the ideas for inspiration when you have a little extra time. In addition, I (Jean) suggest ideas tailored to each chapter at the end of the Day 1 lesson. Here are this chapter's suggestions:

- Color Karla's full-page illustration at the end of this chapter while repeating the words of the verse aloud. (Bonus: This is a great way to memorize Scripture!)
- Color the sidebar toppers using different color schemes. Pick your favorite to use on the bookmark on this chapter's opening page.
- The bookmark on this chapter's opening page is reproduced at the end of the book. Color and cut it out to use or to give as a gift.
- Choose a verse that stood out to you from what you read today. Follow Karla's instructions at the end of the chapter for designing a bookmark.
- Write a letter about what it means to be adopted into God's family.

The Little Details
The Gospel Beginnings

When writing a biography about someone, how far back should an author go? In modern times, biographies often start with parents. But in ancient times, they might even include genealogies.

The Gospel of Mark begins with the testimony of John the Baptist about Jesus (Mark 1:4). Matthew, written for a Jewish audience, begins with Abraham's day, for all Jews descend from Abraham (Matthew 1:1). Luke was written for a Gentile (non-Jewish) audience and begins with Adam's day, for all humans descend from Adam (Luke 3:38).

But John goes back even further, to the beginning of time.

In the beginning, then, God created everything by his Word.

Jesus Is the Word

In a theologically rich prologue, John lets us know right away that this man he's going to tell us about is no ordinary man.

The Word Was God

> **4.** Read John 1:1-2. (a) When did the Word exist? (b) With whom was the Word? (c) Who was the Word? (d) With whom was he in the beginning?

Even though this Gospel is a biography of a man who lived in John's time, John begins by quoting the first words of the Old Testament: "In the beginning" (Genesis 1:1). He places the Word with God at the beginning of creation and calls the Word *he*.

Genesis tells us that God spoke the universe into existence (Genesis 1:3). Elsewhere, God's word came to prophets (Jeremiah 1:4). Additionally, his word healed and delivered (Psalm 107:20). New Testament scholar D.A. Carson writes, "In short, God's 'Word' in the Old Testament is his powerful self-expression in creation, revelation and salvation, and the personification of that 'Word' makes it suitable for John to apply it as a title to God's ultimate self-disclosure, the person of his own Son."[3]

John also tells us that the Word *was with God* and *was God*. This is not unprecedented. For instance, one prophecy said the descendant of David who would reign forever would be called "Mighty God" (Isaiah 9:6-7).

> **5.** According to John 1:3, what was made through the Word?

In the beginning, then, God created everything by his Word.

The Word Was Life and Light

> **6.** In John 1:4-5 below, circle the two occurrences of life. Draw a star ⭐ around the two occurrences of light. Box the two occurrences of darkness.
>
> In him was life, and the life was the light of men. The light shines in the darkness, and the darkness has not overcome it.

Life and light are themes that thread throughout John's Gospel. In the beginning, God gave life to all creatures on earth. He also gave the stars and planets for light, illuminating our world.

> **7.** Read John 1:6-8. (a) Whom did God send (verse 6)? (b) What was his purpose (verses 7-8)?

These verses speak of John the Baptist, a prophet who called Jews to repent and be baptized. Here the Gospel speaks not just of the lights God created in the beginning but also of the light that dispels spiritual darkness so that people may believe.

> **8.** In John 1:9-11 below, draw a star ⭐ around who was coming into the world. Circle where he was, what was made through him, and what didn't know him (the same word given three times). Underline who didn't receive him.
>
> The true light, which gives light to everyone, was coming into the world. He was in the world, and the world was made through him, yet the world did not know him. He came to his own, and his own people did not receive him.

All things were made through the Word (verse 3), and the world was made through the true light. So the Word is the true light and the light of men (verse 4). *True* here means "real" or "genuine."[5] Isaiah 50:10-11 warns people of the danger of living by their own lights (that is, man-made philosophies) instead of trusting God. It says living by false lights ultimately brings torment.

In John, we see that the true light enters the world, but the world is in rebellion and doesn't recognize him. The light shines on everyone, but some don't receive that light. In particular, the Word's *own people* don't receive him.

The Word Grants the Right to Become Children of God

Now we come to our key verse.

> **9.** Read John 1:11-13. (a) What did the Word give to those who received him and believed in his name (verse 12)? (b) What were they born of (verse 13)?

This is good news indeed. The Word gives the right to become children of God to those who receive him and believe in his name. They become his children by being born of God, not by blood descent from human parents such as Abraham and Sarah (from whom all Jews descend) or even Adam and Eve.

D.A. Carson explains what *receive him* means:

> "*Yet to all who received him…*" Another way of describing these people is to say that they *believed in his name.* The "name" is more than a label; it is the character of the person, or even the person himself. The entire expression does not guarantee that those who exercise such faith are genuine believers…but at its best, such faith yields allegiance to the Word, trusts him completely, acknowledges his claims and confesses him with gratitude. That is what it means to "receive" him.[6]

John still hasn't identified the Word, but he's about to.

believe

The Little Details
Poetry in John

John sometimes uses poetic devices. For instance, John 1:1-3 appears to be a chiasm in which elements equal distance from the center are related:

In the beginning
  was
    the word
      and the word
        was
          with God
          and God
        was
      the word
    This one
  was
in the beginning with God

These verses can also be arranged in a double chiasm:

In the beginning
  was
    the word
    and the word
  was
with God
And God
  was
    the word
    This one
  was
In the beginning
with God[4]

The Word Became Flesh

10. In John 1:14 below, underline what the Word did. Circle what people saw. Double-underline "only Son." Box what the Son was full of.

> And the Word became flesh and dwelt among us, and we have seen his glory, glory as of the only Son from the Father, full of grace and truth.

This verse is packed with theological significance. First, the Word who is God *became flesh*—what we call the incarnation.

Second, the words translated *dwelt among us* are more literally "pitched his tabernacle, or lived in his tent, amongst us."[7] Moses built a tent as a place where God could dwell among his people in a special way. Now Jesus has come in a tent of flesh to dwell among people.

Third, in the phrase *we have seen his glory*, the word *we* refers to the disciples and others who were with Jesus. *Seen his glory* reminds readers that the Israelites saw God's glory on Mount Sinai when God gave the Ten Commandments (Exodus 24:16). Also, when Moses dedicated the tabernacle, God's glory shone in a cloud that filled it (Exodus 40:35). Just as God's glory was visible in the exodus, so God's glory was visible in Jesus.

Fourth, *only son* is sometimes translated "only begotten" (NASB, KJV) because it's a special phrase. It means a father's "one and only, best-loved Son."[9] It's an allusion to Genesis 22:16, where God described Isaac to Abraham as "your son, your only son" even though Abraham had another son.

Finally, *glory full of...grace and truth* alludes to Exodus 34. There, Moses asked God to show him his glory (Exodus 33:18). The Lord passed before Moses in a cloud, proclaiming that he is "abounding in steadfast love and faithfulness" (Exodus 34:6). D.A. Carson explains that the word translated *steadfast love* has to do with graciousness, and the word translated *faithfulness* means "truth" or "faithfulness." So the "two words that John uses, 'full of *grace* and *truth*,' are his ways of summing up the same ideas."[10]

In summary, then, the Word became flesh and tabernacled among people, displaying his glory. Moreover, the Father sent his Son, who is the Word.

11. Read John 1:15-16. (a) What did John the Baptist say about the Word who became flesh (verse 15)? (b) What have we received from the Word's fullness (verse 16)?

John the Baptist was older than Jesus and began ministering before Jesus did, but he insists that Jesus is greater than he, saying "because he was before me," referring to Jesus's pre-existence as well as his greater status.

The Word Is Jesus Christ, Giver of Grace and Truth

12. In John 1:16 below, underline what John says they have all received from the Word's fullness.

> For from his fullness we have all received, grace upon grace.

Grace is unmerited favor, so this is good news.

13. In John 1:17 below, circle what was given through Moses. Draw an arrow from "Moses" to "law." Circle what came through Jesus. Draw an arrow from Jesus to what you circled. Box Jesus's title (the last word).

> For the law was given through Moses; grace and truth came through Jesus Christ.

Now we know the identity of the Word: Jesus. And John gives Jesus the title *Christ*. Just as *Messiah* comes from the Hebrew for "Anointed One," so *Christ* comes from the Greek for "Anointed One." Thus, John means that Jesus is the long-awaited King who will rule forever. He also means that Jesus is a descendant of King David. Therefore, *his own people* who *did not receive him* in verse 11 refers to the Jews.

The Jewish people's identity rested on the Mosaic law. But John contrasts the law coming through Moses with grace and truth coming through Jesus. Jesus is like Moses in that he brings something from God.

14. In John 1:18 below, box who has seen God. Underline who has made God known.

> No one has ever seen God; the only God, who is at the Father's side, he has made him known.

The Lord God made his glory visible to Moses in a limited way, but Moses did not see God's face.[11] God is invisible, though he at times makes his presence known in a way that humans can sense. Such manifestations are called *theophanies*.

Jesus, the only God who is at the Father's side (or in his bosom), has now made God known through the incarnation.

So far, John has given us several pieces of good news. In Jesus, God himself became flesh to dwell with humans and make God known. Jesus gives life and light, and he grants the right to become children of God. Moreover, grace and truth come through Jesus.

In the next lesson, we'll discover what a contemporary prophet said about Jesus.

The Little Details
Bethany Across the Jordan

When we travel, I'm always surprised to find cities with the same name as those in my California county. Apparently, something like that went on in the areas over which Jesus walked.

"Bethany across the Jordan" in John 1:28 is not the same as the Bethany in Judea near Jerusalem where Lazarus lived (John 12:1). This Bethany (or "Bethabara" as it's alternately spelled) is either a place unknown today or an alternate spelling for Batanea. Batanea is the area where Jesus later withdrew when the Jews tried to kill him (John 10:40). It had a different ruler than Judea did.

Day 3

John the Baptist Testifies About Jesus

We read John's prologue yesterday and learned that Jesus is God, Jesus is with God, and Jesus was in the beginning with God. We also learned that he grants the right to become a child of God to those who believe on his name.

15. ♥ (a) Have you received Jesus and believed on his name so that you can have the right to become a child of God (John 1:12)? (b) If not, what questions or obstacles hold you back?

> In Jesus, God himself became flesh to dwell with humans and make God known.

John the Baptist was a prophet who called Jews to repent from sin and turn to God because something important was about to happen. He had a huge following that attracted the

The Little Details
Priests, Levites, and Elijah

John the Baptist makes *straight the way of the Lord* by preaching, "Repent, for the kingdom of heaven is at hand."[12] Proverbs 11:5 calls the way of the righteous *straight*. Droves of people confessed their sins to John and asked him to baptize them.[13]

In John 1:19, priests and Levites came to question John. John 1:24 explains that the Pharisees had sent them. So who were they?

Levites were from the tribe of Levi. Male Levites who descended from Aaron (the first high priest) could be priests. Other Levites assisted in duties related to the temple, including worship. In Jesus's day, some were temple police.

The Baptist's father was a priest, though the New Testament never mentions John serving as a priest.

While the Baptist does not connect himself with Elijah (John 1:21), the angel who told his father about his future said that he would go before the Lord "in the spirit and power of Elijah" (Luke 1:17). Jesus later said, "John the Baptist...is Elijah who is to come" (Matthew 11:12-14).

attention of the Jewish leaders in Jerusalem. Jerusalem was the site of the temple and the former site of King David's throne.

Jesus Is Greater Than John the Baptist

The Gospel author has already said that the Baptist bore witness as to who Jesus was. Now he explains what the Baptist testified.

> **16.** Read John 1:19-21. What three people did John the Baptist say he was not?

Priests are descendants of the first high priest, Aaron, a Levite. They offer sacrifices. *Levites* are descendants of Levi but not Aaron. They care for the temple and assist with worship. Some priests and Levites wonder if John the Baptist fulfills any prophecy.

The Christ was the descendant of David whom the prophets said would one day rule as a righteous king forever. *Elijah* was an ancient prophet who was taken to heaven in a chariot of fire; after the Jews returned from exile, the prophet Malachi prophesied that Elijah would come before the day of the Lord.[14] *The Prophet* is the prophet like Moses whom Moses prophesied would come.[15]

> **17.** Read John 1:22-23. (a) What was the voice crying out (verse 23)? (b) What prophet was John the Baptist quoting?

John quotes Isaiah 40:3, which we read in the Day 1 lesson. There, God spoke comforting words to exiled Israelites, letting them know he would pardon their sins, bring them out of exile, and take them back to the promised land in a new exodus. He foretold a voice calling for the highway to be prepared for God's arrival. John the Baptist claims to be that voice.

> **18.** Read John 1:24-25. (a) What Jewish sect was involved in questioning John (verse 24)? (b) What did they want to know (verse 25)?

Verse 24 can be interpreted as either the Pharisees sent the questioners in verse 25 (ESV, NASB) or the Pharisees are the questioners (NIV, KJV). Many Jews highly respect the Pharisees for their strict adherence to both the Mosaic law and oral traditions with many more rules. Pharisees control what is taught at most synagogues.[16] Most priests, however, belong to the Sadducees, a sect that rejects the Pharisees' oral traditions.

One reason they ask why John baptizes people is that, at this time, converts to Judaism usually baptize themselves.[17] Those born Jewish typically feel no need for baptism. Yet John is baptizing Jews for repentance.

19. Read John 1:26-28. (a) What did John baptize with (verse 26)? (b) How did John feel about the one who was coming (verse 27)? (c) Where did the questioning take place (verse 28)?

The Pharisees thought of themselves as righteous because they adhered to strict rules. In contrast, John declared himself not worthy of being even the lowest slave to the one coming. New Testament scholar Gerald L. Borchert explains the significance of untying sandals:

> The Baptizer considered himself unworthy even to perform the most menial or degrading task of a slave—namely untying the sandals—for God's anointed one. In the rabbinic tradition the teacher could demand that his students should willingly serve the teacher except in acts of touching his feet.[18]

Jesus Is the Lamb of God

The next day John told his followers who Jesus was.

20. In John 1:29-31 (HCSB) below, underline what John says Jesus is and does. Box why Jesus surpasses John. Circle why John baptizes.

> The next day John saw Jesus coming toward him and said, "Here is the Lamb of God, who takes away the sin of the world! This is the One I told you about: 'After me comes a man who has surpassed me, because He existed before me.' I didn't know Him, but I came baptizing with water so He might be revealed to Israel."

Lamb of God could refer to several Old Testament references to lambs:

- The Passover lamb that saved firstborn sons from death (Exodus 12:3)
- The purification offering (or sin offering) that commoners gave for unintentional sin (Leviticus 4:32)
- The suffering servant who would be led to slaughter like a lamb as an offering for others' guilt (Isaiah 53:7,10)

That John says Jesus takes away the sin of the *world* fits in with Old Testament prophecies about the suffering servant: "I will make you as a light for the nations, that my salvation may reach to the end of the earth" (Isaiah 49:6).

Jesus Baptizes with the Holy Spirit

21. Read John 1:32-34. (a) How did God show John that Jesus was the one who ranked before him (verses 32-33)? (b) With what would Jesus baptize (verse 33)? (c) What was John's witness about Jesus (verse 34)?

The Pharisees thought of themselves as righteous because they adhered to strict rules.

The Little Details

Jay Sklar: Sin

The essence of sin is to break the Lord's laws, instead of keeping them. The results of sin are always catastrophic, both for sinners and for the world: for sinners, because their relationship with the Lord, their King and Creator, is now ruptured, and alienation replaces warm fellowship; for the world, because sin destroys the type of community the Lord intended, one in which people experience his love, joy, peace, goodness and justice. Sin is an acid that mars and destroys whatever it touches. The Lord is not being a killjoy by forbidding sin; he is being a loving Saviour.[19]

Seeing the Holy Spirit descend on Jesus might have reminded the Baptist of several Old Testament passages. God promised to pour his Spirit on

- a righteous descendant of David who would be king (Isaiah 11:1-2);
- the righteous suffering servant (Isaiah 42:1); and
- an anointed one who would bring good news and liberty (Isaiah 61:1).

The Baptist says Jesus will baptize people with the Holy Spirit. This is in keeping with prophecies that say God will one day pour out his Spirit on people. For example, Ezekiel 36:25-27 prophesies that God will clean people, give them a new heart and spirit, and put his Spirit within them so they can obey him.

John the Baptist testifies that Jesus is the *Son of God* (ESV) or *God's Chosen One* (NIV). Ancient texts differ slightly. *Son of God* is a title of anointed kings (more on this in the next lesson), while *God's Chosen One* refers to the suffering servant whom God chose and anointed with his Spirit.[20]

So far we've seen that John the Baptist testified that Jesus outranks him, that Jesus is the Lamb of God who takes away the sin of the world, and that Jesus will baptize people with the Holy Spirit. In the next lesson, the baptizing prophet will tell us even more about Jesus.

Day 4

Jesus Gains Followers

In the last lesson, we began looking at what John the Baptist testified about Jesus.

Jesus Is Teacher

The next day, the Baptist points out Jesus to two of his followers.

> 22. Read John 1:35-39. (a) What did John call Jesus (verse 36)? (b) What did Jesus ask the two men following him (verse 38)? (c) When they asked where he was staying, what did Jesus reply (verse 39)?

John's two followers trust his testimony and follow Jesus. They call Jesus *Teacher* and tell him they want to know where he's staying. It's about 4:00 p.m.

Jesus Is the Messiah

Next, one of John the Baptist's disciples tells his brother about Jesus.

> 23. Read John 1:40-42. (a) What was the name of one of John's disciples who followed Jesus (verse 40)? (b) What did he tell his brother, Simon (verse 41)? (c) What did he do next (verse 42)? (d) What did Jesus call Simon (verse 42)?

John's two followers trust his testimony and follow Jesus.

One of the two disciples staying with Jesus is Andrew. The other is unnamed, but it's likely that he's this Gospel's author, John. Not only does the passage read like eyewitness testimony, but John never names himself in this Gospel, whereas the other Gospels speak of him frequently.[21]

In Jesus's day, Jewish men go by their given name plus their father's name: *Simon son of John*. Jesus says Simon will be called *Cephas*, which is from the Aramaic for "rock." John translates Cephas to the Greek *Peter* for us. By giving Peter a new name, Jesus tells Peter what he will become.

24. ❤ (a) Who is someone you tried to bring to Jesus? How did that person respond? (b) Who is someone you would like to bring to Jesus?

Jesus Is the Ladder to Heaven

The next day brings two more followers.

25. Read John 1:43-44. What did Jesus say to Philip (verse 43)?

The Greek is unclear as to whether Jesus or Andrew decide to go to Galilee and find Philip. Either way, Jesus says to Philip, "Follow me."

26. Read John 1:45-46. (a) Whom did Philip find (verse 45)? (b) who did Philip say had written about Jesus (verse 45)? (c) When Nathanael expressed doubt, what did Philip say (verse 46)?

Philip presents evidence that Jesus fulfills the Old Testament prophecies. When his friend doubts, he invites him to simply come and check it out for himself.

27. Read John 1:47-49. (a) What did Jesus say about Nathanael when he saw him (verse 47)? (b) After Jesus's response, what did Nathanael conclude (verse 49)?

The text doesn't tell us what Nathanael did that Jesus knows about. But the fact that Jesus knows about it is enough to convince Nathanael that Jesus is a prophet, and he concludes that Philip is right. Nathanael probably uses *Son of God* as a title; all kings descended from King David held the title "son of God" (2 Samuel 7:14). It reflected that they were lesser kings submitted to a greater King, the Lord God.

The Little Details
Kings as Sons of God

If you've not studied how the Old Testament reveals Jesus, it may surprise you that the kings descended from David were called sons of God. In the ancient Near East, some kings were subordinate to other kings. The greater king was the king of kings, or suzerain. His subordinate kings were his vassals. The greater king called his vassals *sons* and the lesser kings called their suzerain *father*. King David was suzerain to several kings but was himself vassal to God, the King of kings.

God said of David's future son Solomon, "I will be to him a father, and he shall be to me a son" (2 Samuel 7:14). This reflected the vassal relationship the kings were to have with the Lord. The title "son of God" foreshadowed the King who was literally the Son of God, Jesus.

The Little Details
The Call of the Twelve

John describes how five men came to follow Jesus. Later, Jesus chose 12 among his large following to be disciples in a special way.

Matthew 4:18-22 tells us that after Jesus moved to Capernaum, he approached two pairs of brothers as they fished and told them, "Follow me, and I will make you fishers of men" (verse 19). The first pair was Simon Peter and Andrew. The second was James and John. That these men were already attached in some way to Jesus explains why they were willing to drop everything, including their livelihoods, to follow him when he later called them to be part of his 12 disciples.

In Matthew 10:1-4, Jesus sent 12 of his followers to go out in pairs to preach the good news that the kingdom of heaven is at hand. These 12 (or "the Twelve") are called *apostles*, which means "those sent out on a mission."[22]

28. Read John 1:50-51. (a) What would Nathanael see (verse 50)? (b) What did that include (verse 51)?

Jesus says "Truly, truly" to Nathanael, emphasizing his statement's importance and truthfulness. *You will see heaven opened* means he will see revelations. Thus, Jesus promises even more evidence that he is the fulfillment of Old Testament prophecies.

Jesus quotes Genesis 28:12. There, Jacob saw angels ascending and descending on a ladder that reached from Bethel (which means "house of God") to heaven. Jesus claims, then, that he "is the link between heaven and earth, the realms above and below, between God and humanity."[23]

Jacob was deceitful and a cheat at the time he saw this revelation, but God changed him into an honest man and renamed him Israel. In contrast, Nathanael is a true *Israelite indeed, in whom there is no deceit.*

Jesus Is the Son of Man

Jesus calls himself *Son of Man*. This title has theological significance, for the prophet Daniel spoke of "one like a son of man" who came "with the clouds of heaven" and "was given... everlasting dominion" (Daniel 7:13-14). But at the same time, it's vague enough that the significance can be missed. That way Jesus doesn't stoke political fires. Many want a Messiah (Christ) who will overthrow Rome. Thus, if Jesus identifies himself as the Messiah too soon, people will pressure him to meet expectations that differ from his intended plan.

29. ♥ Share one doubt you had about Jesus before coming to Christ and how God helped you past that. Or, if you're not a Christian, write one question you have about who Jesus is.

In the passages we read in this lesson, Jesus is Teacher, Messiah, and Son of Man. He connects heaven and earth. He is also a prophet who can see hidden things and foretell the future. He is someone who says, "Follow me." In the next lesson, we'll see Jesus give another sign to his followers about who he is.

Jesus Begins to Minister

So far, we've met five of Jesus's new followers: an unnamed follower, Andrew, Simon Peter, Philip, and Nathanael. Jesus and his followers head to Cana (Nathanael's hometown) for a wedding.

Jesus Gives Signs Like Moses Gave

In Jesus's day, weddings are often weeklong celebrations. The bridegroom's family is responsible for all the costs, including providing food and wine for the guests.

> 30. Read John 2:1-5. (a) What did Jesus's mother tell him (verse 3)? (b) What did Jesus ask her (verse 4)? (c) What else did Jesus say (verse 4)?

On the third day means two days after the prior event and allows time for travel. That Jesus, his mother, and his followers are all invited to the same wedding suggests it's for someone close to them all. Jesus's mother is concerned lest the bridegroom's family suffer shame. So she approaches Jesus for help. Jesus addresses her as *woman*, which sounds strange today but was not unusual then. Jesus's father apparently has passed away, and so she turns to her son for help.

Having begun his public ministry, Jesus begins to draw apart from his family. Still, Mary's request apparently reminds Jesus of prophecies about abundant wine flowing when the Messiah comes and rules.[24] He notes that his *hour has not yet come*—that is, the hour of that kingdom. At that hour, the Messiah will be the bridegroom who supplies all the wine (Hosea 2:16-20; Revelation 21:9).

Nonetheless, Jesus's mother expects he will help, and she tells the servants to do whatever he asks.

> 31. Read John 2:6-10. (a) What happened to the water in the stone jars (verse 9)? (b) How was the bridegroom saved from shame (verses 9-10)?

The stone jars held 16 to 27 gallons of water each. The Jews used the water to cleanse themselves before eating. Jesus replaced the water with wine, saving the bridegroom's face but also removing the water for purification.

> 32. In John 2:11 below, circle what changing the water into wine was the first of. Box what it manifested. Underline what it caused the disciples to do. Turn to the **8 Signs** chart at the back of the book. Note that this first sign is filled in for you.
>
> This, the first of his signs, Jesus did at Cana in Galilee, and manifested his glory. And his disciples believed in him.

The Little Details

"My Hour Has Not Yet Come" (John 2:4)

If you've read John's Gospel, you know that Jesus's *hour* is the time when he leaves the earth (John 13:1). So what does his hour have to do with supplying wine?

Jesus's parables often featured everyday events to communicate spiritual truths. Wine links with his hour in two ways.

First, at his last supper with his disciples, Jesus gave them wine as part of the institution of the new covenant, and he told them he would not drink wine again until he drank it with them in the Father's kingdom (Matthew 26:26-29). So Jesus may have been referring to it not being his time to offer the wine of the new covenant.

Second, Jesus elsewhere compares the kingdom of heaven to a wedding and himself to a bridegroom (Matthew 9:15; 22:1-14; 25:1-13). Indeed, Revelation 19:7-9 describes the marriage supper of the Lamb, wherein Jesus is the bridegroom and the church his bride. As bridegroom, he will then be responsible for the marriage supper, but he was not responsible for it at the wedding in Cana.

The Little Details
Capernaum and the Temple Cleansing

Early in Jesus's ministry, King Herod imprisoned John the Baptist. When Jesus heard of the arrest, he moved to Capernaum (Matthew 4:13). Capernaum was a village of about a thousand people in Galilee,[25] about a three-day journey from Jerusalem in Judea.[26]

Jesus cleansed the temple a second time during the last week of his ministry (Matthew 21:12). The two cleansings' dialogues and details differ. Analytic philosopher Lydia McGrew writes of one difference: "John alone reports that the leaders ask Jesus for a sign of his authority to cleanse the Temple (John 2.18). It is more difficult to imagine their doing this at the end of Jesus' ministry. John in particular emphasizes their hostility due to the raising of Lazarus. They would hardly in that case have wanted Jesus to do *more* signs in Passion week, which would draw the people to him all the more. In the Synoptics they are entirely hostile to him during Passion week…and are trying to trap him, not to induce him to perform signs."[27]

Chapters 2 to 12 in John are often called the "book of signs" because John lists seven signs in them (a final sign comes later). A sign signifies something is likely. For example, a ring on someone's left ring finger is a sign that the person is likely married.

Because that's what he did throughout the Old Testament, the Jews of Jesus's day expect God to provide signs showing that messengers he sends are from him. For instance, Moses turned water into blood. Likewise, Jesus turned water into wine. By doing this, Jesus *manifested his glory* and caused his disciples to believe in him.

Jesus's Body Is a Temple

> **33.** Read John 2:12-13. (a) Where did Jesus's family and his disciples go after the wedding (verse 12)? (b) What event caused Jesus to go to Jerusalem (verse 13)?

Jews celebrate Passover on the full moon near the end of March and the beginning of April. God commanded his people to celebrate it every year so they would always remember how the destroyer passed over the homes that had lamb's blood painted on its doorframes when he killed the firstborn males in the Egyptian homes.

> **34.** Read John 2:14-17. (a) What did Jesus say the moneychangers and sellers were doing (verse 16)? (b) What did the disciples remember (verse 17)?

In Jesus's day, when Jewish men travel from other countries to the temple for Passover and the weeklong feast that immediately follows, they need money to pay a temple tax and to buy animals to sacrifice. If they come a distance, it's convenient to exchange currency and purchase animals in Jerusalem. Thus, the priests have permitted moneychangers and animal sellers to set up in the outer court of the temple. The outer court is where Gentiles (non-Jews) can worship. But the moneychangers and livestock sellers have made it into a market. Jesus drives out the larger animals with a whip and tells those who sell birds to take them away.

Jesus's disciples remember Psalm 69:9: "For zeal for your house has consumed me." King David wrote this psalm. That's significant because the prophets called the future righteous Messiah "David," meaning David was a type of the future Messiah.[28]

A *type* is a person, institution, or event that foreshadows something significant in the future. English Bible translations use a variety of words to describe such people and things, including *portents*, *patterns*, *copies*, *shadows*, and *types*. Thus, the disciples saw King David's zeal for God's house as foreshadowing Jesus's zeal.

35. Read John 2:18-22. (a) What do the Jews want Jesus to show them (verse 18)? (b) What sign does Jesus give them (verse 19)? (c) Of what temple was Jesus speaking (verse 21)? (d) When did his disciples remember what he said (verse 22)? (e) What was the result of their remembering (verse 22)?

The Jews demand a sign that shows Jesus's authority to cleanse the temple. They misunderstand Jesus's answer, for he speaks of the temple of his body, not of the temple with the courtyard in which they stand.

Then John tells us something amazing: *When therefore he was raised from the dead!* John alerts us now that this man Jesus will die and be raised from the dead in a trio of days.

Jesus Is the Knower of People

By turning water into wine, Jesus disrupts Jewish purification rituals. By overturning the moneychangers' tables, he disrupts a Jewish feast. Indeed, this man Jesus is heading for conflict with the religious leaders.

36. Read John 2:23-25. (a) Why did many believe in Jesus's name at the Passover Feast (verse 23)? (b) What did Jesus know (verses 24-25)?

Even though John doesn't list them here, he explains that Jesus gave more signs while he was in Jerusalem. The result: *Many believed in his name.*

The Little Details
Lydia McGrew: The Significance of 46 Years
Historically, this reference to forty-six years points quite strongly to the *beginning* of Jesus' ministry. A location in time at the Passover of the year A.D. 28 is the most common scholarly estimate based on this statement by the Jewish leaders, calculating from the time when Josephus records that Herod began to rebuild the Temple, probably sometime between 20 and 19 B.C. If one counts parts of years as years (e.g., parts of the years of Herod's reign or parts of the Jewish year), the reference to forty-six years would place the conversation even earlier. The reference to forty-six years also fits well with Luke's statement that John the Baptist came baptizing "in the fifteenth year of the reign of Tiberius Caesar" (Luke 3.1); the beginning of John the Baptist's ministry, of course, would have occurred even earlier than this first Passover of Jesus' own public ministry. It is almost impossible to see this reference to forty-six years as fitting into a Temple cleansing at the end of Jesus' ministry.[29]

The Good News

In the first two chapters of John, we learned much good news. Jesus is God who became flesh. He gives light to the world and offers people the right to become children of God. Grace and truth come through him. He is the Lamb of God who takes away the sin of the world. He baptizes people with the Holy Spirit. Jesus is Teacher, Son of God, Messiah, and Son of Man. Like Moses, he gives signs that God sent him. His body is a temple. He can see hidden things and at times knows the future. He says, "Follow me." And he will die and raise himself from the dead.

37. ♥ Which of these items of good news means the most to you today? Why?

In John 2:25, the apostle told us that Jesus "knew what was in man." In our next chapter, we'll see what that means when Jesus gives good news to both the elite and the outcast.

Praise God for something you saw of his character this week. **Confess** anything that convicted you. **Ask** for help to do something God's Word calls you to do. **Thank** God for something you learned this week.

Jesus is Teacher, Son of God, Messiah, and Son of Man.

Karla's Creative Connection

I love how John jumps right into his story of Jesus with "In the beginning..." describing Jesus as the Word that was with God and was God. It takes me back to the first verse of Genesis, where we're told that "in the beginning God created the heavens and the earth." But God didn't create everything all at once; it was a process, a day-by-day adding of a new layer of design and creativity until the moment he looked at all he had made and declared it was very good.

Made in his image, we are much like God in this way. Creativity is a process, and this week I want to share my creative process in designing the bookmarks you see throughout this Bible study.

Typically, I read and meditate on a passage of Scripture and then choose one verse that jumps off the page at me or speaks to my heart in the moment. As I write out the verse, reading it several times, I look for and circle or underline key words and phrases I want to emphasize, as you can see in the example below.

But to (all) who [did receive him], who [believed in His name,] he gave the right to become [children of God.]

I first sketch out the size of the bookmark and simply write the verse with my key words and phrases in larger letters to determine spacing and how much room I have to play with. This stage sometimes includes a lot of erasing, but that's part of the fun. In the next sketch you can see how I start playing with borders and banners to again bring greater attention to these key points in the verse. At this stage I might do two or three more sketches before moving to the third one you see here.

This is where the fun really begins! I start refining the spacing, deciding on the particular styles of banners and borders, playing with the lettering, and adding as many embellishments as I can to dress up the design. And then, in the last sketch, you can see that I've refined it to the point where I'm ready to ink it or trace it into my Bible.

I use this process when creating Bible art because it helps me slow down, focus on the truth of what the verse is saying to me, and enjoy my time in God's presence. I hope it will do the same for you!

Karla

but to ALL who did receive him who believed in His Name he gave the right to become children of GOD

John 1:12

Chapter 2

John 3:1–4:54
The Good News

What is the good news?

Worship Which Way?

My Mexican American mother was raised Catholic, but she was intrigued by her grandmother in Mexico. She claimed she was a witch, and Mom liked witchcraft's offer of power and fortune-telling. My father was raised as an atheist and dabbled in ESP (extrasensory perception), thinking he could read minds. He gave me science fiction books about researchers discovering how to harness the power of the mind.

I suppose the reason my dad agreed to attend church after he and my mother married was that she was Catholic. Until I was about seven we went to a Protestant church that met at a drive-in theater. Then one Sunday he drove us to a park instead. He said we wouldn't attend church anymore because God didn't exist and everything our Sunday school teachers had told us was a lie. When I protested, he said I could believe in God if I wanted, but that would be stupid. Nonetheless, I didn't think it was stupid, and I decided to learn about God when I was older.

I didn't remember much of what my Sunday school teachers taught, but I did remember some of the songs, like "Jesus Loves the Little Children." Whether it was the music or the lessons, something made me think it was possible that God might like me. I hoped so—because my parents often said they didn't.

Around age 12, I found a television show called *Dark Shadows*. Its tales of witches, vampires, ghosts, and werewolves spellbound me. I watched it every day after school, drawn to the witches' power to protect themselves. I didn't know if witchcraft was real, but I wanted to find out.

Then after I had watched *Dark Shadows* for a couple of years, my girlfriend Linda told me she thought I was too obsessed with it. She said I was starting to act like one of the witches. Also, she wasn't sure whether witchcraft was compatible with Christianity. Hence, she suggested I give up *Dark Shadows* for Lent as a sign that God was more important.

Previously I had asked Linda how to get to heaven. She was the one I mentioned in this book's Introduction who told me the good had to outweigh the bad at the end of my life. I was convinced I would go to hell because my mom had been telling me I was bad since I was four. I prayed and asked God to let me live long enough to work off all the bad in my life. Linda said giving up *Dark Shadows* would be a good deed that made up for bad

The Little Details

Jay Sklar: Atonement as Ransom

The key Hebrew term [for atonement] is *kipper*…It is clear that the term is related to the Hebrew word for "ransom" (*kōper*)…In the Old Testament, a "ransom" has the following characteristics:

1. it is a legally or ethically legitimate payment;

2. it delivers a guilty party from a just punishment that is the right of the offended party to execute or to have executed;

3. it is a lesser punishment than was originally expected;

4. it is up to the offended party whether or not to accept the payment;

5. and its acceptance serves both to rescue the life of the guilty and to appease the offended party, thus restoring peace to the relationship.

This means that, in at least some instances, atonement is characterized by the payment of a ransom (sacrifice) on behalf of the guilty party (the sinner) to the offended party (the Lord). This understanding seems to work best in contexts of sin, in which the sinner is obviously in danger of the Lord's wrath and in need of ransoming.[10]

deeds. So I gave it up for Lent. By the end of the 40 days, I was surprised at how free I felt. I gave it up completely.

But Jesus didn't leave people like me wondering how to approach God. In today's passage, on the one hand he'll chide a religious scholar for not understanding finer points of the Old Testament better. On the other, he'll gently correct someone who rejects most Scripture. Best of all, he'll offer eternal life to both.

God's Word to Us in the Old Testament

John assumes his readers know four things the Old Testament teaches about eternal life, plus a little about two groups of people. Let's take a brief look at those.

Sin Brought Death, but God Left Hope for Eternal Life

Genesis tells us that God placed Adam and Eve in a garden where they enjoyed intimate fellowship with him. He gave them a holy commission: reign over the earth and fill it with people bearing God's image.[1] They could eat freely from the fruit of all the trees but one: the tree of the knowledge of good and evil. That tree would bring **death**. But they ate, and the sentence of death descended on humankind.

Having corrupted themselves, they passed that corruption to their offspring.[2] So instead of filling the earth with holy descendants bearing God's image, they filled it with descendants who filled the earth with violence.[3] Still, the hope of life remained, for the garden's tree of life still stood even though cherubim barred the way to it.[4]

The Law of Moses Showed Sin Separated from God but Left Hope for Eternal Life

After the Lord God freed the Israelites from the land of slavery, he offered them a covenant. He would be their King, and they would live in his land. He would commission them with showing the world God's ways so others could know him.[5] Everyone agreed to the covenant. But the intimate relationship Adam and Eve had with God before the fall was still missing, for seeing God's glory and hearing his voice left the people fearing they would die.[6]

The Lord God provided instructions for living as his holy people with him in their midst. The law of Moses (as we call his instructions) showed that **sin not only brought death; it defiled and separated all people from God**. They could not draw near to God in such a state.

But God graciously provided people a way to deal with sin so they could fellowship with him. He gave them the blood of certain animals to offer on his altar to atone for sins.[7] **Atonement paid a ransom of the blood of a perfect animal in place of their own life,**[8] and **it cleansed sin's defilement**. Then they could draw near in worship and fellowship.[9]

These sacrificial laws assured those who had sinned unintentionally or who had made amends for intentional sin that they were forgiven. At the same time, since no one could bring a fellowship offering without first bringing sacrifices to pay sin's penalty and **purify** them, it was clear that **all sinned and needed God's forgiveness**.[11]

The law also showed that contact with things related to **death** defiled people and objects. This often required purifying with **water** or the **water of cleansing** before one could worship at the tabernacle.[12]

The law explained that **people cannot approach God in their own way**. Instead, it described acceptable and unacceptable worship practices. It forbade using other religions' practices to worship God.[13] It also forbade making idols, worshiping idols, astrology, witchcraft, and fortune-telling.[14] (My friend Linda was right!)

Moreover, the five books of Moses showed the law's limitation: It could not make people obey it. In fact, as Moses led the people to the promised land, they rebelled many times. After one such rebellion, poisonous serpents appeared, killing many. The Lord told Moses, "Make a fiery serpent and set it on a pole, and everyone who is bitten, when he sees it, shall live."[15] So Moses made and **lifted up a bronze serpent**. Those bitten by a serpent who **looked** at the bronze serpent survived.

The tabernacle's layout limited full access to God. People could offer sacrifices and worship God in the courtyard, and priests could serve in the larger room of the tabernacle, called the Holy Place.[16] But only the high priest could enter the curtained-off Most Holy Place, and he could do that just once a year.[17] Since the Most Holy Place served as a footstool for the divine King,[18] this demonstrated that **people needed holiness to approach God**, but a restoration of the intimate fellowship Adam and Eve had enjoyed with him was not yet available. **Embroidered cherubim on the curtain, however, reminded them that the way to eternal life still existed**.[19]

The Psalms Declare That No One Deserves Eternal Life

Eventually, the people settled in the promised land. King David (who was also a prophet[20]) wrote that the "children of man...have all fallen away; together they have become corrupt; there is none who does good, not even one."[21]

David noted that although animal sacrifices could ransom life temporarily, nonetheless, no one could ransom others in a way that let them live forever: "Truly no man can ransom another, or give to God the price of his life, for the ransom of their life is costly and can never suffice, that he should live on forever and never see the pit" (Psalm 49:7-9). Still, what humans could not do on their own, God could do: "But God will ransom my soul from the power of Sheol, for he will receive me" (verse 15). *Sheol* is the grave or death.

God Promises to Cleanse, Give His Spirit, and Raise the Dead

As mentioned in the last chapter, eventually the people abandoned their covenant with God. In fact, they treated sacrifices as a way to get away with sin.[22] But the sacrificial system had no provision for unrepentant, intentional sin.[23] As Moses warned would happen, God exiled the people. Then God sent one of the exiles—Ezekiel—a message.

 Take a moment to pray for insight as you read God's Word.

1. Read Ezekiel 36:22-29. (a) What will God sprinkle people with to clean them (verse 25)? (b) What will he give them (verse 26)? (c) Why will he put his Spirit in people (verse 27)?

Next, God showed he intended to deal with sin's curse of death. Ezekiel saw a valley of dry bones come to life. God said, "You shall know that I am the LORD, when I open your graves, and raise you from your graves" (Ezekiel 37:13). Thus, amid the unfaithfulness of God's people came a message of **hope for life after death**.

Judea was in the south and included Jerusalem and the temple. It was roughly where the former kingdom of Judah was.

Samaria was north of Judea, roughly where the southern part of Israel had been. The inhabitants were a mixed race, being partly Jewish. They worshiped the God of the Pentateuch and other gods.

Galilee was north of Samaria, roughly where the northern parts of Israel had been. After the exile, both Jews and Gentiles lived there. During the days of the second temple, the Jews there returned to Jewish customs and obeying the law of Moses.

Perea was on the other side of the Jordan River from Judea and Samaria, roughly where the eastern parts of Israel had been. The Gospels call it **beyond the Jordan**. Like Galilee, it contained both Jews who had returned to Jewish customs and Gentiles. John baptized Jesus in Perea (John 1:28-31).

Many Jews looked up to the Pharisees with their strict rules.

The Lord continued, "I will save them from all the backslidings in which they have sinned, and will **cleanse** them; and they shall be my people, and I will be their God" (Ezekiel 37:23). At that time, "**David my servant shall be their prince forever**" (verse 25). By calling the future ruler David, he showed that David was a type of the future king.

How the Samaritans and Pharisees Came to Be

When the people abandoned God, the Lord exiled them temporarily. First, all but the poorest people in Israel left while people from other lands settled in their place. The newcomers intermarried with the Israelites who remained and brought their religious practices with them. The mixed descendants became known as **Samaritans**.

Later, God exiled Judah for 70 years. Although some returned, foreigners still ruled.

As the people awaited their promised king, Judaism broke into sects. One sect—the **Pharisees**—memorized extra rules meant to put a hedge around the law so people wouldn't break it. Many Jews looked up to the Pharisees with their strict rules.

God's Word to Us in John

We're about to meet a respected Pharisee, some followers of John the Baptist in Judea, a Samaritan outcast in Samaria, and Jews in Galilee. Jesus has good news for them all.

> 2.   ♥ Read John 3:1–4:54. What stands out to you? Why?

We've seen that sin's penalty is death, but God offers atonement. Next we'll dive into the details of the good news Jesus shares with a man who thought he was very good.

Pam's Heart-to-Heart with the Great I Am—"I Am the Son of God"

As for me, the Father chose me and sent me into the world.
How, then, can you say that I blaspheme because I said that I am the Son of God?
John 10:36 GNT

Jesus claimed to be the Son of God, and God confirmed Jesus was his Son:

> At that time Jesus came from Nazareth in Galilee and was baptized by John in the Jordan. Just as Jesus was coming up out of the water, he saw heaven being torn open and the Spirit descending on him like a dove. And a voice came from heaven: "You are my Son, whom I love; with you I am well pleased" (Mark 1:9-11 NIV).

Jesus embodied the divine DNA—and Christ walked out his heavenly identity! On a recent prayer walk, my husband and I recalled precious days as we parented three sons. The highlights were all connected to watching these young men grasp their identity in Christ, then walk it out.

> I have no greater joy than to hear that my children are walking in the truth (3 John 1:4 NIV).

When Brock was a baby, Bill was a youth pastor. One day I was praying for our son, "Lord, it seems that some kids at 18 soar and succeed, and others stumble and fall. What's the difference?" I began to list the traits, qualities, and skills of successful kids. Many of our own family traditions began from that prayer. Let me share it through the lens of an important day in our family.

For our twenty-fifth wedding anniversary, we gave our sons a tie tac with our family moniker (a crest or coat of arms) we had designed when they were babies. It's an heirloom that can be passed down from generation to generation, symbolizing the values of the Farrel family. (In our book *10 Best Decisions a Parent Can Make*, we describe and show a picture of our crest and tell readers how to design their own.)

Our moniker is a circle, and inside are three *L*'s that stand for **L**earner, **L**eader, and **L**ove God. These are the three core values we prayed our kids would hold on to.

Learner: Competitors willing to do the hard work to learn and become excellent.

Leader: Difference-makers in their spheres of influence using their own unique leadership style, leading rather than following the crowd.

Love God: Owners of their own faith and people who walk out their own personal relationship with God.

Each year from the time our oldest was four, we hosted a Learner and Leaders Who Love God Day, where we negotiated privileges and responsibilities, selected one leadership trait to focus on for each son that year, and gave a gift that applauded the uniqueness (passion, calling, platform) we saw God building in each of their lives. (We included a privileges and responsibilities/chores list in *10 Best Decisions a Parent Can Make*.)

Also in our crest is a cross with a star rising from it, representing our desire to see them seek God's vision for their life. We wanted the source of all their hopes, dreams, and desires to come from God's heart. We believe if young children, tweens, or teens develop a vibrant relationship with God, it will be easier for them to discern the life path God created for them.

The two interlocking hearts represent integrity and commitment. When a Farrel speaks, we want their words to be truth, and we want to be known as a family that keeps all of our commitments, especially the marriage covenant.

The verse inscribed with the crest is the motto by which we raised our sons: "Those who honor God, God honors" (1 Samuel 2:30 paraphrased).

Each fall for over 20 years, on Learner and Leader Who Loves God Day, we had a fun family activity someplace like an amusement park, lake, beach, or favorite restaurant. We'd complete the Learner and Leader contract for each child and choose one verse to pray over his life for the year and one leadership trait to focus on and equip that child to live out. Because one of the traits is a love for God's Word, we taught each son how to select his verse for the year by using internet Bible study tools.

Also each year, we selected a Learner and Leader Who Loves God gift for each child. The gift was three things:

Personal: Something according to that child's needs and unique strengths.

Practical: Something that child would need and was part of the family budget.

Prophetic: Something that encouraged the promise and potential of that child's giftedness and calling.

Now, decades later, our three sons are all adults, and they all walk with Jesus and serve God. They and their wives have their own family missions, mottos, and monikers. Our grandchildren have their own Learner and Leader Who Loves God days! If you're raising children, set your own family fun day to celebrate and equip *your* Learners and Leaders Who Love God! (If you're grandparents, take your grown kids out for coffee and ask, "How can we walk alongside you well as you raise our wonderful grandkids?") Ask God to give you creative ideas to help those you love walk out their identity that reflects the Son of God. As you do this study, consider each answer you give and design, color, or create a gift of legacy for the ones you love.

Experiencing Scripture Creatively

If you have extra time, consider these suggestions for creatively engaging with verses from this week's reading. The appendix has even more ideas.

- Find or take a digital photo of a sunrise. Using Canva or any photo editing software, type John 3:21 onto the photo. Share on social media or with friends. Go to www.DiscoveringTheBibleSeries.com for more instructions.

- Pick your favorite phrase from a verse that stood out to you in today's reading. Follow Karla's instructions at the end of this chapter for making a banner using that phrase. Create the banner in your Bible near the verse, in a journal, or in a margin of this book.

- Color Karla's full-page illustration at the end of the chapter while repeating the words of the verse aloud. (When you're finished, check to see if the activity enabled you to memorize the verse.)

Day 2

Good News for a Pharisee

Yesterday we read that sin defiled people, separated them from God, and brought death. But God provided atoning sacrifices people could offer to receive forgiveness. They did not, however, fully bridge the gap between people and God. Neither did they end death. Still, there were clues that God had a plan to reverse sin's curse. For example, Ezekiel prophesied that the Lord would raise people from their graves, cleanse them, and give them a Messiah to rule them forever.

Because of this, most Jews in Jesus's day believed the Messiah would rule an earthly kingdom at the end of the age. They thought all but the worst Jews would be admitted.[24] Jesus does have good news about that kingdom, but first there's bad news.

First, the Bad News

Jesus is still in Jerusalem[25] when a Jewish leader comes to see him.

> 3. Read John 3:1-2. (a) To what Jewish sect does Nicodemus belong (verse 1)? (b) Why does he think God is with Jesus (verse 2)?

Nicodemus belongs to the strict Jewish sect, the Pharisees. That means he follows both the law of Moses and the hundreds of oral traditions the Pharisees added to the law. He is also a ruler. So other Jews look up to him as a righteous, moral man of God.

He calls Jesus *Rabbi* and acknowledges him as *a teacher*. *Rabbi* literally translates to "my great one," but students commonly called their teachers by that title.[26] Nicodemus does not recognize Jesus as the Christ or the prophet like Moses. Still, he expresses that he and those he represents—either other Pharisees or other rulers—think God must have sent Jesus because of the signs he gives.

> 4. Read John 3:3-4. (a) What does Jesus say is the requirement to see (or experience) the kingdom of God (verse 3)? (b) Does Nicodemus agree (verse 4)?

Jesus's proclamation shocks Nicodemus. Surely of all Jews, Nicodemus is good enough to see God's coming kingdom. He is faithful to the law's instructions for purification. Why would he need to do something as outlandish as this seems?

We Must Be Born Again to Enter God's Kingdom

> 5. Read John 3:5-8. (a) Of what must one be born to enter God's kingdom (verse 5)? (b) What is born of the Spirit (verse 6)? (c) The same Greek word is translated "wind" and "Spirit" in verse 8. How are wind and Spirit alike?

The Little Details
Born of Water and Spirit

The first time I read John 3:5, I thought *water* referred to amniotic fluid! But New Testament scholar D.A. Carson points out that the Greek grammar is speaking of one birth that is of both water and Spirit.

Some think this refers to water baptism, but the Old Testament does not speak much about water baptism. So since Jesus expected Nicodemus to know what he was talking about (John 3:10), he must be referring to something in the Old Testament.

The Bible has many passages on the importance of both water for cleansing and spirit for life, but Ezekiel 36 is the clearest. Plus, it's followed by the imagery of resurrection in chapter 37.

Still, there were clues that God had a plan to reverse sin's curse.

It's unclear whether Jesus's words end at verse 15 (NIV) or 21 (ESV). If they end at verse 15, then what follows are John's thoughts on what transpired.

In the Old Testament, water cleansed from impurities and God's Spirit gave life. In Ezekiel 36:25-27, God said he would sprinkle water on the people to clean them from all their uncleanness and idolatries. Then he would give them a new, transformed heart and spirit. He would also pour his Holy Spirit within them to enable them to obey his commands, the same Holy Spirit who brings life to dry bones in Ezekiel 37. Jesus says Nicodemus should not marvel, for just as we see the effects of the wind but not the wind, so we see the effects of the Spirit but not the Spirit.

6. Read John 3:9-11. (a) Does Nicodemus agree with Jesus (verse 9)? (b) Why does Jesus say Nicodemus should understand him (verse 10)? (c) Both the references to "you" in verse 11 are plural. How does Jesus say Nicodemus and those he's with react to the testimony from Jesus and his Father?

Nicodemus has been using *we* to refer to the group he represents. Perhaps he thought Jesus would want the group's instruction. Now Jesus imitates his *we*, likely referring to himself and the Father. Although Nicodemus calls Jesus Rabbi and acknowledges that God sent him, he's not ready to receive Jesus's teaching without challenge.

Jesus Instructs on Heavenly Things

Jesus isn't meeting with Nicodemus to seek instruction but rather to instruct. Nicodemus doesn't understand the Old Testament's teaching about the need for a better cleansing, a heart transformed from stone to flesh, a new spirit, and God's Spirit indwelling and enabling obedience.

7. Read John 3:12-13. (a) Jesus has told Nicodemus earthly things (he must be born again on earth). What was Nicodemus's response (verse 12)? (b) Why should Nicodemus believe Jesus about heavenly things (verse 13)?

Jesus calls himself *Son of Man* and claims to have descended from heaven. That's why Nicodemus should believe him. It's quite a claim, and if it weren't for Jesus's signs, it wouldn't be believable. Indeed, Jesus can see that this Pharisee does not believe him.

Jesus Offers Eternal Life to Those Who Believe in Him

8. Read John 3:14-15 below. Underline what Moses did. Draw an arrow from that to what Jesus will do. Circle what those who believe in Jesus may have.

   And as Moses lifted up the serpent in the wilderness,
   so must the Son of Man be lifted up,
   that whoever believes in him may have eternal life.

Moses *lifted up the serpent* of bronze on a pole so that those dying from a poisonous

Jesus calls himself *Son of Man* and claims to have descended from heaven.

serpent's bite could look to the bronze serpent and live. Jesus says he likewise must be *lifted up* so that those dying from another Serpent's sting may look to him and live eternally. In other words, the bronze serpent was a type of Jesus.

Lifted up also alludes to the prophet Isaiah's prophecy of a future righteous, suffering servant who will be lifted up, will sprinkle many, and will bear people's sin in his death (Isaiah 52:13-15; 53:12). But none of the Jews think the Christ and the suffering servant are the same person. How can a servant who dies be a Christ who rules forever? Nicodemus needs to ponder Jesus's words more.

The bad news is that Nicodemus's high moral standing and goodness aren't enough to receive eternal life. The good news is that this man who gives signs that he is from God also says those who believe in him may have eternal life.

God Gives His Son Jesus Out of Love

9. Write out John 3:16 below.

God created the world and placed humans in it. But humans turned from him and his commands on how to live a blessed life. Instead, they embraced wars, rape, infanticide, murder, lies, and idolatry. Yet God still loved the world. So he gave his only Son to be lifted up in order that people who believe in him might have eternal life. Indeed, the new birth is into eternal life.[27]

Jesus's Purpose Is to Save from Condemnation

10. Read John 3:17-18 below. In the first sentence, box what God didn't send Jesus to do. Underline the reason God sent Jesus. In the second sentence, double underline the standing of those who believe in Jesus. Box the standing of those who don't believe in Jesus.

> For God did not send his Son into the world to condemn the world, but in order that the world might be saved through him. Whoever believes in him is not condemned, but whoever does not believe is condemned already, because he has not believed in the name of the only Son of God.

The whole world stands condemned because of sin. But God sent his Son to save those who believe in his Son and all he represents from condemnation.

Jesus Is the Light Who Exposes Works as Evil or True

11. In John 3:19-20 below, circle what has come into the world. Underline the reason people love darkness. Box the deeds of those who hate the light. Underline the reason they avoid the light.

> And this is the judgment: the light has come into the world, and people loved the darkness rather than the light because their works were evil. For everyone who does wicked things hates the light and does not come to the light, lest his works should be exposed.

The Little Details
Only Son

An important phrase in John 1:14 and 3:16 can be missed in English translations. The ESV translates it *only Son.* The NIV uses *one and only Son.* The NASB says *only begotten Son.*

The phrase alludes to verses where God asks Abraham to offer to him "your son, your only son" (Genesis 22:2,12,16). Isaac was not Abraham's only son, but he was the only son of the promise. God stayed Abraham's hand and substituted a ram for the life of the young man, who was between 15 and 30 years old.

Hebrews 11:17-19 says Abraham's receiving Isaac back was a type of the Father receiving Jesus back via resurrection. In Hebrews 11:17, the ESV calls Isaac Abraham's *only son,* the NIV his *one and only son,* and the NASB his *only begotten son.*

John uses this special phrase because he wants his readers to notice the link and realize that the two prophets, Abraham and Isaac, acted out a future monumental event: the Father offering his Son, Jesus.

Jesus is the light shining in the darkness (John 1:5). Light exposes evil. Yet most people prefer to justify their deeds and see themselves as good rather than come to the light.

> **12.** In John 3:21 below, circle who comes to the light. Underline why.
>
> But whoever does what is true comes to the light, so that it may be clearly seen that his works have been carried out in God.

It remains to be seen whether Nicodemus will look past his good deeds into his heart.

> **13.** ♥ Do you regularly pray for God to search your heart and show you anything he finds offensive (Psalm 139:23-24)? If you do, how has that helped you grow as a Christian? If you don't, what keeps you from doing so?

In this lesson, we read that Jesus told Nicodemus that neither his ethnicity as a Jew nor his adherence to high moral standards was enough to enter the kingdom of God and receive eternal life. That's the bad news.

But if he believed in Jesus's name and looked to Jesus when Jesus was lifted up, he could have eternal life. Moreover, Jesus could instruct on heavenly things because he came down from heaven. In fact, Jesus is the Son of God whom God gives out of his love for the world. His purpose was not to condemn, but to save, which was also good news. Still, Jesus was the light, and that meant he exposed all works for what they really were. That was bad news for the wicked but good news for those walking in truth.

In the next lesson, we'll read good news from John the Baptist.

Day 3

Good News for the Baptist's Followers

We saw in Day 2's lesson how Jesus shared good news with a highly respected Jewish teacher who thought his goodness and ethnicity made him acceptable to God.

Next we'll see John the Baptist share good news with some of his followers. The Baptist's followers are Jews who have repented of sin and are trying to live a godly life. They believe John is a prophet.

Jesus Rises in Popularity

> **14.** Read John 3:22-24. (a) Where were Jesus and his disciples (verse 22)? (b) Who else was baptizing (verse 23)? (c) What hadn't happened yet (verse 24)?

His purpose was not to condemn, but to save, which was also good news.

Jesus has left Jerusalem, and both he and John the Baptist are in Judea's countryside some time before John the Baptist's imprisonment (an event all the Gospel's first readers would have known about).

> **15.** Read John 3:25-26. (a) What were John's disciples discussing (verse 25)? (b) What were they disturbed about (verse 26)?

Purification has to do with the laws about how to clean what is ceremonially unclean. An unnamed Jew argues with John's followers over purification, probably because various Jewish sects disagreed with each other over baptism practices.[28] Somehow that discussion leads John's followers to resent how many people are now going to Jesus rather than to John for baptism.

Jesus Is the Christ and the Bridegroom

John the Baptist responds to his disturbed disciples.

> **16.** Read John 3:27-29. (a) What is necessary for us to receive a ministry (verse 27)? (b) What had John told his followers (verse 28)? (c) To what did John liken himself and Jesus (verse 29)?

John the Baptist's followers are jealous for his sake. They may not have thought through what it meant when their beloved leader said he was not the Christ.

> **17.** ♥ (a) Write out John 3:30 below. (b) To whom does "he" refer? (c) What ministry have you been given from heaven? (d) If you're envious of someone else's ministry, how can you apply John 3:27-30 to it?

John the Baptist possesses insight and humility. He knows who he is in God's sight. He knows what God has assigned him to do. He does it wholeheartedly and shows no jealousy that another now has a bigger following while his own following shrinks. Most important, he points his followers to Jesus.

It might not feel like it now, but this is good news for John's followers. He can't give them what they truly need, but he can point them to the one who will.

Jesus Is Above All

It's unclear whether verses 31-36 are John the Baptist's words (NASB) or John the apostle's (ESV, NIV). Either way, they expand on and explain the Baptist's teaching.

The Little Details
Ministry Before the Baptist's Imprisonment
John 3:22-23 notes that the discussion that follows takes place in Judea before John the Baptist's imprisonment. That means this Gospel is telling us of events that happened prior to what the other three Gospels narrate about Jesus's public ministry, for they begin in Galilee after the Baptist's arrest (Matthew 4:12; Mark 1:14; Luke 3:20).

The fact that the Gospel writer knew of events that happened before Jesus selected 12 disciples in Galilee for special training is more evidence that the apostle John is the unnamed disciple in John 1:35-40. There, Peter and the unnamed disciple hear the Baptist's testimony about Jesus and follow him. In fact, the other Gospels tell us that Peter and John were often together.

John the Baptist possesses insight and humility. He knows who he is in God's sight. He knows what God has assigned him to do.

18. Read John 3:31-33. (a) Who is above all others on earth (verse 31)? (b) When that person tells of the heavenly things he's seen and heard, how do most react (verse 32)? (c) What do those who receive his testimony do (verse 33)?

Jesus comes from heaven and is above all people, including John. John can baptize with water but not with the Holy Spirit. He can also call people to repent and point them to Jesus as the Christ, but he himself does not come from heaven. Only Jesus can reveal what he has seen and heard from above. Still, although Jesus teaches the things of heaven, most reject his words. Those who receive them, though, certify God's truthfulness.

Jesus Has the Spirit of the Lord

19. Read John 3:34-35. (a) Why does the one God has sent (Jesus) utter the words of God (end of verse 34)? (b) What has the Father given the Son (verse 35)?

The Father sent Jesus, and Jesus utters the words of God for the Father gives him the Spirit without measure. The Father has, in fact, given all things to his beloved Son.

We already saw that John the Baptist testified, "I saw the Spirit descend from heaven like a dove, and it remained on him" (John 1:32). The outpouring of the Spirit on Jesus without measure fits with the description of the Christ in Isaiah 11:2: "And the Spirit of the LORD shall rest upon him, the Spirit of wisdom and understanding, the Spirit of counsel and might, the Spirit of knowledge and the fear of the LORD."

Remember, *Messiah* and *Christ* both mean "Anointed One." Isaiah 61:1 describes the coming Messiah as anointed by the Spirit of the Lord:

> The Spirit of the Lord GOD is upon me, because the LORD has anointed me to bring good news to the poor; he has sent me to bind up the brokenhearted, to proclaim liberty to the captives, and the opening of the prison to those who are bound.

Additionally, the outpouring of the Spirit on Jesus suits Isaiah's description of a righteous, suffering servant: "Behold my servant, whom I uphold, my chosen, in whom my soul delights; I have put my Spirit upon him; he will bring forth justice to the nations" (Isaiah 42:1). Still, Jews in Jesus's day don't see how the Messiah who reigns forever can also be the dying suffering servant.

Jews in Jesus's day don't see how the Messiah who reigns forever can also be the dying suffering servant.

Jesus Offers Eternal Life

> **20.** Read John 3:36. (a) What do those who believe in the Son have? (b) What will those who don't obey the Son not see? (c) What will happen to them instead?

We need to know the bad news before we can appreciate or even want the good news. The bad news is that all have sinned and stand condemned. The Baptist's followers had repented from their sin when John baptized them, but that wasn't enough to see eternal life. John baptized them in preparation for the coming of the Messiah. Now the Messiah has arrived. Now they need to believe in the Son so the purification the baptism pointed to would become a reality in their lives.

Day 4

Good News for the Outcast

We've seen there's good news for the religious leader and the laypeople who turned from sin. They need more than what the law of Moses offers. They need Jesus.

Now we'll see that there is even good news for the ungodly who hold erroneous beliefs about God, just as I once did.

Jesus Comes to Samaria

> **21.** Read John 4:1-5. (a) Why did Jesus leave Judea (verses 1-3)? (b) Through where did he have to pass (verse 4)?

Jesus may have left Judea to avoid conflict with the Pharisees. As he heads toward Galilee, where he grew up, he passes through Samaria.

As mentioned on Day 1, the Samaritans are part Jewish. They use a Samaritan version of the Pentateuch (the first five books of the Old Testament). However, they combine religious practices from other nations with their form of Judaism, including at times worshiping other gods. In Jesus's day, they lived in the Roman district of Samaria, sandwiched between Judea to the south and Galilee to the north.

Jesus Is the Word Become Flesh

> **22.** Why was Jesus sitting by the well (John 4:6)?

When the Word became flesh, he took on physical weaknesses. In the next scene, it's about noon, the hottest part of the day.

> We need to know the bad news before we can appreciate or even want the good news.

The Little Details
D.A. Carson: Living Water

The metaphor speaks of God and his grace, knowledge of God, life, the transforming power of the Holy Spirit; in Isaiah 1:16-18; Ezekiel 36:25-27 water promises cleansing. All of these themes are picked up in John's use of "water" or "living water" in this gospel...In this chapter, the water is the satisfying eternal life mediated by the Spirit that only Jesus, the Messiah and Saviour of the world, can provide.[30]

- - - - - - - - - - - - - - - -

The offer of living water that quenches thirst and wells up to eternal life is good news.

- - - - - - - - - - - - - - - -

23. Read John 4:7-9. (a) For what did Jesus ask (verse 7)? (b) Where were his disciples (verse 8)? (c) Why was the woman surprised at Jesus's request (verse 9)?

In Jesus's day, many Jews refuse to eat or drink from Samaritan dishes because they think doing so will make them unclean. Some Jews will eat Samaritan dry foods while others avoid all food from Samaria.[29] That Jesus's disciples are buying food in Samaria shows they do not follow the strictest customs.

Jesus Offers Living Water

24. Read John 4:10-12. What would Jesus offer the woman if she asked (verse 10)?

Living water sometimes refers to springs, but that's not what Jesus means. Jesus likely refers to Jeremiah 2:13: "For my people have committed two evils: they have forsaken me, the fountain of living waters, and hewed out cisterns for themselves, broken cisterns that can hold no water."

25. Name two ways the water Jesus offers differs from well water (John 4:13-14).

The offer of living water that quenches thirst and wells up to eternal life is good news.

Jesus Reveals He Is a Prophet

26. Read John 4:15-18. (a) How does Jesus test the woman (verse 16)? (b) What does Jesus know about the woman (verse 18)?

It's no surprise that the woman wants this water! But Jesus's reply tells us why she came to the well at noon rather than with other women in the morning. She is a social outcast among the townspeople. Still, Jesus's words encourage her to talk.

27. Read John 4:19-20. (a) What did the woman perceive about Jesus (verse 19)? (b) To what did she change the subject (verse 20)?

Since the Samaritans use the Pentateuch, they expect the prophet like Moses to come and reveal many things. The Samaritans call the prophet like Moses "Taheb" and believe that "water shall flow from his buckets" (Numbers 24:7).[31] The woman asks Jesus about one of the main conflicts between Jews and Samaritans. That is, the Samaritans had built a temple on Mount Gerizim, but the Jews destroyed it, saying only the temple in Jerusalem is legitimate.

Jesus Reveals the Essence of True Worship

28. Read John 4:21-24. (a) How did Jesus let the woman know that her religious beliefs were mistaken (verse 22)? (b) What is God (verse 24)? (c) How must his worshipers worship him (verse 24)?

The Samaritans do not know the God they claim to worship, while the Jews possess the saving revelation. But a change is coming, and in fact, it has arrived, for *God is spirit*: He is invisible and unknowable unless he chooses to reveal himself. And he has chosen to reveal himself through Jesus, the Word who became flesh to dwell among us. True worship will soon cease at the Jerusalem temple, though, and it will be replaced with *worship in spirit and truth*. Such worship will come from those born of the Spirit because they know the One who is full of truth (John 1:14; 3:6).

Jesus Reveals He Is Messiah (and Taheb)

29. Read John 4:25-26. (a) Who does the woman say is coming (verse 25)? (b) Who does Jesus say he is (verse 26)?

The woman uses the Jewish title *Messiah*. To the Samaritans, the Taheb is a prophet who reveals truth and is equivalent to the Jewish Messiah. In contrast, the Jews expect the Messiah to be a ruler rather than a teacher. But John has already told us Jesus is both revealer and Messiah (John 1:17-18). With tenderness and compassion, Jesus reveals himself to her: "I who speak to you am he" (4:26). He has not revealed that to Jews yet in this Gospel, for the title *Messiah* carries too many political expectations that Jesus has yet to dispel.

30. ♥ What is your response to the good news that Jesus is willing to correct false beliefs and offer eternal life even to those with immoral pasts?

Jesus knows the Samaritan woman's mistaken beliefs and sinful past, yet he still offers her living water that wells up to eternal life. He gently corrects her errant beliefs and honors her with the revelation of who he is. What good news this is: God's gift isn't limited to good Jews. He reaches out to the lost and invites them to know him.

The Little Details
"Worship in Spirit and Truth" (John 4:23)

Jesus said, "The hour is coming when neither on this mountain nor in Jerusalem will you worship the Father" (John 4:21). Soon after Jesus spoke those words, it became impossible to worship at the Jerusalem temple. Here's why.

After Jesus's resurrection, Jews in Jerusalem rebelled against Rome, hoping to put in place another messiah to rule them. Rome crushed the rebellion. In AD 70, Rome demolished the temple, just as Jesus foretold in Luke 21:6.

Now those who belong to Christ are "a dwelling place for God by the Spirit" (Ephesians 2:22). Paul wrote, "For God's temple is holy, and you are that temple" (1 Corinthians 3:17).

Jesus knows the Samaritan woman's mistaken beliefs and sinful past, yet he still offers her living water that wells up to eternal life.

Day 5

Good News for Two Cities

In our last lesson, we read about Jesus telling a Samaritan woman that he is the Messiah. Now we'll see how the residents of two towns react to Jesus's good news.

Jesus Comes to Sychar of Samaria

31. Read John 4:27-30. (a) Why did the disciples marvel (verse 27)? (b) What did the woman tell the townspeople (verses 28-29)? (c) How did they react (verse 30)?

Rabbis don't usually teach women, so the disciples are amazed. But Jesus doesn't care what other rabbis do; he teaches women and men alike. The woman leaves her water jar and gets the townspeople so they can meet him.

32. Read John 4:31-34. What was Jesus's food (verse 34)?

In the Old Testament, the righteous man Job said, "I have treasured the words of his mouth more than my portion of food" (Job 23:12). In Moses's day, God explained that he fed the people manna in the wilderness so they would learn that "man does not live by bread alone, but man lives by every word that comes from the mouth of the LORD" (Deuteronomy 8:3). Jesus lives this out.

33. ♥ How can you apply John 4:34 to your own life?

Our spirits need food just as our bodies do.

34. Read John 4:35-38. (a) What kind of fruit is the reaper gathering (verse 36)? (b) What will the disciples reap (verse 38)?

Our spirits need food just as our bodies do.

Four months passed between planting certain seeds and harvesting grain. Here, Jesus declares the harvest is ready. But he's speaking of a spiritual harvest and means that John the Baptist and all the Old Testament saints had sown spiritual seeds. Now in a Samaritan town, souls are being reaped. In eternity, both sower and reaper will rejoice. Likewise, Jesus's disciples will reap where others have already planted.

Jesus Is the Savior of the World

35. Read John 4:39-42. (a) What first caused the Samaritans to believe in Jesus (verse 39)? (b) What happened that showed Jesus had cleared away the usual animosity between Jews and Samaritans (verse 40)? (c) What further convinced the Samaritans to believe (verse 41)? (d) Who did they know he was (verse 42)?

They welcome the good news that Jesus is *the Savior of the world*, not just of Jews.

Jesus Comes to Cana of Galilee

After two days in Samaria, Jesus continues his journey to Cana in Galilee, the same city where he turned water into wine.

36. Read John 4:43-45. (a) What did prophets lack in their hometowns (verse 44)? (b) Why did the Galileans welcome Jesus (verse 45)?

Jesus leaves Samaria, where people fully embrace him as Savior of the world, and comes to Galilee, where he now resides. The Galileans welcome him but as a miracle worker rather than Messiah. Once again, John refers to the signs Jesus gave at the Passover Feast that John did not record for us.[32]

37. Read John 4:46-48. (a) Why did the official from Capernaum come to Cana (verses 46-47)? (b) What did Jesus say (verse 48)?

The Galileans welcome Jesus because they want to see more signs like those he gave at the feast. It's not his teaching or his person that they seek but his power. Thus, their weak faith disappoints Jesus. Indeed, the Samaritans had honored him more as a prophet than the Galileans with whom he has lived for years, proving the proverb that says *a prophet has no honor in his own hometown.*

Jesus Heals from Afar

38. Read John 4:49-50. (a) What does the official ask Jesus to do (verse 49)? (b) What does Jesus do instead (verse 50)? (c) How does the official respond (verse 50)?

It's not his teaching or his person that they seek but his power.

Jesus doesn't always do things the way people ask.

> **39.** Read John 4:51-53. (a) What happened to the official's son (verse 51)? (b) When (verse 53)? (c) How did the official and his household respond (verse 53)?

The official and his household in Capernaum believe in Jesus. But there's no mention of what else happened in Cana or of anyone there believing in him at this time.

> **40.** In John 4:54 below, circle what John calls the healing. Record "Healed the official's son" on line 2 of the **8 Signs** chart at the back of this book.
>
> This was now the second sign that Jesus did when he had come from Judea to Galilee.

The healing is the second sign in Cana of Galilee.

> **41.** ♥ Describe a time God answered a prayer request differently from the way you asked him to answer. What benefits did God's way have over your way?

The Good News

In John 3–4, we discovered that Jesus came to earth not to condemn but to save. Still, he is the light who exposes deeds as either evil or true. He is the Christ and is above all. Jesus teaches even those with false beliefs and immoral lives the truth about himself. In fact, he's the Savior of the world, not just of good Jews. We also discovered that everyone—even those considered the most moral people—must be born again to enter God's kingdom. No one is good enough on their own. But God loves the world and gave his Son so that those who believe in Jesus may have eternal life.

> **42.** ♥ Which of these items of good news means the most to you today? Why?

Jesus teaches even those with false beliefs and immoral lives the truth about himself. In fact, he's the Savior of the world, not just of good Jews.

The Samaritans thought the prophet like Moses was equivalent to the Jews' Messiah. But the Jewish leaders disagreed. In the next chapter, we'll see how Jesus demonstrates that he is indeed both.

> **Praise** God for something you saw of his character this week. **Confess** anything that convicted you. **Ask** for help to do something God's Word calls you to do. **Thank** God for something you learned this week.

Karla's Creative Connection

As I shared last week, one of the first things I do when illustrating a Bible verse is to read it several times, looking for the key words or phrases I want to emphasize. Doing this not only helps me begin to break the verse into sections to illustrate but, more importantly, gives me time to think about the power and importance of those particular words.

We can make a word or phrase pop on the page in several ways, such as with the style or size of the lettering, but one of my favorites is to use banners. For this week's bookmark, wrapping the world with a banner declaring God's love was perfect. A simple flat banner emphasized the truth that the good news is available to "whoever" believes. And I couldn't resist creating a special banner to celebrate the gift of "eternal life."

Banners can range from super simple to complex. They may look intimidating at first, but their construction is simple once you look at how they're created step by step. Following the steps below, draw out your banner with a pencil first so you can erase any "dotted lines" after you've gone over it with a pen or marker. With a little practice, you'll become a pro banner maker in no time!

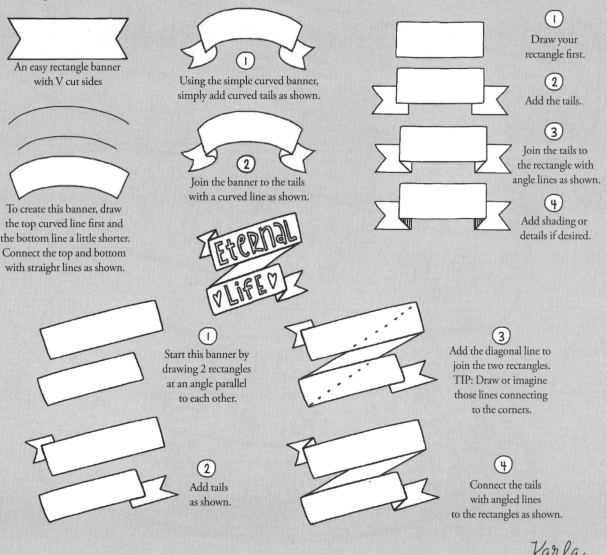

An easy rectangle banner with V cut sides

To create this banner, draw the top curved line first and the bottom line a little shorter. Connect the top and bottom with straight lines as shown.

1. Using the simple curved banner, simply add curved tails as shown.

2. Join the banner to the tails with a curved line as shown.

1. Draw your rectangle first.

2. Add the tails.

3. Join the tails to the rectangle with angle lines as shown.

4. Add shading or details if desired.

1. Start this banner by drawing 2 rectangles at an angle parallel to each other.

2. Add tails as shown.

3. Add the diagonal line to join the two rectangles. TIP: Draw or imagine those lines connecting to the corners.

4. Connect the tails with angled lines to the rectangles as shown.

Karla

everyone who LOOKS to the SON and believes in Him shall have eternal life and I will raise them up at the last day

John 6:40 NIV

Chapter 3

John 5:1–6:46
Expectations Meet Reality

Why do people reject the good news?

Day 1

The Prophet Like Moses

As I shared in the Introduction to this book, when I was 14, a teenage boy told me I needed to accept Jesus as Lord in order to go to heaven. I thought that was crazy. I told him I could see someone like Moses or David being the way to heaven because they were great leaders. But Jesus was just a shepherd who liked children and couldn't get along with adults, so they killed him.

Obviously, not being raised in the church left me with misunderstandings.

A few months later, I got hold of a New Testament and started reading it from the beginning. By the time I got to John's Gospel, I thought my opinion of Jesus was justified. After all, he argued with everyone and constantly claimed to know more than others, so of course no one liked him. I didn't either.

I expected Jesus to be a certain way, and my expectations colored what I read. But what I believed clashed with Jesus's teaching in John 5, which we'll read today.

Indeed, his teaching clashed with most of his listeners' expectations about the Messiah and the prophet like Moses. Just as my preconceived notions kept me from seeing who Jesus really was, so did theirs.

God's Word to Us in the Old Testament

Chapter 1 mentioned that Moses promised that one day God would send a prophet like him. In chapter 2, we read that the Samaritans thought this prophet and the Jews' Messiah were the same person. Some of the ordinary Jews thought they might be the same person too. However, the Jewish leaders taught that they were different people. Still, Jesus revealed he was the Messiah to the Samaritan woman. In today's reading, Jesus will show that he is also the prophet like Moses, so let's read about him.

Moses Prophesied About a Future Prophet Like Moses

Here's what Moses said about this prophet in Deuteronomy 18:15, 17-19:

> The Lord your God will raise up for you a prophet like me from among you, from your brothers—it is to him you shall listen…And the Lord said to me, "…I will raise up for them a prophet like you from among their brothers. And I will put my words in his mouth, and he shall speak to them all that I command

51

The Little Details

Psalm 78:23-25:

Yet he commanded the skies above and opened the doors of heaven, and he rained down on them manna to eat and gave them the grain of heaven. Man ate of the bread of the angels; he sent them food in abundance.

him. And whoever will not listen to my words that he shall speak in my name, I myself will require it of him."

We've already seen some similarities between Moses and Jesus. For example, just as Moses turned water to blood as a sign God sent him, so Jesus turned water to wine as a sign God sent him. Just as Moses said he would lead people to the earthly promised land, so Jesus says he is leading people to another promised land: the kingdom of God. Additionally, Moses led much like a king; Jesus has revealed he is the Jews' longed-for king—the Messiah.

Here are other events in Moses's life that will relate to what we read about Jesus today.

- God gave Moses the **ability to perform certain miracles as signs that God truly had sent him**.
- God answered Moses's prayer for God to **heal a person**.
- Moses was a **judge** who not only **judged people's** disputes but also **judged how the law should apply to people's lives**.
- Moses **delivered God's messages** to the people at a **mountain**.
- **God communicated with Moses more directly than he did with others**.
- Moses showed **control over a sea** by parting the Red Sea.
- God through Moses gave the Hebrews **bread from heaven**.[1]

Let's read more about that last item because it figures prominently in John's Gospel.

 Take a moment to pray for insight as you read God's Word.

1. Turn to Exodus 16. (a) What did God call the food he gave the people (verse 4)? (b) Why did he send the people out to gather it (verse 4)? (c) What should the people know when they see the food (verse 12)? (d) What did the people call the food (verse 31)?

Eventually, the people **grumbled** that they were tired of manna. But it sustained them until they reached the promised land, at which point it stopped appearing.[2] Psalm 78 later describes the miraculous meals as **bread from heaven** (see sidebar).

The Law of Moses Commanded Rest on the Sabbath

On the way to the promised land, Moses gave the Lord's Ten Commandments to the people on stone tablets. The fourth is "Remember the Sabbath day, to keep it holy. Six days you shall labor, and do all your work, but the seventh day is a Sabbath to the LORD your God. On it you shall not do any work."[3]

This commandment meant the Jews **rested on the Sabbath** (sundown Friday to sundown Saturday) to keep it holy—that is, set aside for the Lord. This was a **sign** of their covenant with God: Instead of a signature on paper, they showed they accepted God's covenant by resting each Sabbath (Exodus 31:13). God in his love gave them something beneficial as a sign of their covenant relationship with him.

God in his love gave them something beneficial as a sign of their covenant relationship with him.

The Prophet Daniel Prophesied a Future Resurrection

Centuries later, the prophet Daniel lived in exile. There, the Lord gave him a vision about the time of the end.

> **2.** Read Daniel 12:1-2. (a) Where are the names of the people who will be delivered written (verse 1)? (b) To what will the dead ("those who sleep in the dust of the earth") awaken (verse 2)?

God revealed to Daniel that **he will resurrect all the dead to one of two destinies**.

The Pharisees Interpreted the Law of Moses

As mentioned in chapter 2, the **Pharisees** had **oral traditions** that interpreted the law of Moses. These **included what people could and could not do on the Sabbath**.

God's Word to Us in John

In today's chapters, the Sanhedrin is the highest Jewish tribunal. Its members come from two sects, Sadducees and Pharisees. The Pharisees are looking for a Messiah who will rule as king but will allow them to have authority over spiritual matters. They don't want a king who is also the prophet like Moses. After all, Moses was the supreme judge over all spiritual matters in his day.

> **3.** ♥ Read John 5:1–6:46. (We're stopping in the middle of a conversation.) What stands out to you? Why?

Did you notice how Jesus differed from many expectations? In the next daily lesson, we'll dive into the details of the healing at the pool.

> **4.** ♥ What mistaken notions did you initially have about Jesus? How did you discover your mistake?

The Little Details
Messianic Expectations in Jesus's Day

Pharisees were mostly middle-class businessmen and a few priests who had a system of oral traditions meant to be a hedge around the Mosaic law. For example, they interpreted how far one could walk without breaking the Sabbath. They believed God equally inspired the Old Testament and their oral law, called the *tradition of the elders*. They hoped their righteousness would cause God to send the Messiah.[4]

Sadducees were wealthy, aristocratic priests who may have accepted the Old Testament as we have it today but believed the later writings were subordinate to the five books of Moses. They were not looking for an anointed king (messiah).[5]

Zealots were activists who believed God would send a king (messiah) when the people took up arms against Rome.[6]

Did you notice how Jesus differed from many expectations?

Pam's Heart-to-Heart with the Great I Am—"I Am the Bread of Life"

Then Jesus declared, "I am the bread of life. Whoever comes to me will never go hungry,
and whoever believes in me will never be thirsty."
John 6:35 NIV

Do you have a favorite bread? In the Holy Land, I discovered the sweet challah with honey and the savory laffa, hot from the pan with olive oil. The bread common in the life of Jesus was probably unleavened, baked in an oven, and flat like a large, thick pancake. To eat it you'd break or tear it.

Jesus claimed the title *bread* from the Greek *ártos*, which means "(figuratively) divine provision; all the sustenance God supplies to yielded believers scene-by-scene to live in His preferred-will."[7] The day before he shared this name, he fed 5,000 plus with nothing more than a little boy's lunch! "In Jesus's hands not enough became more than enough."[8] We each choose what will fill our lives—that which nourishes and keeps us healthy or "fast food" that looks or tastes good but has nearly no lifegiving value. Life with Jesus is satisfying.

Christ also says if we believe with absolute trust, a fully persuaded confident faith in him, we will never thirst. Thirsting by biblical definition is a painful feeling of want or a longing for something to quench the pain. Only Jesus, the Living Water, truly refreshes, supports, and strengthens the soul (John 4:10). Jennifer Kennedy Dean, in her book *Prized*, elaborates: "He [Christ] never creates us with a need that He himself is not the supply."[9]

Scene-by-Scene Provision

In the Lord's prayer, Jesus taught us to ask, "Give us this day our daily bread" (Matthew 6:11). And in a previous Bible study, *Discovering Joy in Philippians*, we spent time processing the comfort of Philippians 4:19 (NIV): "And my God will meet all your needs according to the riches of his glory in Christ Jesus."

I was recently a guest on a podcast where the host asked me to share miracles of God's provision, and I referred to many as "manna" or bread from heaven. Jesus was also connecting himself to God, who led the Israelites out of bondage and provided for them the *bread of life* in the wilderness (Exodus 16:8).

In that interview, I shared so many miracles that time ran out before I could recount them all! In our book *A Couple's Journey with God*, my husband and I share a list of times we trusted God early in our marriage. Our Bread of Life laid a proven track record to help us gain a strong foundation for the faith of our fledgling family:

- We married at age 20 with only part-time jobs and no college diplomas yet. God provided for our needs.

- Bill quit his job and we lived on just my salary so he could finish two years of college in just one packed academic year.

- We had only $10 for a week's worth of groceries and God had us win four bags full in a grocery store sweepstakes we had not even entered! (Later we found out our Sunday school class all wrote our names on their entries.)

- We went without a car for almost an entire year (while working several part-time jobs, volunteering as youth leaders, and carrying full-time college class loads), rode our bikes, and trusted God would somehow provide a car. Our youth group was praying and bought us a bumper sticker that read "I believe in miracles." Nine months later over 150 kids helped place that sticker on a car provided through one of their families for $67!

- We set off for Talbot seminary and Biola University to get training for ministry knowing our part-time job incomes would fall short, and God sent financial support from the parents of the kids we'd mentored.

- We started a family, then bought and remodeled our first home—on a youth pastor's salary.

- We took a cut in pay for Bill to take a senior pastor position at age 28, so two friends pitched in to cover the car payments until it was paid off or we grew the church budget.

- I was a reentry college student, our church was under 100 people, and we had two little kids when my car died. Then a Christian businessman gave us his "old" nice car.

- Wanting our roots to be deep in the community, a church member loaned us money for a property down payment, and together with church members, we hammered up a home in San Diego—and repaid the loan.

- We started our writing and speaking ministry, and God blessed it so we could in turn bless others as we had been blessed.[10]

We call God's provision "God-math." We married young, followed God with whole hearts, worked extremely hard (and still do), and have the delight of experiencing him! Pray bold, God-sized, send-manna-from-heaven prayers not only for you but for all who need the Bread of Life in this world. And when God asks you to be a part of the answer, give the blessing in his name.

Pam

Experiencing Scripture Creatively

- Find or take a digital photo of a graveyard. Using Canva or any photo editing software, type John 5:28-29 on the photo. Share on social media or with friends.

- Follow Karla's instructions at the end of this chapter for writing *hope* in faux calligraphy. Copy it next to the most hopeful verse in your Bible from today's reading.

- Bake or buy special bread to share with your small group as you discuss Jesus as the bread of life.

The Little Details

When Did John Write His Gospel?

Scholars have different opinions about when John wrote his Gospel. They date it after the writing of the other three Gospels, between AD 55 and 95.

John 5:2 reads, "Now there is in Jerusalem by the Sheep Gate a pool." Some scholars argue that this is strong evidence that the Gospel was written prior to AD 70, when Rome destroyed Jerusalem and the temple complex.

Others think John's remark about Jesus's prophecy of Peter's future martyrdom places the Gospel after Peter's crucifixion in AD 64 or 65 (John 21:18-19). They also see John's mention of only the Pharisees as support for a date after the temple's destruction because the Pharisees were the only sect that survived.[11]

One would think that everyone would cheer this amazing healing of one incapacitated for so long.

The Healer

In the Old Testament, God struck the prophetess Miriam with leprosy as punishment for her sin, but Moses prayed for her and God healed her. If Jesus were the prophet like Moses, we would expect God to answer his requests to heal people as well, even those whose illness was a consequence of sin, like Miriam's. And that's what we'll see in today's passage as Jesus approaches an invalid who doesn't know Jesus can heal.

Jesus Is Healer of the Lame

Jesus departed Galilee again.

5. Read John 5:1-2. (a) To where did Jesus return (verse 1)? (b) In verse 2, which of the following did John write?

☐ There is

☐ There was

John's detail about the pool being in existence at the time of his writing suggests that John may have written this Gospel before AD 70 (see sidebar).

6. Read John 5:3-6. (a) How many years had the man been lying there (verse 5)? (b) What did Jesus ask him (verse 6)?

Not everyone who is ill wants healing.

7. Read John 5:7-9. (a) What three things did Jesus tell the man to do (verse 8)? (b) What happened (verse 9)? (c) What day of the week was it?

The Sabbath is the last day of the week for Jews and a day of rest. One would think that everyone would cheer this amazing healing of one incapacitated for so long. Indeed, this miracle seems to fulfill prophecy: "'Behold, your God...will come and save you.'...Then shall the lame man leap like a deer" (Isaiah 35:4,6).

8. Read John 5:10-13. (a) Why did the Jews tell the healed man he shouldn't carry his bed (verse 10)? (b) Why didn't the man know Jesus's name (verse 13)?

The *Jews* rebuke the man for carrying his bed because *it is not lawful*. The law of Moses doesn't forbid carrying a bed; it forbids work on the Sabbath. But the Pharisees have many rules defining work, and these rules include a prohibition against carrying a bed. So by *Jews*, John here means the Pharisees among the Jewish leadership.

Rather than rejoice over the healing, they demand to know who broke their rules.

Jesus Removes Sin's Consequence

9. Read John 5:14-15. (a) What did Jesus tell the man to stop doing (verse 14)? (b) What did the man do (verse 15)? (c) Jump ahead momentarily and read John 6:2. Then turn to the **8 Signs** chart and write "Healed the sick" on line 3.

While not every illness is a result of sin, Jesus ties this infirmity to sin, just as Miriam's leprosy was a result of sin. D.A. Carson writes, "The unavoidable implication is that the bad thing that has already happened was occasioned by the sin which the person must not repeat."[12] The good news, then, is that Jesus can restore those suffering from sin's consequences.

Jesus Is the Son of God Who Rejects Human Traditions

The man responds by telling the indignant Jews that Jesus is the one who healed him and told him to carry his bed. He appears more interested in ingratiating himself to the Jewish leaders than in giving thanks to the one who healed him.

10. Read John 5:16-17. (a) Why did Jews persecute Jesus (verse 16)? (b) What did Jesus respond when they confronted him (verse 17)?

The Pharisees had taken upon themselves the authority to interpret how the law of Moses should apply to people's lives. But Jesus rejects the rules they added to the law. He bases his rejection on the fact that his Father—God—still works on Sabbaths, so he should too. Now, the Pharisees agree that God works on the Sabbath, else the world would fall apart.[13] But they don't think people should. Plus, Jesus's argument angers them because he calls God his Father.

11. In John 5:18 below, underline the two reasons the Jews sought to kill Jesus. Number them in the margin.

    This was why the Jews were seeking all the more to kill him, because not only was he breaking the Sabbath, but he was even calling God his own Father, making himself equal with God.

The Pharisees expect a Messiah who will comply with their interpretation of how to apply Moses's law. But Jesus doesn't do that. Instead, he claims to be God's Son, which would make him greater than Moses, who was merely God's servant.[14]

The good news, then, is that Jesus can restore those suffering from sin's consequences.

The Little Details
D.A. Carson: Work on the Sabbath

The Old Testament had forbidden work on the Sabbath. But what is "work"? The assumption in the Scripture seems to be that "work" refers to one's customary employment; but judging by Mishnah (*Shabbath* 7:2; 10:5), dominant rabbinic opinion had analyzed the prohibition into thirty-nine classes of work, including taking or carrying anything from one domain to another (except for cases of compassion, such as carrying a paralytic). By Old Testament standards, it is not clear the healed man was contravening the law, since he did not normally carry mats around for a living; according to the "tradition of the elders" the man *was* breaking the law, since he was contravening one of the prohibited thirty-nine categories of work to which the law was understood to refer. It is not yet Jesus who is charged with breaking the law...though that will come (v. 18): for the moment, it is the healed man who must face the indignation of *the Jews*—here referring to the religious authorities in Jerusalem.[15]

Jesus's Authority Comes from God

> **12.** Read John 5:19-20. (a) Why did Jesus do what he was doing (verse 19)? (b) What is Jesus's relationship to God the Father (verse 20)? (c) What else were the Jews who questioned him going to see (verse 20)?

Jesus claims he does *only what he sees the Father doing*. Therefore, he sees the Father healing and imitates him. He says the Father loves him, something the Pharisees doubt since they judge him sinful for flouting their rules. Finally, he assures them they will see *greater works* so they *may marvel*. In other words, just as Moses had given signs that God had sent him, so Jesus gives signs that the Father has sent him.

Jesus Is the Giver of Life

What type of works will they see so that they marvel?

> **13.** In John 5:21 below, circle what the Father does. Underline what Jesus does.
>
> For as the Father raises the dead and gives them life, so also the Son gives life to whom he will.

Jesus claims to be able to give life, something that is God's prerogative alone: "See now that I, even I, am he, and there is no god beside me; I kill and I make alive; I wound and I heal; and there is none that can deliver out of my hand" (Deuteronomy 32:39). Certainly, giving life to the dead would powerfully testify that God sent Jesus.

Jesus Is the Ultimate Judge

> **14.** Read John 5:22-23. (a) To whom has the Father given all judgment (verse 22)? (b) Why (verse 23)? (c) If you don't honor the Son, who else don't you honor (verse 23)?

In Moses's day, Moses was the ultimate judge who judged not only the Israelites' disputes but also how to apply God's commands (Exodus 18:13,16). But Jesus claims to be a judge with more authority than even Moses had. He also claims that the Father gave him all judgment so that all may honor him. That implies that not honoring him could have negative consequences come the judgment.

> **15.** ♥ What about you? Do you honor God's Son? Why or why not?

In today's lesson, we saw Jesus heal the lame in fulfillment of prophecy. He heals even when infirmity is the result of sin. He claims to be God's Son. He rejects the rules the Pharisees insist properly interpret Moses's law and claims his authority comes from God. He says he'll show them greater works, for he can give life, something the Jews believe only God can do. This miracle worker also asserts that God has given him all judgment so that all will honor him.

Jesus isn't finished explaining his authority, and we'll pick up that topic again in the next lesson.

Day 3

The Son's Authority

Jesus has healed a lame man on the Sabbath. He told the man to get up, pick up his bed, and walk even though he knows that the Pharisees teach that carrying a bed breaks the Sabbath. When questioned, he tells the Pharisees that he's imitating his Father. And he claims the Father has given him all judgment.

Jesus Links Eternal Life to Judgment

Jesus now links eternal life to the judgment the Father has given him.

> **16.** In John 5:24 below, double underline the first two words. Circle the two actions one takes to have eternal life. Box what such a person does not come into. Underline what that person has passed from and to.
>
> Truly, truly, I say to you, whoever hears my word and believes him who sent me has eternal life. He does not come into judgment, but has passed from death to life.

Jesus starts with a double *truly*, letting us know what follows is important to grasp. He says when we hear his words and believe his Father who sent him, we have eternal life. In other words, when we hear and believe, eternal life begins in us.

Judgment in this verse means negative judgment or condemnation. We won't come into condemnation at the judgment on the last day but have passed out of death into life. That's good news. However, the flip side is that those who reject Jesus will face judgment and condemnation.

> **17.** Read John 5:25-27, which begins with another double *truly*. (a) What will happen to those who hear the Son of God's voice (verse 25)? (b) What does the Son have (verse 26)? (c) What authority does the Son have (verse 27)?

Jesus says he is both the *Son of God* and the *Son of Man*, and that the Father has given him authority to *execute judgment*. Jesus here claims far greater authority than the Pharisees claim for themselves. He claims even greater authority to judge than Moses had. He not only interprets how to apply the law but grants life and executes judgment.

The Little Details
D.A. Carson: Judgment Versus Condemnation

There exists a certain tension between 3:17 and 5:22, but it is more formal than real. The Father does not send the Son into the world to condemn (*krinō*) the world, but he does entrust all judgment (*krisis*) to the Son. The resolution turns in part on the semantic range of *krinō* and its cognates: it can refer to a (usually judicial) principle of discrimination, or to outright condemnation. John 3:17 speaks of the latter; John 5:22 refers more broadly to the former—though, clearly, any judicial discrimination issues in *some* condemnation. More importantly, John 3:17 refers to the *purpose* of the Son's coming: it was *not* to bring condemnation. By contrast, John 5:22 refers to the distinctive roles of Father and Son: the Father entrusts all judgment to the Son. That leaves room for the *purpose* of the Son's coming to be primarily salvific (3:16,17), even though all must face him as their judge, and even though the inevitable *result* of his coming is that some will be condemned.[16]

The Little Details
What Happens When People Die?

When people die, their bodies remain on earth where they decay and return to the dust from which they came. But their souls temporarily go to one of two places. The souls of some go to a place called Hades or Sheol (Psalm 16:10; Luke 16:23). The souls of others go to a place Jesus calls paradise, where they await the resurrection (Luke 16:22; 23:43; 2 Corinthians 12:2-4).

God will resurrect all people, reuniting souls with resurrected bodies. Then comes the judgment (Revelation 20:11-13). Those whose names are not entered in the Book of Life enter the lake of fire, which is also called the second death and hell (Revelation 20:14-15).

Then God will either create a new heaven and earth or renew the current heaven and earth (Revelation 21:1). Those whose names are written in the Book of Life come to the new (or renewed) earth to dwell forever with God, reigning under Jesus (Revelation 21:3; 22:5).

Jesus executes judgment because he is the light that people flee for darkness (John 3:19). He executes judgment because he is the *Son of Man* who is able to relate. Finally, he executes judgment because he is the *Son of Man* who receives everlasting dominion, as Daniel 7:13-14 describes (emphasis mine):

> Behold, with the clouds of heaven
> there came one like a **son of man**,
> and he came to the Ancient of Days
> and was presented before him.
> And to him was given dominion
> and glory and a kingdom,
> that all peoples, nations, and languages
> should serve him;
> his dominion is an everlasting dominion,
> which shall not pass away,
> and his kingdom one
> that shall not be destroyed.

18. In John 5:28-29 below, circle who will hear Jesus's voice. Underline where those who have done good will go. Box where those who have done evil will go.

Do not marvel at this, for an hour is coming when all who are in the tombs will hear his voice and come out, those who have done good to the resurrection of life, and those who have done evil to the resurrection of judgment.

Jesus says the dead will hear his voice and arise to one of two places. He is talking about the final resurrection and judgment of which we read in Daniel 12:1-2 on Day 1. His are audacious claims, so Jesus backs them up by citing witnesses.

Witnesses Support Jesus's Claims

If God is not with Jesus, how can he heal? If his claims are not true, why does God allow him to heal an invalid? The healing bears witness that God sent Jesus.

The Healing Bears Witness

19. (a) Was Jesus healing people on his own (John 5:30)? (b) Why was Jesus's judgment just?

Jesus states the obvious: A human can't miraculously heal another person on his own. The healing is a sign God has sent him. Not only that, but God speaks to him so he can judge according to what he hears. And personal desires aren't clouding his judgment as they are the Pharisees' judgment. Instead, he seeks the Father's will, not his own.

John the Baptist Bore Witness

20. Read John 5:31-33. (a) If Jesus were the only one making these claims about himself, what would be the conclusion (verse 31)? (b) To whom had they talked who had also testified about who Jesus was (verses 32-33)?

They had sent for John the Baptist and heard what he said about Jesus (John 1:19-28). After all, most believe John was a true prophet.

21. Read John 5:34-35. (a) Why does Jesus remind them of John's testimony (verse 34)? (b) What had John the Baptist been (verse 35)? (c) How had they reacted to John (verse 35)?

John 3:24 describes events that happened before John's imprisonment. Here, Jesus says John the Baptist *was* a lamp. That suggests the Baptist is at this point in prison or dead. His beheading in prison was common knowledge to the author's first readers.

John the Baptist had testified that Jesus ranked before him because he existed before him, even though John was older (John 1:15). He said that Jesus was the Lamb of God who takes away the sin of the world (John 1:29); the one who baptizes with the Holy Spirit (1:33); the Son of God (1:34); and the Christ, or Messiah (3:28).

Jesus said John was a lamp: someone who lights the way for others by teaching God's truth. Jesus points out that the Jews to whom he is speaking had rejoiced in John's words for a time. So why then are they now rejecting John's testimony about Jesus?

John is not the only witness to who Jesus is, however.

The Father Bears Witness

22. Read John 5:36-38. (a) What greater testimony than John did Jesus have (verse 36)? (b) Who else bore witness about Jesus (verse 37)? (c) Why did Jesus's opponents not believe Jesus's words (verse 38)?

The miraculous works that the Father gives Jesus to do (such as healing the invalid) testify that he comes from God. In fact, the Father himself bears witness about Jesus, but the Pharisees reject his witness because, unlike Moses and Jesus, they haven't heard the Father's voice and don't have the Father's word abiding in them.

> The miraculous works that the Father gives Jesus to do (such as healing the invalid) testify that he comes from God.

The Little Details

D.A. Carson: Others Who Claimed to Be the Messiah (John 5:44)

The reason why Jesus's interlocutors were eager to accept messianic claimants who came in their own name but were unwilling to receive the one who came in the Father's name is now made clear. Like most people then and now, they were heavily dependent on accepting *praise* (*doxa*) *from one another*; they made *no effort to obtain the praise* (*doxa*) *that comes from God*...Inevitably, that meant they were open to messianic claimants who used flattery or who panted after great reputations or whose values were so closely attuned to their audience that their audience felt they were very wise and farsighted; they were not open to the Messiah that Jesus was turning out to be, one who thought the only *doxa* ("glory"/"praise") worth pursuing was the glory of God.[17]

If they sought glory from God rather than from people, their eyes would open to the witness of Scripture, their hearts to the word of God, their minds to the evidence of the signs, and their ears to the testimony of John the Baptist.

The Scripture Bears Witness

The Scripture—God's words—also bears witness.

> **23.** Read John 5:39-40. (a) What else bears witness about Jesus (verse 39)? (b) What are those talking to him refusing to do (verse 40)?

The Pharisees had searched the Scriptures to find the path to eternal life, but when the Scriptures pointed to Jesus, they refused to come to him. Therefore, God's words in the form of Scripture do not abide in them. Because Jesus ignores the Pharisees' rules surrounding the Sabbath, they set aside the evidence Scripture provides.

Jesus Discerns His Listeners' Problem

Why did the Jewish leaders ignore all the evidence about who Jesus is?

> **24.** Read John 5:41-44. (a) From whom does Jesus not seek glory (verse 41)? (b) What does Jesus know about his listeners (verse 42)? (c) Jesus says he came in his Father's name, but what is the result (verse 43)? (d) What causes their unbelief (verse 44)?

Jesus names the crux of the problem: They seek glory from people rather than from God. Jesus ignores the rules on which they pride themselves, and that stings their pride. He neither praises them nor seeks their favor, and that offends them. He claims a more intimate relationship with God, and that incenses them as blasphemy.

If they sought glory from God rather than from people, their eyes would open to the witness of Scripture, their hearts to the word of God, their minds to the evidence of the signs, and their ears to the testimony of John the Baptist.

Jesus Names the Jews' Accuser

> **25.** In John 5:45-46 below, circle the name of the one who will accuse them at the judgment. Underline the reason.
>
> Do not think that I will accuse you to the Father. There is one who accuses you: Moses, on whom you have set your hope. For if you believed Moses, you would believe me; for he wrote of me.

Moses wrote that one day God would send a prophet like himself and that the people must listen to him (Deuteronomy 18:15). Here before them stands one who gives many indicators that he is that prophet. If they truly believe Moses, they will believe Jesus. D.A. Carson writes, "If scrupulous adherence to the law brings people to hope for salvation in the law itself and to reject the Messiah to whom the law pointed, then the law itself, and its human author, Moses, must stand up in outraged accusation."[18]

Their reaction to a miraculous healing and their rejection of what that healing signifies cast light on Jesus's words to Nicodemus: "And this is the judgment: the light has come into the world, and people loved the darkness rather than the light because their works were evil" (John 3:19-21).

> 26. ♥ What can you do to be sure you're not studying Scripture simply to know Scripture but studying it to know the Giver of Scripture?

To sum up, Jesus claims he is the ultimate judge, but those who believe in him pass from death to life. They are not condemned. Witnesses provide evidence that Jesus is who he claims to be: Miraculous healings, John the Baptist's testimony, the Father's words to those who listen, and Scripture all testify. But those who seek glory from people rather than from God ignore evidence that might lose them human favor. In the next lesson, we'll see Jesus offering even greater evidence that he is the prophet like Moses.

 Day 4

The Bread of Life

People need water to live. So when Jesus told the Samaritan woman that he offered water that gives eternal life, he meant he had something necessary for her to live. In the passages we'll read today, Jesus compares himself to another of life's essentials: food. He also offers more signs that he is the prophet of which Moses spoke.

Jesus Demonstrates He Is the Prophet Like Moses

After Jesus heals the lame man, the Jewish leaders hesitate to embrace him because he told the man to carry his mat on the Sabbath, something the Pharisees forbid. But the crowds are impressed and respond differently—at least at first.

Like Moses, Jesus Leads His Followers to a Mountain

> 27. Read John 6:1-4. (a) Where did Jesus go (verse 1)? (b) Why did a crowd follow (verse 2)? (c) Where did Jesus sit (verse 3)? (d) What feast was at hand (verse 4)?

After the angel passed over the Israelites protected by lambs' blood, Moses led the people to a mountain in a wilderness. Here near the feast that celebrated that deliverance, Jesus leads Israelites to another mountain in a wilderness. John does not want us to miss the Passover connection as he introduces the next narrative.

The Little Details
What Moses Wrote About Jesus (John 5:46)

Genesis 3:15: God promises Eve an offspring who will bruise the head of the serpent who deceived her. Jesus was born of a woman and destroyed the devil's works (Hebrews 2:14; 1 John 3:8).

Genesis 22: The prophets Abraham and Isaac act out a father giving his son as an offering. Abraham receives his son back as a type of the Father receiving his Son back by resurrection (Hebrews 11:17-19).

Exodus 12: The Passover lambs save from death as a type of Jesus (1 Corinthians 5:7).

Leviticus 5: The sin sacrifices foreshadow Jesus's sacrifice (John 1:29). Indeed, the entire sacrificial system points to Jesus.

Numbers 21:9: When venomous serpents bite the Israelites, they can live by looking to the bronze serpent that Moses lifted up. The bronze serpent foreshadowed Jesus being lifted up to give life to all who look to him to save them from death.

Deuteronomy 18:15: Jesus is the prophet like Moses prophesied in this verse.

The Little Details
Why Jesus Asked Philip

In John 6:5, Jesus asks Philip where to buy bread. The reason he asked Philip is found in Luke. Luke 9:10 identifies the village to which Jesus withdrew before feeding the crowd as Bethsaida, a village on the Sea of Galilee. That was Philip's hometown (John 1:44). Thus, Jesus asks Philip where to buy food because he was from the area. This is an example of the different Gospels supporting and explaining each other.

That Luke explains John is called an *undesigned coincidence*. Such coincidences are strong evidence for the historic reliability of the Gospels. In her book, *Hidden in Plain View*, Lydia McGrew writes, "The evidence from undesigned coincidences would be difficult to fake, and it would be even more unlikely to come about by sheer chance in non-factual or manipulated stories."[19]

- -

Just as Moses showed control over the Red Sea by parting its waters shortly after the original Passover deliverance, so now Jesus shows control over the Sea of Galilee.

- -

28. Read John 6:5-9. (a) What did Jesus ask Philip (verse 5)? (b) What did Andrew say a boy had (verse 9)?

Jesus asks Philip where to buy bread because Philip comes from the area.

Like Moses, Jesus Miraculously Feeds Israelites

29. Read John 6:10-13. (a) How many men were there (verse 10)? (b) What did Jesus do before he distributed bread (verse 11)? (c) Why did Jesus want the fragments gathered (verse 12)? (d) How many baskets did they fill from fragments (verse 13)?

With women and children, the crowd may have been as large as 20,000. The number of men is significant because of what they will try to do shortly. That they gathered 12 baskets of fragments is significant too: Jesus amply supplies what the 12 tribes of Israel need.

Like Moses's Followers Believed God Sent Him, the Crowds Conclude That God Sent Jesus

When Moses displayed the signs the Lord gave him, the people believed God sent him and worshiped the Lord (Exodus 4:30-31).

30. In John 6:14 below, circle the word *sign*. Underline what the people concluded from it. Turn to the **8 Signs** chart in the back and write "Multiplied bread and fish" on line 4.

> When the people saw the sign that he had done, they said, "This is indeed the Prophet who is to come into the world!"

The people immediately connect Jesus feeding them miraculously with Moses feeding the Israelites in the wilderness miraculously. Therefore, they conclude God sent him and he must be the prophet like Moses.

31. In John 6:15 below, underline the reason Jesus withdrew.

> Perceiving then that they were about to come and take him by force to make him king, Jesus withdrew again to the mountain by himself.

Some of the people think the prophet like Moses will surely free them from subjugation to Rome just as Moses freed the people from subjugation to Egypt. Unlike the Jewish leaders, members of this crowd have no trouble connecting the prophet like Moses to the Messiah. That's why they want to crown Jesus king and revolt against Rome immediately. If he refuses, the 5,000 men could rebel anyway, crown him, and force his hand. But that is not in God's plan for Jesus, so he withdraws alone.

32. ♥ Describe a time when others wanted you to do something you didn't believe God wanted you to do. How did you get out of it? How did the others react?

The Little Details
The Sea of Galilee
The Sea of Galilee gradually became known as the Sea of Tiberias because of a city by that name on its west shore. The city was named after the Roman emperor Tiberias Caesar.[20]

Like Moses, Jesus Displays Power over a Sea

33. Read John 6:16-19. (a) What part of the day was it when the disciples started rowing (verse 16)? (b) How far had they rowed across the sea when Jesus came to them (verse 19)? (c) What was their reaction when they saw Jesus (verse 19)?

Just as Moses showed control over the Red Sea by parting its waters shortly after the original Passover deliverance, so now Jesus shows control over the Sea of Galilee. John is piling up the evidence that Jesus is the prophet like Moses.

Like Moses, Jesus Delivers His Followers Through a Sea

34. Read John 6:20-21. (a) What did Jesus say to his disciples (verse 20)? (b) What happened as soon as he entered the boat (verse 21)? (c) Turn to the **8 Signs** chart and write "Walked on water" on line 5.

The disciples are about three miles across the lake when they see Jesus. Jesus says, "It is I," which can be translated "I am," perhaps alluding to the name by which the Lord identified himself to Moses. Jesus enters the boat, and immediately they are at their destination. Just as Moses took his followers miraculously through a sea to their destination, so now Jesus takes his disciples miraculously through a sea to theirs.

The Crowds Seek Jesus

The next day, the crowds look for but can't find Jesus.

35. Read John 6:22-24. What did the crowds do when they realized Jesus was gone (verse 24)?

The crowds seek the miracle worker.

36. Read John 6:25-26. (a) According to Jesus, what was not the reason the crowds sought him (verse 26)? (b) What was their reason (verse 26)?

Just as Moses took his followers miraculously through a sea to their destination, so now Jesus takes his disciples miraculously through a sea to theirs.

The crowds want to know when Jesus managed to leave. Jesus ignores their question and responds to the intention of their hearts. They don't seek him because the signs point to who he is—the prophet like Moses. Rather, they seek him because he filled their bellies. They want the gift rather than knowledge of the Giver.

In this lesson, we saw Jesus demonstrate that he is the prophet of which Moses spoke. Just as bread from heaven miraculously fed those following Moses, so bread and fish miraculously feeds those following Jesus. The crowd concludes that God sent Jesus, but when they decide to force Jesus to become king, he withdraws from them. Just as Moses had power over the Red Sea and parted its waters to deliver his followers through it, so Jesus has power over the Sea of Galilee and walks on its waters before delivering his disciples through it. In the next lesson, Jesus will explain what the multiplied bread means.

Day 5

The Giver or the Gift

In the last lesson, Jesus told the crowd that they sought the signs rather than what the signs signified. In other words, they wanted the gifts over the Giver.

Like Moses, Jesus Teaches the People

Here is another way John shows Jesus is the prophet like Moses.

> **37.** In John 6:27-29 below, box what Jesus told the crowds not to work for. Underline what they should work for instead. Double underline what they must do to be doing the works of God.
>
> "Do not work for the food that perishes, but for the food that endures to eternal life, which the Son of Man will give to you. For on him God the Father has set his seal." Then they said to him, "What must we do, to be doing the works of God?" Jesus answered them, "This is the work of God, that you believe in him whom he has sent."

The people seek food that won't last, but Jesus tells them to seek food that endures to eternal life: believing in the one the Father sent. What God wants is faith.

> **38.** Read John 6:30-31. (a) What do the people want Jesus to do before they believe him (verse 30)? (b) To what bread do they refer (verse 31)?

Formerly, God gave bread from heaven (manna) that gave temporary life to people. Now, God gives bread from heaven (Jesus) who will give eternal life to people.

On the day before, Jesus gave a sign that he is the prophet like Moses, and they claimed to believe he was. Still, he fed only 5,000 once, while the manna fed more than 600,000 for 40 years.[21] They counter that if he's the prophet like Moses, ought he not give greater signs?

Jesus Is the Bread of Life

The crowds want more of what they saw the day prior.

39. Read John 6:32-34. (a) Who gave bread from heaven in the desert (verse 32)? (b) Who is the bread of God (verse 33)? (c) What do the people want (verse 34)?

Jesus says it was his Father who gave the bread from heaven called manna. But that bread from heaven merely foreshadowed him. Formerly, God gave bread from heaven (manna) that gave temporary life to people. Now, God gives bread from heaven (Jesus) who will give eternal life to people. But his listeners misunderstand him. Since they know he can multiply bread, they ask him to do so always.

40. In John 6:35 below, circle the words "I am." Underline what Jesus calls himself. In the **7 "I Am" Statements** chart at the back of the book, notice that what you underlined and the verse reference are filled in for you.

    Jesus said to them, "I am the bread of life."

This is one of the seven great "I am" statements in John's Gospel. In these, Jesus tells people who he is by using a reference to God's name for himself: I AM. Here, he calls himself the bread of life. As bread enables earthly life, so Jesus enables eternal life.

41. Read John 6:35-36. (a) What will happen to those who come to Jesus (verse 35)? (b) What will happen to those who believe in him (verse 35)? (c) Did the people believe in Jesus (verse 36)?

Unlike the former bread from heaven, which had to be eaten daily, people need to come to Jesus but once. Coming to Jesus satisfies the hunger for life.

Nonetheless, Jesus refuses their request to provide literal bread, whether manna or barley. What he gave them the prior day was a sign that God sent him and that they ought, therefore, to believe his message.

But while they are ready to believe he is the prophet like Moses and the Messiah, they aren't ready to believe he is the bread of life.

Jesus Receives All Who Come to Him

Still, Jesus encourages them to believe.

42. In John 6:37 below, underline who will come to Jesus. Double underline Jesus's response to those who come to him.

    All that the Father gives me will come to me, and whoever comes to me I will never cast out.

That's good news: Jesus welcomes and keeps those who come to him.

The Little Details
D.A. Carson: "Shall Not Hunger"
So the hungry and thirsty person who comes to Jesus finds his hunger satisfied and his thirst quenched. This does not mean there is no need for continued dependence upon him, for continued feeding upon him; it does mean there is no longer that core emptiness that the initial encounter with Jesus has met. The consummating satiation occurs when those "who have washed their robes...in the blood of the Lamb" stand "before the throne of God" and experience the oracle: "Never again will they hunger; never again will they thirst" (Rev. 7:14-16).[22]

But while they are ready to believe he is the prophet like Moses and the Messiah, they aren't ready to believe he is the bread of life.

Jesus Offers Eternal Life to Those Who Believe in Him

Jesus explains the life he offers.

> **43.** Read John 6:38-40. (a) From where did Jesus come (verse 38)? (b) Why (verse 38)? (c) What was God's will (verse 39)? (d) What will those who believe in the Son have (verse 40)? (e) What will Jesus do for them (verse 40)?

Jesus does not offer barley loaves that sustain for mere hours. Rather, he offers eternal life—a divine prerogative. Indeed, he will raise all who believe in him into eternal life.

Like Moses's Followers, Jesus's Followers Grumble

The crowd grows annoyed that Jesus won't give them the bread they asked to have.

> **44.** Read John 6:41-43. (a) How do the Jews respond to Jesus's offer of eternal life (verse 41)? (b) What does Jesus command (verse 43)?

Since they know who his parents are, the people scoff at Jesus's claim to have come from heaven. Just as their forefathers grumbled when they didn't get food when and how they wanted it in the desert, so the Galileans grumble over Jesus's refusal to feed them as they want and at his insistence that he came from heaven to give life. The grumbling of Moses's followers was a great sin that prevented many from entering the promised land (Numbers 14:27-30). Now Jesus cautions his followers not to grumble.

Jesus Will Raise to Life Those Who Come to Him

> **45.** Read John 6:44-46. (a) What must happen before one can come to Jesus (verse 44)? (b) How will that happen (verse 45)? (c) Who is the only one who has seen God (verse 46)?

God will draw people to Jesus by giving them insight or understanding, perhaps as they read Scripture, pray, or listen to someone. Jesus paraphrases Isaiah 54:13 to explain what he means. Still, that's not the same as seeing God, which is another reason they should listen to Jesus's words and pray for insight from God.

God will draw people to Jesus by giving them insight or understanding, perhaps as they read Scripture, pray, or listen to someone.

The Good News

Jesus heals a lame man but rejects the Pharisees' ban against carrying a mat on the Sabbath. He seeks glory from God, not people. He claims his authority comes from God and that he is both the giver of life and the ultimate judge. His miraculous signs, John the Baptist's testimony, the Father, and the Scripture all bear witness to who he is. He demonstrates that he is the prophet like Moses by multiplying food and exerting power over a sea. He claims to be the bread of life.

46. ♥ Which of these items of good news means the most to you today? Why?

In this chapter, we saw that the leaders of the Pharisees opposed Jesus because he rejected the rules they had added as a hedge around the law of Moses. In the next chapter, we'll finish reading Jesus's discussion on the bread of life, and we'll see him use another Jewish feast to demonstrate how the Old Testament points to him.

Praise God for something you saw of his character this week. **Confess** anything that convicted you. **Ask** for help to do something God's Word calls you to do. **Thank** God for something you learned this week.

Karla's Creative Connection

Shortly after I heard the good news of the gospel and put my faith in Jesus, I took a calligraphy class at a nearby community college. I spent hours practicing each letter of the alphabet, and I had no idea that it was the beginning of a lifelong love affair with hand lettering and the perfect avenue for sharing my newfound love for God's Word. Fast-forward to today and you can see my love for both is still alive and well. But my hand lettering now includes a variety of fun and creative styles.

One of my favorite lettering styles is faux calligraphy, and I'm excited to share the basics of it with you here. The word *faux* literally means "fake," so faux calligraphy is simply a technique you can use to fake or imitate the look of traditional or brush calligraphy with its classic contrast of thick and thin strokes. It's easier than you might think, and you can use any writing instrument, including a pen, a pencil, or a marker, so let's get started.

Because our faith in the good news gives us hope for eternal life in Christ, let's use the word *hope* for our example.

Write your word in cursive, making sure your letters and loops are nice and open. My natural tendency is to write vertically but you can add as much slant as suits you.

As you write your words, begin to pay close attention to the downstrokes, where your hand moves in a downward direction, because you only add thickness to the downstrokes and the upstrokes stay thin.

Next, add a second line parallel to the downstrokes. Note that these lines mimic the curve of the downstrokes and, if two letters are too close together, you can add your new line to whichever side works best.

Now just fill in the spaces you created and you'll see how closely your lettering resembles traditional calligraphy! In this step, you can also adjust the thickness to keep them consistent.

Any cursive writing can be transformed into this beautiful letterform with a little practice, so please remember that it's about the process, not perfection! You can even start using it today to address envelopes, create titles in your planner, letter with chalk on your blackboard, or combine it with other hand lettering to create your own Bible journaling designs.

Karla

Chapter 4

John 6:47–8:36
Finding Truth

How did Jesus correct misconceptions about who he was?

Day 1

Rethinking Expectations

When I was a young teenager sitting on the lawn of my front yard reading a paperback New Testament, John 5–8 challenged everything I believed about the Bible and Jesus. I believed a good God would want to let people know how to reach him in a way that didn't depend on just hearsay. I thought God would want to put such an important message into written form because an all-powerful God would be able to keep the message intact through the ages. I believed the Bible was likely that medium.

But I also believed Jesus was an angry, argumentative cynic who couldn't get along with anyone. When I read the first three Gospels, I reconciled those two beliefs by picturing God as like my Mexican American grandfather: loving but fooled by my parents' lies and thus blind to their flaws. I thought God was likewise blind to his Son's flaws. I realized that made him less powerful, yet it seemed the only way to resolve these issues.

John 5:23 blew that all away: "Whoever does not honor the Son does not honor the Father who sent him." I thought, *But I don't honor the Son. I don't even like him. How can it be that not honoring the Son means I'm not honoring the Father?*

I needed more information, so I read through the chapters we'll read today.

The Good News Challenges Expectations

Just as the good news in John's Gospel challenged my beliefs about Scripture and Jesus, so the same good news challenged what the people in Jesus's day believed about Scripture and the Messiah.

- The Jewish leader and Pharisee Nicodemus thought the miraculous signs Jesus offered indicated God sent him, but Nicodemus wasn't immediately ready to abandon his preconceptions about what the Messiah would be like.

- When a Samaritan woman saw evidence that Jesus was a prophet, she allowed him to correct her beliefs and embraced his claim to be the expected Prophet and Messiah.

- Pharisees took offense at Jesus healing a man and telling him to carry his mat on the Sabbath. They held on to their belief that the Messiah would uphold the Pharisees' oral traditions and rejected the miracle as evidence of anything.

- A crowd believed that Jesus's miraculous feeding was a sign that he was the

The Little Details
The Water Ceremony at the Feast of Booths

During the Feast of Booths, the morning celebrations included a **water ceremony.** The high priest led a procession to the Pool of Siloam, where he drew **water** and carried it in a golden pitcher to the altar amid trumpet blasts and choir songs. The people shouted thanks to God as they raised citrus in one hand and shook a bundle of sticks tied with palm in the other. They thanked God for giving their forefathers **water** in the wilderness and for giving them **rain** and fruit. They prayed for **rain** the next year because the dry summer has left their cisterns nearly empty, reminding them of their forefathers' need for water in the desert.[4] As the priest **poured the pool water** and wine out to the Lord, they looked forward to the day when the Lord would **pour out his Spirit** (Joel 2:28-29).

They repeated this ceremony every day for six days. Then on the seventh day, they repeated it seven times.[5]

prophet like Moses. They wanted to force him to be king and lead a revolt against Rome. But they were confused when Jesus neither rebelled against Rome as they expected the Messiah to do nor fed them daily like Moses had.

1. ♥ What about the good news has challenged your beliefs or currently challenges the beliefs of someone you know?

God's Word to Us in the Old Testament

The chapters we'll read in John today refer to significant Jewish customs we haven't yet looked at together. So let's read about them now. Once again, I've bolded the text you'll encounter in John's Gospel.

The Lord Gave Abraham Circumcision as a Sign of a Covenant

God made a covenant with Abraham in which he promised to give his descendants the promised land. The sign of the covenant was that all the males of his household had to be circumcised, and all future **boys must be circumcised at eight days old.**[1]

Later, Moses led Abraham's descendants to the promised land. One of the laws God gave them was that they must continue to **circumcise baby boys at eight days old**.[2] This signified that they were part of God's covenant with Abraham.

Sadly, centuries later the people performed circumcision as a mere rite devoid of its meaning. Jeremiah prophesied judgment on "all those who are **circumcised merely in the flesh**" and were "**uncircumcised in heart**."[3]

The Lord Gave the Israelites the Feast of Booths for Remembrance

As Moses led the people **out of slavery** through the wilderness, they built **booths** (or **tabernacles**) for shelter at night. The presence of the Lord guided them as a pillar of cloud during the day and a **pillar of light at night**.[6]

In the desert, they needed food and water. So the Lord gave them **bread from heaven**, which they called **manna**.[7] When they ran out of **water**, the Lord told Moses, "Behold, I will stand before you there on the rock at Horeb, and you shall strike the rock, and **water shall come out** of it, and the people will drink."[8]

So the people would never forget how God took care of them, the Lord commanded them to celebrate the **Feast of Booths** (the **Festival of Tabernacles** in the NIV) every fall in the promised land. They built **booths** out of branches and palm leaves to live in for one week.[9] They also brought branches and provisions for a seven-day feast. All week, they celebrated how God had given rain and a harvest of grapes, olives, and citrus. On the eighth day, they moved back into homes for a final celebration commemorating the Israelites' arrival in the promised land.

During the days of the second temple, the joyous celebration of God's provision of **water**, harvest, and the pillar of **light** that guided the exodus, as well as his **future pouring out of his Spirit**, grew elaborate. In fact, mornings began with a spectacular **water** ceremony, and evenings ended with dancing and singing at an extravagant **light** ceremony (see sidebars).

God Promised "I Am He Who Blots Out Your Transgressions"

In addition to reading about the customs surrounding circumcision and the Feast of Booths, we'll read more references to Isaiah. In Isaiah, the Lord gave seven dramatic "**I am he**" statements that declare his power to save. We'll look at two that follow the first mention of the suffering servant.

> 2. In Isaiah 43:10 below, underline why the Lord chooses people to be his witnesses and his servants (begin with the word *that*). Box *believe*. Circle "I am he."
>
> "You are my witnesses," declares the LORD, "and my servant whom I have chosen, that you may know and believe me and understand that I am he. Before me no god was formed, nor shall there be any after me."

In one of the "I am he" statements in Isaiah, the Lord foretells what he will do about Israel's sin problem.

> 3. In Isaiah 43:25 below, circle "I am he" and underline two things the Lord will do.
>
> "I, I am he who blots out your transgressions for my own sake, and I will not remember your sins."

God's Word to Us in John

In today's reading, we'll finish the bread of life conversation and then see how Jesus uses the water and light ceremonies to declare good news.

> 🗨 Take a moment to pray for insight as you read God's Word.

> 4. ♥ Read John 6:47–8:36. What stands out to you? Why?

In this lesson, we saw that God instituted circumcision as a sign of his covenant with Abraham and his descendants. Later, he continued that sign in the law of Moses by requiring baby boys to be circumcised at eight days old. The Lord declared that he chose the people of Israel to know and believe and understand that "I am he." He said that "I, I am he" who will one day remove his people's sins.

In the next lesson, we'll see Jesus continue to demonstrate that he is the prophet like Moses.

The Little Details
The Light Ceremony at the Feast of Booths

The nightly celebrations during the Feast of Booths included a **ceremony of lights**. In the temple's court of women towered four giant, golden candlesticks topped with four golden bowls each. Younger priests scrambled up ladders and poured oil into the bowls to feed the lamps. Then they lit the **lights** in remembrance of the **pillar of light** that guided their forefathers in the wilderness. The Mishna records that the light was so bright that it illuminated every courtyard in Jerusalem.

The people took **torches** in their hands, and everyone danced and sang as the temple orchestras played harps, lyres, cymbals, and trumpets.[10]

The Lord declared that he chose the people of Israel to know and believe and understand that "I am he." He said that "I, I am he" who will one day remove his people's sins.

Pam's Heart-to-Heart with the Great I Am—
"I Am the Gate of the Sheep"

Therefore Jesus said again, "Very truly I tell you, I am the gate for the sheep.
All who have come before me are thieves and robbers, but the sheep have not listened to them.
I am the gate; whoever enters through me will be saved.
They will come in and go out, and find pasture.
The thief comes only to steal and kill and destroy;
I have come that they may have life, and have it to the full."
John 10:7-10 NIV

A rule on the farm I grew up on was repeated over and over: "Shut and *lock* the gate behind you!" Livestock and people were in danger if animals wandered onto the road.

When Jesus explains, "I am the gate for the sheep," he pictures the Holy Land sheep pen enclosures made of piled rocks with bushes, thorns, or sticks along the top to protect the sheep from wild animals. In these pens, the shepherd himself sits in the entrance. Jesus makes it clear that a person must *enter* through him to be saved. In addition, the sheep go in and out through the Shepherd to access the nourishing pasture.

I appreciate how clear Jesus makes the decision to enter through him by explaining what is on each side of him, the Gate. Those who claimed to be Messiah before Jesus were sneaky thieves and violent robbers, marauders, and bandits. Then Jesus points to *the* Thief (the devil) who comes to steal (in secret), kill (butcher and slay), and destroy (utterly obliterate).

In contrast, Jesus comes to give life to the full: abundant, more than enough, greater, continually ample, preeminent, and passing all expectations. As a child, I entered through the Gate to gain salvation, but it was in college that I grasped the vital watershed decision of daily choosing to follow the Shepherd while turning my back on the temptations of Satan.

The contrast of good versus evil appears many times in Scripture. Below, in gray pencil, color what to remove from your life. Then in a bright color, circle what activities and traits to keep.

> You must no longer walk as the Gentiles do, in the futility of their minds...They have become callous and have given themselves up to sensuality, greedy to practice every kind of impurity. But that is not the way you learned Christ!...As the truth is in Jesus, to **put off your old self**, which belongs to your former manner of life and is corrupt through deceitful desires, and to be renewed in the spirit of your minds, and to **put on the new self**, created after the likeness of God in true righteousness and holiness.

> Therefore, having put away falsehood, let each one of you speak the truth with his neighbor, for we are members one of another. Be angry and do not sin; do not let the sun go down on your anger, and give no opportunity to the devil. Let the thief no longer steal, but rather let him labor, doing honest work with his own hands, so that he may have something to share with anyone in need. Let no corrupting talk come out of your mouths, but only such as is good for building up...Let all bitterness and wrath and anger and clamor and slander be put away from you, along with all malice. Be kind to one another, tenderhearted, forgiving one another, as God in Christ forgave you (Ephesians 4:17-32, emphasis added).

> Put to death therefore what is earthly in you: sexual immorality, impurity, passion, evil desire, and covetousness, which is idolatry...But now you must put them all away: anger, wrath, malice, slander, and obscene talk from your mouth. Do not lie to one another, seeing that you have **put off the old self** with its practices and have **put on the new self**...

Put on then, as God's chosen ones, holy and beloved, compassionate hearts, kindness, humility, meekness, and patience, bearing with one another and, if one has a complaint against another, forgiving each other; as the Lord has forgiven you, so you also must forgive. And above all these put on love, which binds everything together in perfect harmony. And let the peace of Christ rule in your hearts...And be thankful. Let the word of Christ dwell in you richly, teaching and admonishing one another in all wisdom, singing psalms and hymns and spiritual songs, with thankfulness in your hearts to God. And whatever you do, in word or deed, do everything in the name of the Lord Jesus, giving thanks to God the Father through him (Colossians 3:5-17, emphasis added).

The **acts of the flesh** are obvious: sexual immorality, impurity, and debauchery; idolatry and witchcraft; hatred, discord, jealousy, fits of rage, selfish ambition, dissensions, factions, and envy; drunkenness, orgies, and the like. I warn you, as I did before, that those who live like this will not inherit the kingdom of God.

But the **fruit of the Spirit** is love, joy, peace, forbearance, kindness, goodness, faithfulness, gentleness and self-control. Against such things there is no law. Those who belong to Christ Jesus have crucified the flesh with its passions and desires (Galatians 5:19-24 NIV, emphasis added).

What choices and actions will help you enter through Jesus, the Gate, and live that abundant life? What measures will help you *lock* the gate behind you?

Pam

Experiencing Scripture Creatively

- In your Bible next to John 8:32 or in a journal, write the word *abide* in block letters, following Karla's instructions at the end of this chapter.

- If you've camped in tents before, discuss with children what it's like to return home after camping. (Or if you own a tent, set it up in the yard. Live in it for an afternoon or a day.) Discuss how camping in a tent is different from living in a home. Then discuss how living on this earth in our current temporary bodies is different from living in the new heavens and earth with our resurrected immortal bodies (1 Corinthians 5:1-4).

Words of Eternal Life

In the last chapter, we read that the crowd grumbled over Jesus saying, "I am the bread that came down from heaven."[11] Jesus responded that all those who hear and learn from the Father will come to him. Let's jump back in where we left off.

Jesus Is the Living Bread from Heaven

> **5.** Read John 6:47-51. (a) What will those who believe him have (verse 47)? (b) What happened to those who ate manna in the wilderness (verse 49)? (c) What does Jesus call himself in verse 51? (d) What is the bread he will give (verse 51)?

Jesus begins with the literal statement *whoever believes has eternal life.* Then he extends his previous metaphor: *If anyone eats of this bread, he will live forever.* This tells us that *believes* (verse 47) is equivalent to *eats of this bread* (verse 51).

He explains that manna did not grant eternal life. But Jesus does, and he will do so by giving his *flesh*. Of course, we know what the crowd doesn't yet know: "And the Word became flesh and dwelt among us" (John 1:14).

Jesus Will Raise to Life Those Who Believe in Him

> **6.** Read John 6:52-55. (a) What did Jesus say the people must do to have life (verse 53)? (b) What will Jesus do for such people (verse 54)? (c) Why (verse 55)?

I will raise him up on the last day is God's prerogative. Let's examine this.

> **7.** Compare John 6:40 with John 6:54 below (emphases mine). Notice that the italicized portions say the same thing in a slightly different way. Draw an arrow from the underlined portion of verse 40 to the underlined portion of verse 54.
>
> *"Everyone who <u>looks on the Son and believes in him</u>*
> *should have eternal life, and I will raise him up on the last day"* (John 6:40).
>
> *"Whoever <u>feeds on my flesh and drinks my blood</u>*
> *has eternal life, and I will raise him up on the last day"* (John 6:54).

Jesus returns to his metaphor. The person who *looks on the Son and believes in him* (verse 40) becomes the person who *feeds on my flesh and drinks my blood* (verse 54). His *flesh is true food* and his *blood is true drink* because they sustain life eternally rather than just briefly as the wilderness manna and water did.

He explains that manna did not grant eternal life. But Jesus does, and he will do so by giving his *flesh*.

Those Who Abide in Jesus Will Live Forever

The people are aghast. After all, the law forbids even eating meat with blood still in it, let alone drinking blood. In fact, blood is reserved for sacrifices.

> 8. In John 6:56 below, circle *feeds on my flesh* and *drinks my blood*. Underline the last seven words. Draw an arrow from the circled words to the underlined words.
>
> Whoever feeds on my flesh and drinks my blood abides in me, and I in him.

Thus, *feeds on my flesh* and *drinks my blood* are metaphors for *abides in me, and I in him*.

Jesus Claims to Be Greater Than Moses

Moses never offered eternal life as Jesus claims he can offer.

> 9. Read John 6:57-59. (a) What will happen to whoever feeds on (abides in) Jesus (verse 57)? (b) How do those who feed on manna and those who feed on (abide in) Jesus differ (verse 58)? (c) Where was Jesus teaching (verse 59)?

Again Jesus emphasizes that the bread from heaven is not like manna, for those who ate manna still died, whereas those who partake of him will live eternally. Jesus claims to be more than they expected in a prophet like Moses or even in a Messiah. In fact, he claims he'll raise the dead, something only God can do. Moreover, he refuses to feed them always or perform signs when they ask, even though he's clearly capable.

> 10. Read John 6:60-62. (a) Why did many of Jesus's disciples grumble and take offense (verses 60-61)? (b) What might they see the Son of Man doing that could affect their attitude (verse 62)?

Jesus says that if his teaching offends them, what will happen if they see him ascending to where he was? In other words, his means of ascending will either increase the offense or remove it. To where will he ascend? He has just said he is *the bread that came down from heaven* (verse 58). So he appears to be talking about ascending to heaven *where he was before*. But to his hearers, such a claim is outrageous.

Jesus's Words Are Spirit and Life

In response, Jesus explains the same truths another way.

The Little Details
Flesh and Blood

Since Passover is near, "feeds on my flesh and drinks my blood" may also allude to the Passover lambs. The Jews will soon eat the flesh of the sacrificed lambs and drink wine at the Passover meal.

When Jesus at a later Passover eats the Passover meal at the Last Supper, he institutes communion. He gives bread that represents his body and wine, which represents the blood of the new covenant, the blood that he pours out for forgiveness of sins (Matthew 26:26-28). Communion points to the crucifixion, where Jesus gave his body and shed his blood to bring forgiveness of sins. Thus, the Passover lambs all foreshadowed Jesus's sacrifice as the ultimate Passover Lamb (1 Corinthians 5:7).

Again Jesus emphasizes that the bread from heaven is not like manna, for those who ate manna still died, whereas those who partake of him will live eternally.

The Little Details
The Twelve

John assumes as common knowledge that Jesus called 12 of his followers to be with him more closely and to minister in special ways (Matthew 10:1-4). This happened after John the Baptist's arrest (Matthew 4:12).

Jesus says of the Twelve, "One of you is a devil" (John 6:70). D.A. Carson writes that the word *diabolos* "in common Greek means 'slanderer' or 'false accuser,' but in the New Testament it always refers, when it is a substantive, to Satan, the prince of darkness."[12] Satan operates behind Judas.

The good news in the last half of John 6 is that Jesus is the living bread from heaven.

---

11. Read John 6:63-66. (a) Who gives life (verse 63)? (b) What counts for nothing (verse 63)? (c) What did Jesus know from the beginning (verse 64)? (d) What did many disciples do (verse 66)?

According to Jesus, their goal should not be attaining manna and barley loaves, for *the flesh is no help at all.* They need *the Spirit.*

When Jesus denied their request for something that would satisfy only on this earth and directed their eyes to what would give them eternal life, they grumbled. When his teaching became harder, they deserted him. If those who left had believed Jesus could give life, they would have kept following him, hoping to understand later.

12. ♥ What in the Bible didn't you understand when you first heard or read it but now makes sense to you? How did it come to make sense?

Jesus Has the Words of Eternal Life

Jesus now turns to the 12 disciples he's chosen for a special mission.

13. Read John 6:67-71. (a) Why didn't the Twelve leave (verses 67-69)? (b) What did Jesus know about Judas (verses 70-71)?

Many of those following Jesus stopped when he refused to give them what they asked for and his teaching became challenging. When we encounter a prayer answered no or don't initially understand something in the Bible, we have the same choice as his listeners. If, like Peter, we believe Jesus is the Holy One of God who has the words of eternal life, we will choose to persevere.

14. ♥ Without using a name, describe how someone you know left Jesus after not receiving something they prayed for or after encountering something difficult to understand in the Bible.

The good news in the last half of John 6 is that Jesus is the living bread from heaven. Eating of that bread is a metaphor for believing on Jesus and abiding in him. Indeed, Jesus will raise to eternal life those who believe on him and abide in him, which makes him greater than Moses. Moreover, he will offer his flesh and blood for the life of the world. Still more, his words are spirit and life.

The Feast of Booths

It was spring when Jesus fed the 5,000. Now it's fall. The Jewish authorities in Jerusalem want to kill Jesus for what they consider blasphemy.[13] But Jerusalem is where Jews celebrate the annual feasts, including the Feast of Booths in the fall.

Jesus Follows His Father's Timing

Jesus now lives in Capernaum in Galilee,[14] but the temple is in Jerusalem in Judea.

15. Read John 7:1-5. (a) Where did Jesus stay (verse 1)? (b) What feast was about to start (verse 2)? (c) Why did his brothers tell him to go to Judea (verse 5)?

Jews here refers to the authorities in Judea. Jesus's brothers ask him to accompany them to the year's final celebration, the Feast of Booths. Great crowds will flock there. Perhaps they think he should win back the disciples who deserted him or at least win new followers. But they don't understand his mission.

16. Read John 7:6-9. (a) Why did Jesus not go to Judea (verse 6)? (b) Why did the world hate Jesus (verse 7)?

It isn't Jesus's time to go to the feast, though his brothers can go any time. After all, they aren't telling people their actions are wrong, so no one wants to harm them. So Jesus remains behind until his Father tells him to go.

17. Read John 7:10-13. (a) When Jesus went up later, how did he go (verse 10)? (b) What were people saying about him (verse 12)? (c) Why weren't they discussing him openly (verse 13)?

The people's reactions are mixed. Do the signs mean God sent Jesus? Or are the Pharisees right that someone from God wouldn't ignore their Sabbath restrictions?

Jesus Claims His Teaching Is from God

18. Read John 7:14-16. (a) Why did the people marvel at Jesus's teaching (verses 14-15)? (b) From whom did Jesus's teaching come (verse 16)?

It isn't Jesus's time to go to the feast, though his brothers can go any time. After all, they aren't telling people their actions are wrong, so no one wants to harm them.

Jesus Assures Those Who Seek God's Will

The people can't understand how Jesus displays so much learning when he hasn't studied under a rabbi. So Jesus explains his teaching's source.

> **19.** In John 7:17 below, underline the "if" clause (the first eight words). Circle "he will know." Double underline "whether the teaching is from God." Draw an arrow from "know" to "teaching."
>
> If anyone's will is to do God's will, he will know whether the teaching is from God or whether I am speaking on my own authority.

This is great news. Second Chronicles 16:9 promises, "For the eyes of the LORD run to and fro throughout the whole earth, to give strong support to those whose heart is blameless toward him." In John 6:45, Jesus quotes Isaiah 54:13, saying, "And they will all be taught by God." Here, Jesus illuminates these promises. Those who truly want to do God's will shall *know* whether his teaching is from God. God will see to it.

Jesus Warns Those Who Don't Seek God's Will

If God grants insight to those who want to do his will so they know that Jesus's teaching is from God, then how are Jesus's persecutors resisting God's will?

> **20.** Read John 7:18-20. (a) Who speaks truthfully (verse 18)? (b) What weren't the people keeping (verse 19)?

Jesus seeks the Father's glory and teaches what the Father shows him; therefore, *in him there is no falsehood*. The Pharisees teach on their own authority and seek glory and praise for themselves. By seeking to kill Jesus, they plan to break the **Sixth Commandment**: "You shall not murder."[15] Not only that, but not one of them keeps the law of Moses perfectly.

But visitors who don't know that the local leaders want to kill Jesus think he's unjustly paranoid and must *have a demon*.

Jesus Justifies Healing on the Sabbath

Jesus addresses the Jerusalem authorities again.

> **21.** Read John 7:21-24. (a) What do the Jews do on the Sabbath (verse 22)? (b) To what does Jesus liken that (verse 23)? (c) How should they judge (verse 24)?

Jesus here addresses the reason they persecute him: He healed the invalid on the Sabbath. He argues that it's lawful to circumcise an eight-day-old boy on the Sabbath, so if one part of a person's body can be acted upon on the Sabbath, then why not the whole body? Jesus warns them to judge correctly rather than superficially.

Those who truly want to do God's will shall *know* whether his teaching is from God. God will see to it.

The Christ's Origin Is Unknown

Although the out-of-town visitors don't know the authorities' intentions toward Jesus, Jerusalem's citizens do.

> 22. Read John 7:25-27. (a) What did Jerusalem's citizens wonder (verses 25-26)? (b) What confused them (verse 27)?

Some think the Christ will appear suddenly with no one knowing his origin.[16] But Jesus comes from Nazareth, and his family now lives in Capernaum, so they think he can't be the Christ of unknown origin. But John has already told his readers that Jesus was in the beginning with God, so the people don't know his origin as well as they think they do.

> 23. Read John 7:28-31. (a) From whom did Jesus come (verse 29)? (b) Why didn't they arrest him (verse 30)? (c) Why did many believe in him (verse 31)?

What his detractors miss is that Jesus comes from the Father. Still, many see his signs and realize that Jesus could be both the prophet like Moses who will come with signs and the Christ who will reign. These, therefore, believe in him.

> 24. Read John 7:32-36. (a) What did the chief priests and Pharisees do when they heard the crowd muttering about Jesus (verse 32)? (b) Where did Jesus say he was going (verse 33)? (c) What did the Jews guess that Jesus meant (verse 35)?

The *chief priests* are the aristocratic priests of the Sanhedrin. Jesus will soon return to the one who sent him. The Jews wonder if he intends to go to the Jews who didn't return from exile and to the Greeks with them who had converted to Judaism. Of course, John has already informed us that Jesus claims to have come from the Father in heaven (John 6:38). John lets the irony of their misunderstanding stand.

> 25. ♥ Look again at John 7:17. (a) How did that verse display its truth in your life or in the life of someone you know? (b) What comfort does this verse give you?

For those who truly want God's will, there's good news: They will know whether what Jesus teaches is from God. Indeed, that the Jewish leaders want to kill Jesus is proof that they don't want God's will, for the law of Moses forbids murder. Moreover, Jesus justifies

The Little Details
The Dispersion (John 7:35)

When Moses brought the people to the promised land, he warned them that they could remain in the land only if they kept their covenant with God. If they abandoned God, he would exile them from the land.

The promised land became known as the kingdom of Israel. Later, it split into two kingdoms: Israel and Judah.

Eventually, the people abandoned God, and after many warnings, he sent them into exile. Although the exile ended, most Jews had grown comfortable in their new homes and didn't return to rebuild Jerusalem and their old homes.

Those who did return lived in Judea, Samaria, Galilee, and Perea (which John calls "beyond the Jordan"). These four areas cover roughly the area where Judah and Israel used to be.

By "the Dispersion," John means the people who still live outside these areas. Another name for them is "the Diaspora," from the transliteration of the Greek, *diaspora*. The NIV here translates *diaspora* "where our people live scattered."

The Feast's First Day

The priests read Zechariah 14 on the first day of the feast. It includes passages related to Jesus's words. For example, "On that day living waters shall flow out from Jerusalem…And the LORD will be king over all the earth. On that day the LORD will be one and his name one" (Zechariah 14:8-9).

Zechariah also speaks of a day when all nations must go to Jerusalem to keep the Feast of Booths. If they don't, they will have no rain.

healing on the Sabbath from the law of Moses. Still, he's not done teaching at the feast. In our next lesson, we'll see what else he says.

Day 4

The Water and Light Ceremonies

The Feast of Booths contained a huge, joyous celebration. Everyone lived in booths to re-enact the wilderness experience. Each morning they celebrated with a water ceremony and each evening with a light ceremony. Jesus used both these ceremonies to teach about who he was and what he offered.

Jesus Uses the Water Ceremony to Offer Living Water

Against the backdrop of the water ceremony, Jesus again teaches at the temple.

> 26. Read John 7:37-39. (a) What did Jesus offer those who thirst (verses 37-38)? (b) To whom does "rivers of living water" refer (verse 39)?

The *last day of the feast* is either the seventh day of the Feast of Booths or the eighth-day celebration when everyone moves back into their homes to commemorate the Israelites reaching the promised land.

Here, Jesus combines passages that use water to symbolize God's Spirit. For example, Isaiah 44:3 reads, "For I will pour water on the thirsty land, and streams on the dry ground; I will pour my Spirit upon your offspring, and my blessing on your descendants."

After Jesus's dramatic declaration, people turn to one another in wonderment.

> 27. Read John 7:40-43. (a) Who did some people think Jesus was (verse 40)? (b) Who did others think he was (verse 41)? (c) Why did some think he couldn't be the Christ (verses 41-42). (d) What happened as a result (verse 43)?

Some think this is another sign that Jesus is the prophet like Moses; after all, they're celebrating how God through Moses brought forth water from a rock. But others think he is the Christ (Messiah). To that, some respond that Jesus can't be the Christ because of Micah 5:2: "But you, O Bethlehem Ephrathah, who are too little to be among the clans of Judah, from you shall come forth for me one who is to be ruler in Israel, whose coming forth is from of old, from ancient days."

However, this objection is based on two mistakes. First, they assume that Jesus was born in Galilee because he has a Galilean accent and is called "Jesus of Nazareth." But by the time John wrote his Gospel, that Jesus was born in Bethlehem but raised in the Galilean town of Nazareth was common knowledge.[17] So was the fact that both Jesus's earthly parents and the Baptist's prophetess mother all testified that Jesus was born of the Holy Spirit, not of an earthly father.

Second, they overlook the last clause of the prophecy. It says that the ruler (the Christ) "shall come forth" from Bethlehem, but his "coming forth is from of old, from ancient of days." This fits what John already explained: Jesus "was in the beginning with God" and "all things were made through him" (John 1:2-3).

> **28.** Read John 7:44-49. (a) Why didn't the temple officers arrest Jesus (verses 44-46)? (b) What evidence did the Pharisees give that Jesus wasn't who he said he was (verses 47-48)? (c) What was their opinion of the crowd (verse 49)?

But they were mistaken that none of the authorities and leaders were drawn to Jesus. Nicodemus, whom we met in chapter 3, wasn't in agreement with them. Yet so sure were the Pharisees that their oral traditions correctly interpreted the Sabbath commandment that they pronounced the crowd cursed.

> **29.** Read John 7:50-52. (a) What did Nicodemus say (verse 51)? (b) How did the Pharisees reply (verse 52)?

The Pharisees err three more times. First, Nicodemus is correct about the need for a fair trial, yet the Pharisees reject the firsthand testimony of the officers and neglect to hear Jesus themselves. Second, the prophet Jonah came from Galilee,[18] and others likely did too. Third, Isaiah 9:1-2,7 says the Christ "on the throne of David" will be a "great light" in "the land of Zebulun and the land of Naphtali," which are in "Galilee of the nations." The Pharisees' accusation, "Are you from Galilee too?" shows that their contempt for Galileans pollutes their interpretation of prophecy.

Once again, they seek glory from people rather than from God and cling to prejudices. So John lets the irony of their mistakes boldly demonstrate his earlier testimony: "This is the judgment: the light has come into the world, and people loved the darkness rather than the light because their works were evil" (John 3:19).

Jesus Refuses to Condemn an Adulteress Woman

Your Bible may set off the narrative in John 7:53–8:6 in brackets or italics because it doesn't appear here in the earliest manuscripts (see sidebar on the next page).

> **30.** Read John 7:53–8:6. (a) Why did the Scribes and Pharisees bring the woman before Jesus (verse 6)? (b) How did Jesus respond (verse 6)?

This situation has problems. First, why do the authorities bring the woman but not the man? Second, they quote the law of Moses, but they also know that Rome forbids such

Yet so sure were the Pharisees that their oral traditions correctly interpreted the Sabbath commandment that they pronounced the crowd cursed.

The Little Details
The Woman Caught in Adultery

The narrative of the woman caught in adultery is not in the earliest manuscripts. That's why most English translations set John 7:53–8:11 apart in some way.

The ancient manuscripts that do include the narrative usually place it after John 7:52. Sometimes, however, they place it after Luke 21:38, John 7:36, John 7:44, or John 21:2.

New Testament scholar D.A. Carson explains that the "diversity of placement confirms" the narrative does not belong to any of the original Gospel manuscripts. Nonetheless, he writes, "There is little reason for doubting that the *event* here described occurred, even if in its written form it did not in the beginning belong to the canonical books."[19]

John mentions scribes only here. Most scribes were Pharisees. They "were the recognized students and expositors of the law of Moses...and came to assume something of the roles of lawyer, ethicist, theologian, catechist, and jurist."[20]

- - - - - - - - - - - - - - - - - - - -

How easy it is to condemn others and overlook our own sin.

- - - - - - - - - - - - - - - - - - - -

executions by Jews. Thus, they wish to trap Jesus by getting him to speak against either the law or Rome.

But Jesus gives no answer and merely writes on the ground. John does not tell us what he wrote.

> **31.** Read John 8:7-11. (a) What did Jesus finally respond (verse 7)? (b) What happened to the accusers (verse 9)? (c) What did Jesus tell the woman (verse 11)?

Jesus refers to the Old Testament commands that the first to throw stones must be witnesses to the crime but not participants in it.[21] The accusers leave one by one.

How easy it is to condemn others and overlook our own sin. Here, the scribes and Pharisees try to trap Jesus in order to condemn him without recognizing their own complicity. But his remarkable answer turns the situation around.

> **32.** ♥ (a) When you find forgiving someone difficult, do you take time to confess your own sins, especially those similar to what you're trying to forgive? (b) Why does reminding ourselves of our own sin help when we're tempted to condemn another (that is, not forgive them)?

Jesus Uses the Light Ceremony to Declare He Is the Light of the World

During the Feast of Booths came another ceremony, this one at night: the illumination of the temple to symbolize the pillar of fire that led the Israelites at night through the desert. John 8:20 tells us Jesus is teaching in the treasury, which is next to the women's court where the giant menorahs for the light ceremony stand. It is against this backdrop that Jesus again addresses the people.

> **33.** In John 8:12 below, draw a star ⭐ around what Jesus says he is. Underline what one must do to not walk in darkness. Lightly shade "darkness." Draw a star ⭐ around "light of life." Go to the **7 "I Am" Statements** chart at the back of the book and write "Light of the world" next to item 2.
>
> Again Jesus spoke to them, saying, "I am the light of the world. Whoever follows me will not walk in darkness, but will have the light of life."

Jesus alludes to Isaiah's prophecy that God will make the righteous suffering servant a light not just for the Jews but for the world: "I will make you as a light for the nations, that my salvation may reach to the end of the earth" (Isaiah 49:6).

Still, against the backdrop of the Feast of Booths and the lighting ceremony, there's more to Jesus's claim. He's saying he's like the pillar of light. Therefore, just as their ancestors followed the pillar that appeared as a cloud by day and as fire by night lighting their way, so they should now follow him. For as the pillar led the people to the promised land, so Jesus will lead them to eternal life.

Jesus's Judgment Is True

But the Pharisees appear to miss the allusion.

> 34. Read John 8:13-16. (a) What don't the Pharisees know (verse 14)? (b) How are the Pharisees judging (verse 15)? (c) Why are Jesus's judgments true (verse 16)?

The Pharisees react as if every statement Jesus makes must have a witness as in a court hearing. They misunderstand what Jesus said in John 5:31 when he said if he alone testified to who he was, his testimony wouldn't be true. There, Jesus gave multiple witnesses to who he was.

Here, Jesus asserts his testimony is true, for he knows where he's come from and where he's going. Jesus told them he came down from heaven from the Father and will return to him.[22] But the Pharisees don't believe the Father sent him, so they can't know these things. They judge by the flesh—that is, superficially according to instincts and passions. But Jesus judges no one by the flesh. On the contrary, when he judges, his judgment is true.

> 35. Read John 8:17-20. (a) Who bears witness to who Jesus is (verse 18)? (b) Whom do the Pharisees not know (verse 19)? (c) Why did they not arrest him (verse 20)?

Jesus next brings in the law about which they are speaking, which says no one can be convicted of a crime based on only one witness (Deuteronomy 19:15). They're applying the law out of context, but Jesus goes with their premise anyway and says his Father bears witness about him.

Of course, one of the things they hold against him is that he calls God his Father. But they misunderstand and ask where his father is, referring to his earthly parent. The fact that they don't know who his earthly father is shows they really don't know where he comes from despite their earlier claims to the contrary (John 7:27). Jesus points out that if they truly knew him, they would know his Father also.

During the Feast of Booths, Jesus proclaimed good news: Just as God through Moses brought the Israelites water in the exodus from slavery to Egypt, so Jesus offers living water (the Spirit) to all who thirst in the exodus from slavery to sin. And just as the pillar of light guided the Hebrews to the promised land, so Jesus declares he is the light that guides the world to the promised kingdom of God. Nonetheless, this conversation isn't over, so we'll pick it up in the next lesson.

The Little Details
The Feast's Eighth Day

The teacher Ezra led the people to celebrate the Feast of Booths after the return from exile. On the eighth day, the priests led the people in a prayer that included these words that relate to Jesus's teaching:

"You gave them bread from heaven for their hunger and brought water for them out of the rock for their thirst, and you told them to go in to possess the land that you had sworn to give them" (Nehemiah 9:15).

"The pillar of cloud to lead them in the way did not depart from them by day, nor the pillar of fire by night to light for them the way by which they should go. You gave your good Spirit to instruct them and did not withhold your manna from their mouth and gave them water for their thirst" (Nehemiah 9:19-20).

Just as God through Moses brought the Israelites water in the exodus from slavery to Egypt, so Jesus offers living water (the Spirit) to all who thirst in the exodus from slavery to sin.

The Little Details

The 7 "I Am He" Statements in Isaiah

Here is where we find the seven "I am he" statements:

Isaiah 41:4

Isaiah 43:10

Isaiah 43:13

Isaiah 43:25

Isaiah 46:4

Isaiah 48:12

Isaiah 51:12

The Suffering Servant

Where we left off in the last lesson, Jesus is still teaching in the temple treasury. As he continues, he makes assertions with interesting allusions to Isaiah's prophecies.

Jesus Claims "I Am He"

Jesus has just told his hearers that if they really knew him, they would know his Father.

36. Read John 8:21-23. (a) Why is it important that Jesus's hearers believe in him (verse 21)? (b) Where are his hearers from and what are they of (verse 23)? (c) Where is Jesus from and what is he of (verse 23)?

The hour when Jesus departs is approaching, but the Pharisees won't be able to follow him where he's going. They will continue to seek the Messiah (*you will seek me*) but will die in their sins.

37. In John 8:24 below, box "believe." Circle "I am he." Underline what will happen if the people don't believe Jesus's claim. Glance back at your responses to questions 2 and 3 and notice the similarities.

    I told you that you would die in your sins, for unless you believe that I am he you will die in your sins.

Jesus says they will die in their sins *unless you believe that I am he.* Jesus has alluded to Isaiah 40–55 many times, and he's doing so again. Remember the seven "I am he" declarations in Isaiah that we talked about on Day 1? In Isaiah 43:10, the Lord says he chooses witnesses that people may "believe me and understand that I am he," just as Jesus now says. In Isaiah 43:25, the Lord says, "I, I am he who blots out your transgressions." Yet now Jesus says his listeners will die in their sins unless they believe his claim that *I am he.*

38. Read John 8:25-27. (a) What do his hearers ask Jesus (verse 25)? (b) What does Jesus answer (verse 25)? (c) What does Jesus declare (verse 26)? (d) What didn't they understand (verse 27)?

Jesus Likens Himself to the Suffering Servant

Many still don't understand. Next Jesus likens himself to the suffering servant.

Like the Suffering Servant, Jesus Will Be Lifted Up

> **39.** In John 8:28 below, underline when they would know what Jesus was saying. Circle "I am he." Double underline how Jesus speaks.
>
> So Jesus said to them, "When you have lifted up the Son of Man, then you will know that I am he, and that I do nothing on my own authority, but speak just as the Father taught me."

We saw earlier that *lifted up* alluded to the bronze snake that Moses lifted up to grant life to those dying of a serpent's bite. Here where Jesus is drawing from Isaiah, it alludes as well to the fourth servant song: "Behold, my servant shall act wisely; he shall be high and lifted up, and shall be exalted" (Isaiah 52:13).

Like the Suffering Servant, Jesus Speaks as He Is Taught by God

Jesus says that when they have lifted him up, people will know that *I am he* and that he speaks *just as the Father taught me*. This last phrase alludes to the third servant song: "The Lord GOD has given me the tongue of those who are taught, that I may know how to sustain with a word him who is weary. Morning by morning he awakens; he awakens my ear to hear as those who are taught" (Isaiah 50:4).

Like the Suffering Servant, God Is Near Jesus

> **40.** Read John 8:29. (a) Where is God? (b) What hasn't God done? (c) Why?

Jesus says his Father is with him. The third servant song reads, "He who vindicates me is near. Who will contend with me? Let us stand up together" (Isaiah 50:8). This illustrates the attitude Jesus displays. He knows the Father is with him, so he speaks whatever the Father tells him to say.

Like the Suffering Servant, Jesus Does What Pleases God

Jesus claims that he always does what pleases God. The servant songs declare that the servant does all that God says despite suffering that leads to death: "The Lord GOD has opened my ear, and I was not rebellious; I turned not backward."[24]

Like the Suffering Servant, Jesus Offers Freedom

Among the crowd, some respond positively.

> **41.** Read John 8:30. What did many do?

Jesus turns his attention to the listeners who believe the Father sent him.

The Little Details
D.A. Carson: Genuine Faith

To the Jews who have professed faith in him, Jesus, understandably enough, indicates what genuine faith does: it perseveres, it holds tight to Jesus' teaching, with some glorious consequences (v. 32). But such faith costs not less than everything, and the freedom it brings presupposes that life before such faith is pitiful slavery. By sketching genuine faith in such stark terms, Jesus is standing true to a pattern we find elsewhere: he is never interested in multiplying numbers of converts if they are not genuine believers, and therefore he insists on forcing would-be disciples to count the cost...The Evangelist includes all of this material not because he is trying to nurture the faith of fledgling believers, but because he is trying to evangelize Jews and proselytes who must carefully understand what faith in Jesus Christ entails. They, too, must count the cost, and John, like Jesus, must present the gospel in such a way that spurious professions of faith are soon unmasked.[23]

42. In John 8:31-32 below, circle what true disciples do. Underline the two results.

> So Jesus said to the Jews who had believed him, "If you abide in my word, you are truly my disciples, and you will know the truth, and the truth will set you free."

Those who had followed him for a time but turned away when he didn't meet their expectations weren't truly his disciples. True disciples abide in his words. They meditate on them and measure their actions by them. His words then bring them to know truth, and truth brings freedom, just as God told the suffering servant "to say to the captives, 'Come out,' and to those in darkness, 'Be free!'" (Isaiah 49:9 NIV).

43. ♥ Describe a way that abiding in Jesus's words resulted in your knowing the truth and being set free.

Like the Suffering Servant, Jesus Offers Freedom from Sin

Jesus's offer of freedom offends those who don't believe they need him to set them free. They aren't ready to abide in his words.

44. Read John 8:33. What offends Jesus's detractors?

The feast celebrates the Jews' deliverance from slavery in Egypt, but Rome currently rules them. So the Jews aren't talking about political slavery but rather something like spiritual slavery.[25]

45. Read John 8:34-36. (a) To what kind of slavery is Jesus referring (verse 34)? (b) Who is a slave to sin (verse 34)? (c) What is the Son able to do (verse 36)?

Jesus clarifies that he's talking about slavery to sin. He offers to set them free to live as God commands. Freedom from sin is what the suffering servant offers, too, since "his soul makes an offering for guilt" for others and he shall "make many to be accounted righteous, and he shall bear their iniquities" (Isaiah 53:10-11).

Jesus's offer of freedom offends those who don't believe they need him to set them free. They aren't ready to abide in his words.

The Good News

In this chapter, we read that Jesus claimed that just as manna sustained life in the desert, so he is the living bread from heaven who gives eternal life to those who believe and abide in him. He will do so by raising them to life. Jesus also asserted that all who truly want God's will shall know whether what Jesus teaches is from God. Moreover, he offers living water (the Holy Spirit) to all who thirst. Additionally, he declared he is the light of the world. Further, he linked himself to the Lord God's "I am he" statements in Isaiah. Finally, he aligned himself with Isaiah's suffering servant.

46. ♥ Which of these items of good news means the most to you today? Why?

In the next chapter, we'll see opposition against Jesus rise as he continues to align himself with Old Testament Scripture.

💭 **Praise** God for something you saw of his character this week. **Confess** anything that convicted you. **Ask** for help to do something God's Word calls you to do. **Thank** God for something you learned this week.

Karla's Creative Connection

John 8:32 is a powerful and life-changing verse. It quickly reminds us of how much our lives have been transformed by the truth of God's Word. My life transformation started at a little neighborhood Bible study where God's Word introduced me to Jesus and opened my heart to believe in him as my Savior. I also learned that as we continue to abide in Scripture—believing it, studying it, and living it out—we not only grow in our knowledge of who Jesus is and our relationship with him, but we also come to know the truth of who he says we are. And that truth transforms our lives. I'm so thankful that his truth truly does set us free!

As I read and meditated on John 8:32, I wanted to emphasize three key phrases. So I chose to frame them. But I also wanted you to be able to focus on several key words as you color, so I chose to create them with block letters. Coloring words created with block letters gives you time to reflect on their meaning and what God is saying to you through them.

Block lettering is a simple letter form with a whimsical look, and it makes it easy for you to add more color to your design. So let's get started with the word *ABIDE* from this week's bookmark design.

① The easiest way to make block letters is to draw them first with a pencil, making sure to leave plenty of space between each letter.

② Using a fine line marker, outline your pencil letters and erase all your pencil lines. Note how combining upper and lower case letters adds a touch of whimsy!

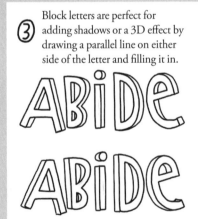

③ Block letters are perfect for adding shadows or a 3D effect by drawing a parallel line on either side of the letter and filling it in.

④ Here is a complete alphabet done in block lettering for you to use as a guide.

This is a fun letter style to combine with the faux calligraphy you learned last week. You can also use this block lettering technique with your cursive writing. Just make sure to open up the letters and the loops and add some extra space between the letters themselves.

Karla

If you ABIDE in my WORD, you are truly MY DISCIPLES, and you will KNOW the TRUTH, and the truth will SET YOU FREE

JOHN 8:31-32

Chapter 5

John 8:37–10:42
The Good Shepherd

What causes spiritual blindness?

I AM the good Shepherd

The good Shepherd lays down His life for the sheep.

John 10:11

Good and Bad Shepherds

On that sunny afternoon when I first read "Whoever does not honor the Son does not honor the Father who sent him" (John 5:23), I was perplexed. I held two conflicting beliefs, and I didn't know how to reconcile them.

I kept reading, hoping for clarification. Then I came to these words of Jesus: "If God were your Father, you would love me, for I came from God and I am here" (John 8:42). This didn't make things better; it made them worse!

I'd been sure the Bible would be God's way of telling me how to reach him. But I wanted a way that didn't involve Jesus. Yet here the Bible plainly said that for God to be my Father, I had to love Jesus. But I didn't love Jesus. Rather, I feared the man I thought he was: cynical, argumentative, narcissistic, dangerous, and trying to obtain followers for himself rather than for God.

I wondered why God cared whether people loved Jesus. I may have asked God why—I don't remember. But this thought came to mind: *If Jesus really is God's Son, then the Father might not like it if people don't like his kid.*

I asked myself, *Do I believe that an all-powerful God can keep the message of how to reach him correct?* I thought for a bit and determined, *Yes, I do.* I decided I would tell God why I feared Jesus that night.

What I didn't realize then was that my past was skewing how I interpreted what I read. You see, when I was five, my father in a fit of temper nearly killed me. At that time in his life, he was cynical, argumentative, and narcissistic (traits he recognizes today and regrets). My parents tried many foolish and sinful ways to coerce me into not showing fear around him. What finally worked was him telling me he could read my mind, and if I so much as thought a bad thing about him, he would "get" me. I was sure he meant he would kill me.

Today I know that many people perceive either the Father or Jesus in a way similar to their early perceptions of a significant male, such as their earthly father. I was as afraid of Jesus as I was of my father—more so, because Jesus was more powerful.

That night in bed, as I began to tell God why I feared Jesus, a strange phenomenon occurred. The room turned red, I heard something like seashore waves, and my body tingled. Thinking it was from Satan, I tried to rebuke it, like I'd read about Jesus doing in the first three Gospels. But then everything worsened. I heard words: "If you stop pursuing

The Little Details
Ezekiel 34:2-5:

Ah, shepherds of Israel who have been feeding yourselves! Should not shepherds feed the sheep? You eat the fat, you clothe yourselves with the wool, you slaughter the fat ones, but you do not feed the sheep. The weak you have not strengthened, the sick you have not healed, the injured you have not bound up, the strayed you have not brought back, the lost you have not sought, and with force and harshness you have ruled them. So they were scattered, because there was no shepherd, and they became food for all the wild beasts.

Throughout history, God showed tender care for people, especially the weak and powerless, by charging certain people to care for others. He often likened these caregivers to shepherds caring for sheep.

---

him now, I'll leave you alone." Terrified, I yelled, "Jesus, save me!" Immediately, the attack ended.

Now I knew beyond a shadow of a doubt that Jesus was not who I'd thought he was. No. He was the Savior.

Jesus said, "If anyone's will is to do God's will, he will know whether the teaching is from God or whether I am speaking on my own authority" (John 7:17). I truly did want to know God's will. And in a special way the Lord God let a mixed-up teenager know that Jesus's teaching was indeed from God.

When I opened my Bible the next day, it was as if the astigmatism distorting my vision had been corrected. As I read, the picture of Jesus revealed in the Bible's pages was of an entirely different person—someone I had just met, someone who actually cared for the lost, the powerless, and the mistreated.

If you, too, have a view of Jesus and the Father distorted by ungodly people in your life, I pray that God will heal your spiritual eyes as well.

God's Word to Us in the Old Testament

Throughout history, God showed tender care for people, especially the weak and powerless, by charging certain people to care for others. He often likened these caregivers to shepherds caring for sheep.

The Lord Called Adam and Eve to Care for Earth's Living Creatures

God placed Adam and Eve in a garden and told them to reign over every living creature (Genesis 1:28). He told them they could eat from all the garden's plants but one: the tree of the knowledge of good and evil. That tree would bring **death**. But a **serpent lied** to Eve, saying it would not bring death, that instead it would give her knowledge like God's. She ate, and the sentence of death descended on the two and their offspring.

Elsewhere, we learn that the serpent is called the **devil** and Satan, both meaning "adversary" or "accuser."[1] He is a fallen angel who accuses humans before God.

"I Am" Called Moses and Aaron to Shepherd His People

The Lord God called to a **shepherd** named Moses from a burning bush, telling him to lead the Israelites out of slavery in Egypt to the promised land. When Moses asked him his name, "God said to Moses, 'I am who I am.' And he said, 'Say this to the people of Israel, "I am has sent me to you"'" (Exodus 3:13-14).

On the way to the promised land, Moses was **leader** and **prophet** while Aaron was **high priest**. God led his people to the promised land "like a flock by the hand of Moses and Aaron" (Psalm 77:20).

The Lord Called David to Shepherd His People

David was another shepherd-leader. He was a **shepherd** boy when a prophet told him he would one day be king. As such, he would **shepherd God's people** (Psalm 78:70-72). When David later considered all the ways the Lord had cared for him, he wrote a psalm that began, "**The Lord is my shepherd**" (Psalm 23:1).

The Lord Said a Future Good Shepherd Would Replace Bad Shepherds

Eventually, the **three types of shepherds** God had placed over his people—kings, priests, and prophets—failed in their duties: "The priests did not say, 'Where is the Lord?' Those

who handle the law did not know me; the shepherds [kings] transgressed against me; the prophets prophesied by Baal and went after things that do not profit" (Jeremiah 2:8).

God saw his people hurting and rebuked the shepherds for caring for themselves rather than for the people. Then he promised, "Behold, **I, I myself** will search for my sheep and will seek them out...And I will set up over them **one shepherd**, my servant David, and he shall feed them: he shall feed them and be their shepherd" (Ezekiel 34:11,23). God would do this because, he said, "**You are my sheep, human sheep of my pasture**, and I am your God" (Ezekiel 34:31).

The Lord Said He Himself Would Shepherd His People and Open Blind Eyes

Isaiah 40:9-11 explains more about God's plan to fix the bad shepherd problem.

> Go on up to a high mountain, O Zion, herald of **good news**; lift up your voice with strength, O Jerusalem, herald of **good news**; lift it up, fear not; say to the cities of Judah, "Behold your God!" Behold, the Lord GOD comes with might, and his arm rules for him...He will tend his flock like a **shepherd**; he will gather the lambs in his arms; he will carry them in his bosom, and gently lead those that are with young.

Here the **good news** is that, sometime after the exile, **God himself** will come and **shepherd** the people. Not only that, but he "'will come and save you.' Then the **eyes of the blind shall be opened**...then shall the **lame** man leap like a deer" (Isaiah 35:4-6). They will recognize God's visitation by these signs.

Moreover, he said that the suffering servant will **open blind eyes** (see sidebar).

God's Word to Us in John

We saw Jesus heal the lame in John 5. In today's reading, we'll finish Jesus's temple conversation and see him react to both physical and spiritual blindness.

> 🗨 Take a moment to pray for insight as you read God's Word.

> 1. ♥ Read John 8:37–10:42. What stands out to you? Why?

In this lesson, we saw that God set shepherds over his people, but eventually bad shepherds used their position for their own benefit rather than to care for those under their charge. So God announced that he would one day set a descendant of David as a good shepherd over his people. He also said that he himself would come and shepherd the people, and that they would know when he arrived when they saw the lame and blind healed.

In our next lesson, we'll finish up Jesus's conversation at the temple and glimpse why the prophecies about the coming of both God and the suffering servant overlap.

Pam's Heart-to-Heart with the Great I Am—"I Am the Good Shepherd"

"I am the good shepherd. The good shepherd lays down his life for the sheep."
John 10:11

I have a legacy of good shepherds in my family for generations back! My great-great-grandparents emigrated from New Zealand—with their flock of sheep! That they disembarked on the Oregon coast and then walked (or herded) the flock all the way to the land they then homesteaded in Idaho is legend in my family.

I grew up playing in the green pastures of my great-grandparents' home, and when they passed away, we bought their farm and I began the life of a shepherdess. I learned about the care of sheep from my mother and grandfather. I saw what it meant to care for sheep: to feed them, card and shear their wool, provide them with water, give them medical care, and do the hard work of helping a ewe bring a precious lamb into the world.

Our flock wore collars with bells to alert us if coyotes, mountain lions, or wild dogs were endangering them. If all was well, the bells sounded like the gentle tingling of a wind chime. But when predators spooked the flock, the clanging was like a fire alarm, and all shepherds jumped into action to protect them.

In this study, we'll look closely at Jesus, our Good Shepherd, who laid down his life in substitutionary death for his flock. But good shepherd also refers to leaders, pastors, or protectors the Lord calls to purposefully place themselves where they can best look after the well-being of the flock.

Here are a few of my favorite Good Shepherd verses (emphasis added):

- "What man of you, having a hundred sheep, if he has lost one of them, does not **leave the ninety-nine…and go after the one** that is lost, until he finds it? And when he has found it, **he lays it on his shoulders, rejoicing**" (Luke 15:4-5).

- He will tend his flock like a shepherd; he will gather the lambs in his arms; he will **carry them** in his bosom, and **gently lead** those that are with young (Isaiah 40:11).

- "I myself will **search** for my sheep…As a shepherd seeks out his flock…so will I **seek out** my sheep, and I will **rescue** them…And I will…**gather** them…and will **bring** them into their own land. And I will **feed** them…with good pasture" (Ezekiel 34:11-14).

When I look back at my and my husband's faith story, I see a Shepherd who sought out his lost lambs. I came to Christ because one of my mom's friends saw that we needed rescuing from the drinking and rage of my earthly dad. Bill came to faith out from a home filled with emotional instability and through the movie *The Exorcist*—he was "scared to life"! The Shepherd carried us to mentors who fed us from the Word, gathered us up, fostered our love, and led us "into our own land."

We have many accounts of God's leading us into our own land from our years of marriage and ministry, but the story that magnifies this (and combines marriage and ministry) is the one about how our bestselling book *Men Are Like Waffles—Women Are Like Spaghetti* was born. The title came about in a God way.

A husband brought his wife into Bill's counseling office, where she began jumping from topic to topic while her husband, like a deer caught in headlights, stared and looked puzzled. From his master's studies, Bill knew the nuances of each gender, so he explained to the man, "Think of her mind like a plate of spaghetti, and if you follow one noodle, it will seem to touch every other noodle. She's making connections to you." Bill then taught him some listening skills, and his wife shared for 55 minutes straight! She added, "That was great! So if I'm spaghetti—what is my husband?"

Bill prayed God would give him a food illustration with compartments, as science indicates women "integrate" and men "compartmentalize." Our boys were making toaster waffles, and Bill thought, *Boxes!* He helped the couple stay in the one compartment that held their biggest disagreement, and they solved the issue in that counseling session.

Bill said to me later, "I think we should share this in the marriage conference this weekend." My response was, "It's kinda corny, but I trust you and I trust God, so yes!"

We went on to write *Men Are Like Waffles—Women Are Like Spaghetti,* and it's nearing 400,000 copies sold in English and has been translated into over 15 languages. There's a married couples' version, a devotional, a DVD series, a singles' version, and a teen version. God has filled our schedule with radio, TV, and speaking at live and virtual events worldwide. Recently, we got a thank-you note from a marriage counselor thanking us for the positive fruit in her own relationship because of our book. She included a photo of her wedding cake topped with an icing design of waffles and spaghetti!

As a lamb, pray to your Good Shepherd, *Gather, rescue, lead, carry, guide, feed, and rejoice over me. Thank you! Amen.*

Pam

Experiencing Scripture Creatively

- With children, act out John 8:27 by blindfolding them one at a time in a safe place and helping them follow you by listening to your voice. Discuss how we follow Jesus's voice by reading or hearing what he says in the Bible.

- Take or find a digital photo of sheep following a shepherd. Using Canva or any photo editing software, write your favorite verse from John 15 on the photo. Share on social media or with friends.

- In your Bible near John 10 or in a journal, follow Karla's instructions at the end of this chapter for drawing a sheep.

Day 2

Jesus the I Am

Previously, we read that Jesus told those who believed in him to abide in his word so they would know the truth and the truth would set them free. This offended some who claimed they were already free because they were descendants of Abraham.

The True Children of God Love Jesus

2. Read John 8:37-41. (a) What does Jesus say is the reason they seek to kill him (verse 37)? (b) If they were Abraham's children as they claimed, what would they be doing (verse 39)? (c) From whom did Jesus hear truth (verse 40)? (d) Whom do the Jews claim is their Father in verse 41?

While those who want to kill Jesus are physically descended from Abraham, they are not his spiritual descendants if they don't act like him, according to Jesus.

While those who want to kill Jesus are physically descended from Abraham, they are not his spiritual descendants if they don't act like him, according to Jesus. They counter with *We were not born of sexual immorality*. That suggests they know that Jesus's mother, Mary, was pregnant before she married Joseph. They then claim that God is their Father, the very claim they were angry with Jesus for making.[2]

> **3.** Read John 8:42-43 below. Circle what Jesus's listeners would do if God were their Father. Box why Jesus came. Underline the reason they don't understand Jesus.
>
> Jesus said to them, "If God were your Father, you would love me, for I came from God and I am here. I came not of my own accord, but he sent me. Why do you not understand what I say? It is because you cannot bear to hear my word."

Now they can't misunderstand who Jesus claims sent him. He gets to the heart of their problem: His detractors can't bear what he has to say, so they seek to silence him.

Jesus Speaks Truth

> **4.** Read John 8:44-45. (a) Who does Jesus say is their father (verse 44)? (b) What is their father like (verse 44)? (c) Why won't they believe Jesus (verse 45)?

The devil...was a murderer from the beginning, and...there is no truth in him refers to Genesis 3:4-5. There, the serpent told Eve that God hadn't told her the truth when he said she'd die if she ate from the forbidden tree. Rather, she would be like God. But the serpent lied, and when she ate, death descended.

Those Who Are of God Hear His Words

> **5.** Read John 8:46-47 below. Underline what Jesus asks since they want to kill him. Circle who hears God's words. Box the reason people don't hear them.
>
> Which one of you convicts me of sin? If I tell the truth, why do you not believe me? Whoever is of God hears the words of God. The reason why you do not hear them is that you are not of God.

They've accused Jesus of breaking the Sabbath and of blasphemy. But they can't prove he has sinned. Jesus states they think they know God, but they don't. They saw Jesus's miraculous signs and they heard his authoritative teaching, but they refuse to listen to him. They don't want to admit they could be wrong about whether healing on the Sabbath is legitimate. Nor do they want a messiah who doesn't submit to their rules.

That he could be the prophet like Moses should give them pause, for Moses was the ultimate authority on how to apply the law in his day. But they do not hear the *words of God* because they *are not of God*. They fulfill what Isaiah prophesied would happen to the suffering servant: "Who has believed what he has heard from us? And to whom has the arm of the LORD been revealed?" (Isaiah 53:1).

They saw Jesus's miraculous signs and they heard his authoritative teaching, but they refuse to listen to him. They don't want to admit they could be wrong about whether healing on the Sabbath is legitimate.

6. ♥ (a) Did pride prevent you from accepting the gospel at any time? Explain.
   (b) Describe a time when pride temporarily kept you from admitting the truth.

Those Who Keep Jesus's Word Will Not See Death

The Jewish leaders revile again.

7. Read John 8:48-51. (a) How do the Jews mock Jesus (verse 48)? (b) Who seeks Jesus's glory and what is he (verse 50)? (c) What did Jesus further claim (verse 51)?

The Jews despise the Samaritans, so here they are saying Jesus not only lacks true teaching (like the Samaritans) but is demon possessed. In other words, since Jesus told them their spiritual father is the devil, they retort that he has a demon.

They dishonor Jesus, but he isn't concerned because the ultimate Judge seeks to glorify him. As the suffering servant says, "But the Lord GOD helps me; therefore I have not been disgraced…and I know that I shall not be put to shame."[3]

But then Jesus claims anyone who keeps his word (believes and obeys it) *will never see death*.

Jesus Knows God

That claim is too much for his detractors.

8. Read John 8:52-55. (a) Why are the Jews upset at Jesus's claim (verses 52-53)? (b) Why does Jesus refuse to glorify himself (verse 54)? (c) What does Jesus say about their relationship to God versus his relationship to God (verse 55)?

This Gospel's prologue tells us who Jesus is. But the Jews who reject Jesus's message don't accept that God sent Jesus, let alone that Jesus was with God and is God. His claim, "If anyone keeps my word, he will never taste death," would indeed make him greater than Abraham and the prophets. They see the implication correctly, but they reject it.

Jesus Claims, "Before Abraham Was, I Am"

In John 8:24, Jesus says, "I told you that you would die in your sins, for unless you believe that I am he you will die in your sins." As we read in the last chapter, Jesus alludes to the many "I am he" statements God makes in Isaiah, such as in Isaiah 43:10. Even though the priests recite these passages during the festival,[4] it's still an allusion that his hearers could miss. Now Jesus makes his claim even clearer.

The Little Details

D.A. Carson: How Abraham Saw Jesus's Day

It is unlikely that Jesus' opponents took umbrage because they heard him ascribing powers of foresight to the patriarch Abraham. It is altogether likely that some of them, at least, believed that Abraham knew in advance of the messianic age. The point of tension arose because of the way Jesus phrases this: not "Your father Abraham rejoiced to see the messianic age," but "Your father Abraham rejoiced to see my day." The "day" or the "day of the Lord" becomes *Jesus'* day. Even if "to see my day" does not mean some prophetic vision of the literal fulfillment of prophecy in Jesus and his ministry, but some vision, however vague, of the promise inherent in the binding of Isaac or (better) of the covenant promising that in him all the nations of the earth would be blessed...the fact remains that Jesus identifies the ultimate fulfillment of all Abraham's hopes and joys with his own person and work.[5]

9. Read John 8:56-59. (a) What did Abraham rejoice at (verse 56)? (b) Why do the Jews scoff at that (verse 57)? (c) What did Jesus say next (verse 58)? (d) How did the Jews react (verse 59)?

You are not yet fifty means both that he's not old enough to have seen Abraham and he's not even old enough to hold many Jewish offices.[6] When Jesus says, "Truly, truly, I say to you, before Abraham was, I am," he uses the name by which God calls himself. With that, Jesus claims not only to be greater than Abraham and the prophets but to be God.

If he were not God, his claim would be blasphemous. They don't believe he is, so they attempt to stone him. But Jesus leaves the temple.

C.S. Lewis sums up the issue succinctly:

> I am trying here to prevent anyone saying the really foolish thing that people often say about Him: "I'm ready to accept Jesus as a great moral teacher, but I don't accept his claim to be God." That is the one thing we must not say. A man who was merely a man and said the sort of things Jesus said would not be a great moral teacher. He would either be a lunatic—on a level with the man who says he is a poached egg—or else he would be the Devil of Hell. You must make your choice. Either this man was, and is, the Son of God: or else a madman or something worse. You can shut him up for a fool, you can spit at Him and kill Him as a demon; or you can fall at His feet and call Him Lord and God. But let us not come with any patronizing nonsense about His being a great human teacher. He has not left that open to us. He did not intend to.[7]

In today's reading, Jesus says that the true children of God will love him because God sent him. He says he speaks the truth and those who are truly of God will recognize that. Further, those who keep his word will not die. But his detractors consider that claim audacious and scorn him for making himself out to be greater than Abraham. Jesus replies that Abraham rejoiced to see Jesus's day. When his detractors say that's absurd since Abraham lived long before Jesus, Jesus claims to have existed before Abraham, and he uses God's own name for himself.

Conflict is rising, and in our next lesson, Jesus will provide more evidence that God sent him.

Day 3

The Shepherd Cares for the Sheep

In John 5, we read that Jesus healed a paralytic on the Sabbath. But when the Jewish leaders rebuked the healed man for carrying his mat, he seemed eager to blame Jesus and ingratiate himself with the leaders. The blind man we'll read about today faces similar challenges but reacts differently.

A Blind Man Encounters the Man Called Jesus

This narrative begins on a Sabbath in Jerusalem.

10. Read John 9:1-3. (a) What ailed the man Jesus saw (verse 1)? (b) What did the disciples think caused this ailment (verse 2)? (c) Were they right (verse 3)?

Although the Bible tells us some ailments do come because of sin,[8] Jesus plainly says that is not always the case.

Jesus Is the Light of the World by Which Others Can See

11. Read John 9:4-5. (a) Since God wanted to display his works in the man, what did Jesus say they must do (verse 4)? (b) What is Jesus while he is in the world (verse 5)? (c) Therefore, what does he mean by "night is coming" (verse 4)?

That Jesus is the light of the world is a fulfillment of one of the suffering servant prophecies: "I will make you as a light for the nations, that my salvation may reach to the end of the earth" (Isaiah 49:6). When he leaves the world, darkness will come. But while he is here, he is its light, and he wants to do all the works of God.

Jesus Heals the Man Born Blind

Jesus next acts out what he means.

12. Read John 9:6-7 below. Underline Jesus's actions. Circle the name of the pool and its meaning. Box how the man came back.

> Having said these things, he spit on the ground and made mud with the saliva. Then he anointed the man's eyes with the mud and said to him, "Go, wash in the pool of Siloam" (which means Sent). So he went and washed and came back seeing.

Having said these things links the healing to *I am the light of the world.* As the sun enables people to physically see, so Jesus enables people to spiritually see. To demonstrate, he enables a blind man to see. After anointing the man's eyes, he sends him to the very pool from which water was drawn during the water ceremonies of the Feast of Booths—the water used to symbolize the coming of the Holy Spirit. The Father sent Jesus, who sent a blind man to a pool called Sent, and the blind man *came back seeing.*

Jesus Fulfills Prophecy About Healing the Blind

The healing fulfills what Isaiah 35:4-5 prophesies will happen when God himself appears. It also shows Jesus fulfilling one of the roles of the suffering servant, which was to "open the eyes that are blind" (Isaiah 42:7).

The Little Details
Contempt for Misfortune

Fear often motivates people to determine the cause of illness or loss. If we think we know why someone faces difficulties, then we can avoid acting similarly.

In the Old Testament, the righteous man Job suffered many hardships. Afterward, his friends insisted God was punishing him for secret sin. Job responded that those not facing difficulties "have contempt for misfortune as the fate of those whose feet are slipping" (Job 12:5 NIV). In other words, the friends allayed their fear of disaster by assuring themselves it only befalls those who have slipped into sin.

That Jesus is the light of the world is a fulfillment of one of the suffering servant prophecies: "I will make you as a light for the nations, that my salvation may reach to the end of the earth" (Isaiah 49:6).

The Little Details
The Blind Men in Matthew

Matthew 20:30 records that when Jesus passed through Jericho, two blind men cried out, "Lord, have mercy on us, Son of David!" Jericho is not far from Jerusalem. Lydia McGrew writes, "The healing of the man born blind recorded in John 9 explains the confidence of the blind men in Jericho. Given the stir it created, Bartimaeus and his companion could easily have heard of it and could have had it in mind when they called out to Jesus as the 'Son of David' for help in Jericho."[9] This is another example of an undesigned coincidence—one Gospel explaining details of another.

13. Read John 9:8-12. (a) Why were the man's neighbors confused (verses 8-10)? (b) How did the blind man refer to Jesus (verse 11)? (c) Jump ahead briefly to read verse 16. On line 6 of the **8 Signs** chart, enter "Healed the man born blind."

At this point, the man knows his healer only as *the man called Jesus.*

The Healed Man Declares Jesus Is a Prophet

The neighbors bring the healed man to the Pharisees among the Jewish leaders.

14. Read John 9:13-17. (a) What day of the week was it when Jesus healed the blind man (verse 14)? (b) When the Pharisees asked again how he was healed, what did the healed man testify (verse 15)? (c) Why were the Pharisees divided (verse 16)? (d) What did the healed man say about Jesus (verse 17)?

The great sign and its connection to prophecy cause some of the Pharisees to waver in their conviction that healing on the Sabbath is wrong. But others cling to their traditions and decide that Jesus *is not from God.* Meanwhile, the healed man has moved from thinking of Jesus as a man to believing him a prophet.

The Healed Man's Parents Protect Themselves Over Their Son

An easy solution for the Pharisees is to doubt the man's testimony.

15. Read John 9:18-23. (a) What did the Pharisees do to confirm the man's story (verses 18-20)? (b) Why were his parents intimidated (verse 22)?

A man could testify for himself at age 13. The leaders of this Jerusalem synagogue have decided that Jesus is not the Christ (Messiah), and therefore they will expel from the synagogue anyone who claims he is. The parents don't want to be banned, so they bow out of the questioning except to confirm their son was born blind.

The Pharisees Pressure the Healed Man

16. Read John 9:24-25 below. Underline what the healed man knows.

> For the second time they called the man who had been blind and said to him, "Give glory to God. We know that this man is a sinner." He answered, "Whether he is a sinner I do not know. One thing I do know, that though I was blind, now I see."

Give glory to God pressures the man to change his testimony. They want to turn him against Jesus as they did the paralytic. But he refuses to agree to anything he doesn't know and repeats his testimony of what happened.

As the sun enables people to physically see, so Jesus enables people to spiritually see. To demonstrate, he enables a blind man to see.

17. Read John 9:26-29. (a) When the Pharisees again questioned how Jesus healed him, what did the man ask (verse 27)? (b) Whose disciples did they claim to be (verse 28)? (c) What did they say they didn't know about Jesus (verse 29)?

Though Jesus has given an astounding sign, the Pharisees do not believe what it signifies. Furious, they revile the man for being a disciple of someone whose origins they don't know, despite earlier claiming they do know where he's from (John 7:27).

The Healed Man Declares God Sent Jesus

The man responds to the angry rebuke with calm logic.

18. Read John 9:30-34. (a) How does the healed man argue that Jesus is clearly from God (verses 31-33)? (b) How do the Pharisees react (verse 34)?

The healed man presents a clear argument that God must have sent Jesus. Otherwise, Jesus could not have performed a miracle never before heard of. They had tried to guide his testimony by saying "Give glory to God"; here, he glorifies God, though not in the way they wished.

That he would dare try to teach the knowledgeable Pharisees, however, offends them. They berate him as one *born in utter sin* and expel him from the synagogue. The self-appointed shepherds haven't heeded God's rebuke in Jeremiah 23:1-2:

> "Woe to the shepherds who destroy and scatter the sheep of my pasture!" declares the LORD. Therefore thus says the LORD, the God of Israel, concerning the shepherds who care for my people: "You have scattered my flock and have driven them away, and you have not attended to them. Behold, I will attend to you for your evil deeds."

They also ignore clear prophecies about the blind seeing when God comes to save and when the suffering servant arrives (Isaiah 35:5-6; 42:7).

The Pharisees intimidated the healed paralytic who wanted their favor. They intimidated the healed man's parents too. But not the healed blind man. Jesus opened not just his physical eyes but his spiritual eyes. He sees truths the studied Pharisees miss.

19. ♥ Think about whom you are most like today: the healed paralytic who quickly abandoned Jesus to gain favor with others, the parents who did not yet have strong enough faith to courageously speak out about Jesus, or the healed blind man who boldly proclaimed what he knew about Jesus despite consequences. What steps can you take to be more like the healed blind man?

The Little Details
Synagogue

In 586 BC, the Babylonians burned down the temple Solomon built and exiled the Israelites. The exiles built *synagogues* ("gathering places") to teach people about God. Worshipers met for teaching and prayer on the Sabbath.

After the exile ended and the Jews built a new temple in Jerusalem, they continued making synagogues. In fact, in Jesus's day Jerusalem had many synagogues. Non-Jews couldn't enter the temple beyond the court of Gentiles, but they could come to the synagogues to learn about God.

Though Jesus has given an astounding sign, the Pharisees do not believe what it signifies. Furious, they revile the man for being a disciple of someone whose origins they don't know, despite earlier claiming they do know where he's from.

The Little Details

Inclusio

At the beginning of this tale, Jesus's disciples asked whose sin caused the man to be born blind (John 9:2). In John 9:34, the Pharisees claim he was "born in utter sin." Putting parallel phrases at the beginning and end of a section is a literary technique called *inclusio*. John uses it frequently in his Gospel.

In the passages we read today, we saw that Jesus is the light by which all others can see spiritual truths. To demonstrate that, he healed a man born blind. In doing so, he fulfilled prophecies about what would happen when God and the suffering servant visit earth. Further, despite the Jewish leaders' pressure, the healed man declared Jesus was a prophet sent by God. Our next lesson has Jesus's response.

Day 4

The Sheep Know Their Shepherd

The blind man's parents didn't support him when he faced opposition. The Jewish leaders cast him out of their synagogue, denouncing him as born in sin. The man might have wondered if God the Father might desert him too.

20. ♥ Name a way your earthly father helped or hurt your view of God as Father.

Jesus Is the Son of Man and Lord

Jesus heard what happened and reached out to the man he'd healed.

21. Read John 9:35-38. (a) When Jesus found the healed man, what did he ask him (verse 35)? (b) What does the healed man want to do (verse 36)? (c) What's the man's reaction when he realizes his healer is speaking to him (verse 38)?

Jesus seeks out the man the Pharisees expelled. Now the formerly blind man sees Jesus for the first time. When he hears that this man talking to him is Jesus, he prostrates himself before his healer in worship. The healed man has moved from knowing his healer as a man called Jesus to knowing him as a prophet, as one sent from God, as the Son of Man, as Lord, and now as one to be worshiped.

Jesus Came for Judgment

Jesus came into the world as the Son of Man. Now he explains why.

22. Read John 9:39-41. (a) How did Jesus respond (verse 39)? (b) What did the Pharisees who overheard him ask (verse 40)? (c) Why did Jesus say their guilt remains (verse 41)?

Jesus came to save, not to condemn. But saving uncovers sin, and those who won't acknowledge their sin remain condemned. The Pharisees think they see by the light of

Jesus opened not just his physical eyes but his spiritual eyes.

their traditions, but their traditions blind them to the Savior. Those who reject him while claiming to see spiritual truths remain spiritually blind: "He sees many things, but does not observe them; his ears are open, but he does not hear."[10]

Jesus Is the Door to the Sheepfold

Because of their reaction, Jesus begins to teach the Pharisees about spiritual leadership using the metaphor of a shepherd leading sheep. In his first example, he speaks of a sheep pen holding sheep owned by several families.

Jesus Calls His Sheep by Name

23. Read John 10:1-6. (a) What are those who don't enter by the door (verse 1)? (b) Who enters by the door (verse 2)? (c) How does the shepherd call his sheep (verse 3)? (d) Why do the sheep follow him but not strangers (verses 4-5)?

In shared sheep pens, a gatekeeper guards the sheep at night. In the morning, each family's shepherd comes to the pen, and the gatekeeper opens the gate for him. The shepherd calls his sheep so he can lead them to pasture. The shepherd's sheep know his voice and follow him, while the other sheep stay in the pen.

Jesus's Sheep Do Not Listen to False Shepherds

Jesus has more to teach about shepherds and sheep.

24. Read John 10:7-8 below. Underline what Jesus says he is. Circle what those who came before him are. Turn to the **7 "I Am" Statements** chart at the back of the book and write "The door of the sheep" next to line 3.

    So Jesus again said to them, "Truly, truly, I say to you, I am the door of the sheep. All who came before me are thieves and robbers, but the sheep did not listen to them."

All those who claimed to be the Messiah before Jesus and all the false shepherds who treat the sheep harshly for their own benefit are but *thieves and robbers*. As such, they aren't going through Jesus, the door. But Jesus's sheep aren't fooled by them, just as the healed man wasn't fooled by the leaders who cast him out.

Jesus Offers Abundant Life

Sheep pass through the gate to find food.

25. Read John 10:9-10. (a) What happens to a sheep (person) who enters by the door (Jesus), according to verse 9? (b) Why do thieves come (verse 10)? (c) Why does Jesus come (verse 10)?

The Little Details
Psalm 23
David was a conscientious shepherd when God sent a prophet to anoint him king. Later, he wrote Psalm 23 about how he saw the Lord as his shepherd: "The LORD is my shepherd; I shall not want. He makes me lie down in green pastures. He leads me beside still waters. He restores my soul" (Psalm 23:1-3). The psalm goes on to describe how the Lord leads, guides, and protects his people as a good shepherd leads, guides, and protects his sheep.

- -

Jesus came to save, not to condemn. But saving uncovers sin, and those who won't acknowledge their sin remain condemned.

- -

The Little Details
Moses's Prayer for a Shepherd

In Numbers 27:15-17, Moses prays, "Let the LORD, the God of the spirits of all flesh, appoint a man over the congregation who shall go out before them and come in before them, who shall lead them out and bring them in, that the congregation of the LORD may not be as sheep that have no shepherd." In the next verse, the LORD appoints Joshua to be this shepherd.

The name Joshua in Greek is Jesus. Thus Moses's prayer's initial fulfillment is a type of the coming greater fulfillment of John 10:9: "I am the door. If anyone enters by me, he will be saved and will go in and out and find pasture."

The current shepherds have treated him as weak, lost, and not worth having in the flock. But Jesus sought him and promised good pasture and abundant life—life at its best, as God always intended for humankind.

Whatever the Pharisees thought of Jesus's message, the healed man surely considers this good news. The current shepherds have treated him as weak, lost, and not worth having in the flock. But Jesus sought him and promised good pasture and abundant life—life at its best, as God always intended for humankind.

Jesus Is the Good Shepherd

Jesus switches metaphors slightly in the next verse.

> **26.** Read John 10:11-13. (a) Who is Jesus (verse 11)? (b) What does the good shepherd do (verse 11)? (c) Why don't hired hands do the same (verse 13)? (d) In the **7 "I Am" Statements** chart, write "Good shepherd" on line 4.

Jesus indicts the Pharisees who cast the healed man out of the synagogue as caring nothing for the sheep. Unlike them, he cares for the sheep enough to lay down his life for them.

Jesus Has Sheep in Other Folds

> **27.** Read John 10:14-16. (a) Whom does Jesus know (verse 14)? (b) Whom do they know (verse 14)? (c) What does Jesus do (verse 15)? (d) What will Jesus bring (verse 16)?

Just as sheep know the voice of their shepherd and follow him, so true believers know the voice of this Shepherd and follow him. Here, the first sheepfold has sheep from Judaism. The sheep *not of this fold* are those from among the Samaritans and the Gentiles. When Jesus brings them together, all will be *one flock*.

Jesus Fulfills Prophecy About God as Shepherd

By healing the man and then seeking him when the Jewish leaders cast him out, Jesus acts as God promised to act in Ezekiel 34:14-16:

> I will feed them with good pasture, and on the mountain heights of Israel shall be their grazing land. There they shall lie down in good grazing land, and on rich pasture they shall feed on the mountains of Israel. I myself will be the shepherd of my sheep, and I myself will make them lie down, declares the Lord GOD. I will seek the lost, and I will bring back the strayed, and I will bind up the injured, and I will strengthen the weak, and the fat and the strong I will destroy. I will feed them in justice.

Jesus Fulfills Prophecy About the Messiah as Shepherd

While these words declare what the Lord GOD himself will do, they continue: "And I will set up over them one shepherd, my servant David, and he shall feed them: he shall feed them and be their shepherd" (Ezekiel 34:23). By claiming to be the good shepherd from Ezekiel 34, Jesus links himself to God as the Shepherd and to the Messiah, the descendant of David.

Jesus Claims Authority to Lay Down and Take Up His Life

28. Read John 10:17-18 below. Underline the reason the Father loves Jesus. Box what no one can do. Double underline what Jesus has the authority to do with his life.

> For this reason the Father loves me, because I lay down my life that I may take it up again. No one takes it from me, but I lay it down of my own accord. I have authority to lay it down, and I have authority to take it up again. This charge I have received from my Father.

To Jesus's listeners, these words are puzzling. They will make sense only later and only to those willing to hear. But his followers can take comfort that God's preordained plan is unfolding. Still, his detractors comprehend Jesus's claims that the Father gave him the authority to both *lay* his life *down* and *take it up again*. These are more divine prerogatives, so they have further reason to reject him.

29. Read John 10:19-21. (a) How did some of the Jews dismiss Jesus (verse 20)? (b) How did others rebut their argument (verse 21)?

Some of them argue similarly to the healed man even though the Jewish leaders had cast the healed man out of the synagogue for it.

30. ♥ Think of someone you shepherd. How can you act as a good shepherd who puts the sheep's needs first rather than as the faithless shepherds who seek power, control, and other's praise?

In this lesson, we saw the Jewish leaders cast a healed man out of the synagogue for saying he believed that God sent Jesus. Afterward, Jesus sought him and found him, just as a shepherd should do. Jesus told the Jewish leaders they were spiritually blind. He also claimed to be the only door to the sheepfold of Jews, and he said he has other folds. Further, he said he is the good shepherd who lays his life down for the sheep. He even alleged he had the authority to both lay down his life for the sheep and take it up again.

In our next lesson, we'll see the Jewish leaders' reaction to Jesus's claims.

Day 5

The Sheep Hear the Shepherd's Voice

So far, Jesus has healed a man blind from birth. When the Jewish leaders cast the man out of the synagogue, Jesus sought him out and accepted his worship. He applied to himself the Old Testament prophecies of God pasturing the sheep and setting a descendant of

The Little Details
D.A. Carson: The Thief
While the thief comes *only to steal and kill and destroy,* Jesus comes *that they may have life, and have it to the full.* This is a proverbial way of insisting that there is only one means of receiving eternal life...only one source of knowledge of God, only one fount of spiritual nourishment, only one basis for spiritual security—Jesus alone. The world still seeks its humanistic, political saviours—its Hitlers, its Stalins, its Maos, its Pol Pots—and only too late does it learn that they blatantly confiscate personal property (they come "only to steal"), ruthlessly trample human life under foot (they come "only...to kill"), and contemptuously savage all that is valuable (they come "only...to destroy"). "Jesus is right. It is not the Christian doctrine of heaven that is the myth, but the humanist dream of utopia."[11]

- -

Still, his detractors comprehend Jesus's claims that the Father gave him the authority to both *lay* his life *down* and *take it up again*. These are more divine prerogatives, so they have further reason to reject him.

- -

The Little Details
The Feast of Dedication (Hanukkah)

From exile, Daniel prophesied this about a future foreign ruler: "Forces from him shall appear and profane the temple and fortress, and shall take away the regular burnt offering. And they shall set up the abomination that makes desolate. He shall seduce with flattery those who violate the covenant, but the people who know their God shall stand firm and take action" (Daniel 11:31-32).

This was fulfilled in 167 BC when Antiochus IV Epiphanes sent forces to massacre Jerusalem. He forbade all Jewish religious practices. He erected an altar to Zeus in the temple and sacrificed swine and other unclean animals there. He claimed to be divine. Some unfaithful Jews sided with him.

But the Maccabees were faithful Jews who successfully fought against him. They cleansed and rededicated the temple to God on December 14, 164 BC. This rededication is celebrated annually as the Feast of Dedication, also known as Hanukkah and the Feast of Lights.

David over his people as shepherd. And he claimed to have the divine prerogative to lay down his life and take it up again.

Jesus Is the Christ

Fall flows into winter, and Jesus is again at the temple, this time to celebrate the Feast of Dedication. It celebrated both deliverance from foreign forces that had defiled the temple as well as the cleansing and rededication of the temple afterward. Jesus walked in the colonnade of Solomon, which provided some protection from cold weather. The celebration of deliverance naturally brings up questions about the deliverance Jews hope for from the Christ.

> **31.** Read John 10:22-26. (a) What did the Jews ask (verse 24)? (b) What did Jesus say bore witness to who he has been saying he is (verse 25)? (c) Why don't they believe (verse 26)?

His works, the signs he's given, and his teaching all point to his being the fulfillment of Old Testament prophecies about the Christ. But the Jews present don't believe he is the Christ. Nonetheless, Jesus will not publicly declare he is the Christ, for that could cause a revolt. Besides, his challengers still wouldn't believe him.

Jesus Gives His Sheep Secure Eternal Life

> **32.** Read John 10:27-29. (a) Who hears Jesus's voice (verse 27)? (b) What does Jesus give them (verse 28)? (c) Can anyone snatch his sheep from him (verse 28)? (d) Why not (verse 29)?

Not only is Jesus the good shepherd, but no thief or wolf or being can snatch from God's hand those who belong to Jesus: "For he is our God, and we are the people of his pasture, and the sheep of his hand."[12] His sheep are secure in his care.

Jesus and the Father Are One

> **33.** Read John 10:30-33. (a) What does Jesus claim (verse 30)? (b) What is the Jews' response (verse 31)? (c) Why (verse 33)?

John has already told us that Jesus is indeed God. But the Jews present don't agree.

Jesus points out that he has shown them *many good works from the Father*, all signs that he comes from God. He gives them another chance to consider whether their objections to his healings point to a problem with their traditions.

Jesus Is the Consecrated One

34. Read John 10:34-36. (a) What are the words Jesus quotes from the Old Testament (verse 34)? (b) What does Jesus say about Old Testament Scripture (verse 35)? (c) In what two ways does Jesus describe himself (verse 36)?

Jesus quotes Psalm 82:6. The Hebrew *ĕlōhîm* can refer to God, angels, false gods, or human leaders. But here it refers to corrupt human leaders. Jesus uses the psalm to calm the situation without getting into the nuances of what the psalm means.

Jesus further says he is the one whom *the Father consecrated and sent into the world*. The Jews are currently commemorating the consecration of the second temple. John 2:21 explains that Jesus's body is the temple. Thus, the consecration of the temple foreshadowed the consecration of Jesus's body as the temple. In other words, Jesus fulfills what the Feast of Dedication celebrates.

The Little Details
"Son of God" (John 10:36)

When the Lord sent Moses to Pharaoh, he told him to say this: "Thus says the Lord, Israel is my firstborn son, and I say to you, 'Let my son go that he may serve me'" (Exodus 4:22-23). Here, God called the nation of Israel his son.

Hosea 11:1 is another instance of God calling the nation his son: "When Israel was a child, I loved him, and out of Egypt I called my son."

But Matthew 2:15 says Jesus as the Son of God fulfills Hosea 11:1. Matthew means that Israel's status as son of God was a type of Jesus's status as Son of God in a greater, more literal way.

Jesus Is the Son of God

As to Jesus calling himself *Son of God*, in the Old Testament, God called the nation of Israel his son (Exodus 4:22). Additionally, the Lord gave the title *son of God* to all the kings descended from David (2 Samuel 7:14; Psalm 2:7, the kings' coronation psalm). If Jesus was the Christ, the Messiah, then the title was legitimately his.

Jesus Offers His Works as Evidence He Is One with the Father

35. Read John 10:37-39. (a) What does Jesus want them to believe (verses 37-38)? (b) Why does he want them to believe (verse 38)? (c) What happened when they tried to arrest him (verse 39)?

Healing the lame and blind are works of the Father. The healed blind man sees that. Jesus encourages these to believe the evidence of the works, for that would be a first step toward knowing and understanding who he is in relation to the Father. But the Jews understand Jesus's claim to deity and seek to kill him.

John the Baptist's Disciples Believe in Jesus

By this time, John the Baptist has been martyred.

36. Read John 10:40-42. (a) Where did Jesus go (verse 40)? (b) Why did many of John the Baptist's former followers believe in Jesus (verses 41-42)?

He gives them another chance to consider whether their objections to his healings point to a problem with their traditions.

These people see Jesus's signs, remember what the Baptist told them, and believe.

The Good News

Jesus claimed to have lived before Abraham's time, and he applied to himself God's name—I AM. He said he is the light of the world and demonstrated the truth of his claim by healing a man born blind. This fulfilled prophecies about what the suffering servant would do and what would happen when God visited earth.

Jesus said he is the gate through which his sheep pass to pasture. He also said he is the good shepherd who lays down his life for the sheep. Further, he claimed the authority to both lay down and take up his life. Indeed, he said he offers secure eternal life. Moreover, he asserted he is one with the Father, who consecrated him. Finally, he said he is the Son of God.

> **37.** ♥ Which of these items of good news means the most to you today? Why?

As Jesus's signs increase, so does opposition by the Jewish leaders. In the next chapter we'll see Jesus's greatest sign to date, one that will bring his public ministry to a close.

> **Praise** God for something you saw of his character this week. **Confess** anything that convicted you. **Ask** for help to do something God's Word calls you to do. **Thank** God for something you learned this week.

Jesus claimed to have lived before Abraham's time, and he applied to himself God's name—I AM.

Karla's Creative Connection

I can so identify with sheep. Before I met the Good Shepherd, I wandered. I went from sheepfold to sheepfold looking for a place to belong. Some shepherds I followed wore robes. Some were mystics. Some psychics. Once a shepherd even came knocking on my door. I was lonely and let her in. But every sheepfold left me weary and wanting, and my wandering continued...until I heard and followed the voice of Jesus, the Good Shepherd, calling my name.

Because Jesus laid down his life for us, you and I belong to him. We are the sheep of his pasture, his beloved, and he is always here for us—protecting, leading, and guiding us in every way. Sometimes we just need to quiet all the other voices around us to hear his.

For example, I had always said, "I can't draw animals," let alone teach someone else how to draw them. And yet here I am today teaching you these simple steps to drawing a lamb, only because I trusted that still, small voice in my heart saying, *Yes, you can*. And I trusted it enough to follow. So thanks to our Good Shepherd, I hope you enjoy learning how to draw this little lamb.

1. For the head, start by drawing a circle and oval in pencil as shown above. 2. Add the shape of the ears. 3. Using a fine-tip marker or pen, outline and add the eye and nose as shown. 4. Erase.

5. In pencil, draw an oval for the body and a cute little tail. 6. Add the legs as shown.

7. Add a curly outline to the body, tail, and legs. 8. Erase the pencil lines, and you have a little lamb.

By the way, if your Good Shepherd has been speaking to your heart, encouraging you to turn an "I can't" into a "Yes, I can," don't be afraid. Follow his voice. He'll guide you every step of the way!

Karla

Chapter 6

John 11:1–12:50
The Resurrection and the Life

What evidence did Jesus offer that he had power over death?

Day 1

Reinforced Resolve

When I told my dad I was a Christian, he grimaced and shook his head. "I could easily talk you out of it," he said, "but I won't." I didn't know how long he would hold back, so I determined to study the evidence for Christianity so I would be ready.

Because of my dad's comments, I hardened my commitment to what I believed the evidence supported. I wasn't going to let him sway me. But not all hardening is good. If you've raised teenagers (or remember being one), you know reminding them not to do something they want to do often hardens their resolve. And that happens with adults too.

Today we'll see what happens when God repeats a message to people who don't want to hear.

God's Word to Us in the Old Testament

Our reading in John today both quotes and alludes to Isaiah, so let's begin there.

The Lord Foretold Hardened Hearts

When God called Isaiah to be his prophet, a godly king ruled in Judah. But the people were becoming more corrupt. Isaiah describes seeing a vision of the glory of the Lord. He writes, "And I heard the voice of the Lord saying, 'Whom shall I send, and who will go for us?' Then I said, 'Here I am! Send me'" (Isaiah 6:8). Here's what happens next (verses 9-10):

> And he said, "Go, and say to this people: 'Keep on hearing, but do not understand; keep on seeing, but do not perceive.' Make the heart of this people dull, and their ears heavy, and blind their eyes; lest they see with their eyes, and hear with their ears, and understand with their hearts, and turn and be healed."

In other words, God will send Isaiah to speak his words, but the message will merely harden their resolve. After all, when people repeatedly hear a message they don't want to hear, they block it. So Isaiah's message will encounter the people's stubbornness and cause spiritual **deafness and blindness**.

When their **opportunity to understand and repent passes**, then their hearts will be hardened until their judgment is complete. What judgment will come? The one Moses

The Little Details
Andreas J. Köstenberger and Scott R. Swain: The Prince of This World

The fourth evangelist acknowledges the presence of "the devil" (13:2), "Satan" (13:27), the "prince of this world" (12:31) or the "evil one" (17:15), though references to demon exorcism are notably absent in John. This suggests that, in John, Satan is pitted against Jesus, and the Spirit Jesus would send subsequent to his departure, but not in the sense of two equally matched dualities of good and evil, but in the sense that Satan opposes the triune God's salvation-historical purposes centred in Jesus' God-glorifying cross-death, his "lifting up."[1]

had warned about: exile. Because his people no longer served their purpose of proclaiming God to the nations, the Lord will exile them.

When the king who ruled when God called Isaiah died, his wayward son took the throne. Isaiah encouraged the young man to trust God, but he instead forsook God. Thus, what God told Isaiah came to pass. Namely, the king heard Isaiah's words but neither believed nor heeded them. In fact, this king placed an altar to another god in the temple and even sacrificed sons to a foreign god (2 Chronicles 28:3).

The Lord forewarned that this wouldn't be the last time people refused to listen to his message, though. He said when he sends the suffering servant with a message, many will refuse to believe it: "Who has believed what he has heard from us?" (Isaiah 53:1). Worse, people will despise and reject the servant (53:3).

The Lord Promised Resurrection

Tucked in among these prophecies, though, is good news: "Your dead shall live; their **bodies shall rise. You who dwell in the dust, awake** and sing for joy! For your dew is a dew of light, and **the earth will give birth to the dead**" (Isaiah 26:19). Thus, the Lord will one day resurrect the dead.

The Lord Foretold How the Messiah Will Come

After a remnant returned from exile, the prophet Zechariah encouraged the people to rebuild the temple. He assured them the promised Messiah would come. Indeed, in Zechariah 9:9, he explained how the king will appear:

> Rejoice greatly, O daughter of Zion!
> Shout aloud, O daughter of Jerusalem!
> Behold, your king is coming to you;
> righteous and having salvation is he,
> humble and **mounted on a donkey,**
> **on a colt, the foal of a donkey**.

The king won't enter Jerusalem on a war horse but shall rule in peace (verse 10).

The Psalms Call for the Lord to Save

Once the people rebuilt the temple, worship leaders put the book of Psalms into its final form. Psalm 118 became a favorite psalm to sing at the celebratory festivals for which people journeyed to Jerusalem. Here are verses 25-26:

> Save us, we pray, O Lord!
> O Lord, we pray, give us success!
> **Blessed is he who comes in the name of the Lord!**
> We bless you from the house of the Lord.

The Greek transliteration of the Hebrew for *save us* is **Hosanna**.

God's Word to Us in John

So far, we've seen Jesus offer significant signs that God sent him, including healing a man paralyzed for decades and another blind from birth. Now we'll read about an even greater sign.

The king won't enter Jerusalem on a war horse but shall rule in peace.

 Take a moment to pray for insight as you read God's Word.

1. ♥ Read John 11:1–12:50. What stands out to you? Why?

The Old Testament prophets promised a righteous king who would rule forever. They said he would come to Jerusalem riding on a donkey colt. But they also foretold that people would continue to reject God's messages, not just from current prophets but also from the suffering servant. Still, amid the sad news of hard hearts came the wonderful message that God would raise people from the dead.

In the next lesson, a messenger will come to Jesus with news that a dear friend is seriously ill. This provides Jesus an opportunity to teach more about the resurrection the Old Testament prophets promised.

The Old Testament prophets promised a righteous king who would rule forever.

Pam's Heart-to-Heart with the Great I Am— "I Am the Resurrection and the Life"

*Jesus said to her, "I am the resurrection and the life. The one who believes
in me will live, even though they die; and whoever lives
by believing in me will never die. Do you believe this?"*
John 11:25-26 NIV

Which woman of the Mary and Martha duo do you most relate to? Let me share two snapshots:

Mary's Moment

As Jesus and his disciples were on their way, he came to a village where a woman named Martha opened her home to him. She had a sister called **Mary, who sat at the Lord's feet listening to what he said**. But Martha was distracted by all the preparations that had to be made. She came to him and asked, "Lord, don't you care that my sister has left me to do the work by myself? Tell her to help me!"

"Martha, Martha," the Lord answered, "you are worried and upset about many things, but few things are needed—or **indeed only one. Mary has chosen what is better, and it will not be taken away from her**" (Luke 10:38-42 NIV, emphasis added).

Martha's Moment

On his arrival, Jesus found that Lazarus had already been in the tomb for four days. Now Bethany was less than two miles from Jerusalem, and many Jews had come to Martha and Mary to comfort them in the loss of their brother. **When Martha heard that Jesus was coming, she went out to meet him**, but Mary stayed at home.

"Lord," Martha said to Jesus, "if you had been here, my brother would not have died. But I know that even now God will give you whatever you ask."

Jesus said to her, "Your brother will rise again."

Martha answered, "I know he will rise again in the resurrection at the last day."

Jesus said to her, "I am the resurrection and the life. The one who believes in me will live, even though they die; and whoever lives by believing in me will never die. Do you believe this?"

"Yes, Lord," she replied, "I believe that you are the Messiah, the Son of God, who is to come into the world" (John 11:17-27 NIV, emphasis added).

Both sisters followed Jesus, each in the way they were created by him. For years, I tried to be the "sit-at-the-feet-of-Jesus-and-soak-it-in" kind of gal—but I have ADHD! It's a miracle that I've written 50 plus books, because to write I fight my own body and mind wanting to move. I write only through Christ's resurrection power.

Our Need for Resurrection

On the prayer cards and emails of our Love-Wise ministry, I daily see women longing for Christ's resurrection power in their marriages, children, finances, businesses, health, ministries, and in their friends and family who need a personal relationship with Jesus.

Let me share the most vivid resurrection story in our family. Our son Zach has in his DNA my ADHD and strong will. As soon as Zach could walk, he could climb over the fence and escape the yard! At three he jumped onto his brother's bike and rode like a pro without training wheels. At four he helped his dad hang siding on the home we were building, and to retrieve a Frisbee, he would hop onto the roof of the church we pastored.

But he leaned to rebellion. While building that same home, I saw him disobey and eat a whole box of chocolate donuts after being told no. When confronted, and as chocolate drooled out of his over-packed mouth, he answered, "I didn't eat those!"

Eventually, Zach harnessed his talent and garnered an athletic college scholarship. To guide him, we used two tools we created: the Frosh Foundation Dinner and Dialogue worksheet to help him in his freshman year of college and the Farrel Family Scholarship Agreement to talk through wise choices. As parents, any financial help we give our college-aged kids comes with scholarship requirements too.

Looking back, the most powerful choice I made as a mom of a prodigal was to claim Christ's resurrection power over Zach's life. On my daily prayer walk, I personalized and prayed a verse for my son:

> ...in the presence of the God in whom he believed, who gives life to the dead and calls into existence the things that do not exist (Romans 4:17).

The turning point came when Bill and I had to put Zach on "academic probation." He had six weeks to get his act together or we were going to cut off all our help for his life. I traveled to meet him in person and asked if I could pray this verse over him. He loves and respects us, so he agreed, and we knelt together. I prayed, then slid the Bible in front of him. As he read the truth, something in him broke: Our son's strength submitted to Christ's resurrection power. He rose a new man.

A few weeks later, Zach called. He told me he'd purchased two copies of *The Purpose Driven Life* and asked if I would be his accountability partner. He chose his own church; got involved with men's ministry; captained his team to numerous national championships; met and married a beautiful, godly woman; has become a fabulous husband and attentive father; and is a successful coach who now speaks for Christian groups and team chapels.

Be like Mary. Sit at Jesus's feet to learn the Word. Be like Martha. Rise to meet Jesus as he brings his resurrection power to your world.

Pam

Experiencing Scripture Creatively

- Paint "I am the resurrection and the life" on a flowerpot. Plant flower seeds in the pot.
- Illustrate John 11:25 in your Bible or in a journal by following Karla's instructions at the end of this chapter for drawing flowers. Draw a seed, a seedling, and then a full-grown flower.

The Little Details

Across the Jordan (John 10:40; 11:6)

If Jesus is in Batanea (a possible site of "Bethany across the Jordan" in John 1:28), then he is a four-day journey from Bethany near Jerusalem. That means he waited until he knew Lazarus had died before making the trip.

On the other hand, if Jesus is closer to the Jordan River in Perea, then he is only a one-day trip away. In that case, the messenger took one day to arrive, Jesus waited two days, and Jesus made the trip in one day. In this scenario, Lazarus died shortly after the messenger left.

Either way, Lazarus did not die because Jesus waited.

The sisters want Jesus to hurry, so it's strange that he delays coming *because* he loves them.

The Glorified Son

Because the Jewish leaders in Jerusalem had tried to arrest and kill Jesus, he went across the Jordan to where John had been baptizing. Meanwhile, something happened in Bethany, less than two miles from Jerusalem in Judea.

Sometimes Bad Things Happen to Bring Great Good

2. Read John 11:1-4. (a) Who was ill (verse 1)? (b) What do you think the sisters expected would happen (verse 3)? (c) What did Jesus say the illness would not end in (verse 4)? (d) What was the illness's purpose (verse 4)?

John assumes his readers have already heard about Mary anointing Jesus and lets them know this is she.

Jesus knows from his Father that "this sickness is not to end in death, but for the glory of God, so that the Son of God may be glorified by it" (John 11:4 NASB). *Glory* is a revelation of God that displays his presence, power, and holiness in a way that humans can experience. His glory either draws people to him or pushes them away.

3. Read John 11:5-6. (a) How did Jesus feel about the siblings (verse 5)? (b) Because of that, what did he do (verse 6)?

The sisters want Jesus to hurry, so it's strange that he delays coming *because* he loves them. But later John will explain how love prompts Jesus.

Jesus Does Not Fear His Enemies

4. Read John 11:7-10. (a) Two days later, where did Jesus want to go (verse 7)? (b) Why were the disciples surprised (verse 8)? (c) What won't the disciples do if they walk in the light rather than in the night (verses 9-10)?

The disciples fear returning to Judea. Jesus calms their fears by reminding them of something he said when they were last at the temple: "As long as I am in the world, I am the light of the world" (John 9:5). They won't stumble if they're walking under his guidance because he does only what his Father tells him. And right now, his Father tells him to go to Judea.

5. Read John 11:11-16. (a) What does Jesus know has happened to Lazarus (verse 14)? (b) Why was Jesus glad he wasn't with Lazarus when he died (verse 15)? (c) What courage does Thomas show (verse 16)?

Has fallen asleep is a euphemism for "has died." It's particularly apt because of Jesus's intention to *awaken him*. But the disciples understand neither what he means by *asleep* nor *awaken*.

Jesus Is the Resurrection and the Life

6. Read John 11:17-19. (a) How long had Lazarus been dead (verse 17)? (b) How far was Jerusalem from Bethany (verse 18)?

Many Jews believed that a person's soul hovered around the body for three days, leaving open the possibility of resuscitation within that period.[2] Jesus arrives, therefore, after all hope of resuscitation is gone.

Bethany is so close to Jerusalem that many from the city travel to comfort the sisters. That shows the family's high standing. Friends, relatives, flute players, and professional wailing women all gather around the two siblings.[3]

7. Read John 11:20-22. (a) What did Martha do when she heard Jesus was on his way (verse 20)? (b) What does Martha believe would have happened if Jesus had been present (verse 21)? (c) What is her profession of faith (verse 22)?

Martha goes to greet Jesus while Mary remains with the guests. Martha is not rebuking Jesus but professing her faith that he would have healed her brother had he been present before Lazarus died. Despite thinking Jesus has arrived too late to save her brother, she still has complete faith that God gives Jesus whatever he asks.

8. Read John 11:23-25. (a) What does Jesus assure Martha (verse 23)? (b) What confidence does Martha express (verse 24)? (c) What does Jesus call himself (verse 25)? (d) Turn to the 7 **"I Am" Statements** chart at the back of the book and write "The resurrection and the life" on line 5.

I am the resurrection and the life. This is an amazing claim.

Many Jews believed that a person's soul hovered around the body for three days, leaving open the possibility of resuscitation within that period. Jesus arrives, therefore, after all hope of resuscitation is gone.

9. Read John 11:25-27. (a) What does Jesus say will happen to those who believe in him (verse 25)? (b) What will happen to those who live and believe in him (verse 26)? (c) What three titles does Martha give Jesus (verse 27)?

Martha confesses her belief in Jesus. He is Lord. He is the Christ, the expected King who will rule forever. And he is the Son of God.

10. ♥ Read Jesus's words to Martha in John 11:25-26 as if he is speaking to you. Answer his question: "Do you believe this?"

In this lesson, we saw that Jesus says he is the resurrection and the life. In the next lesson, we'll see Jesus demonstrate not only what he means by *I am the resurrection and the life* but also his great love for Lazarus, Martha, and Mary.

Day 3

The Giver of Life

In our last lesson, we read that Martha's loss and grief did not sway her from her belief in Jesus as the Christ and the Son of God. After speaking to him, she goes to summon her sister Mary.

Jesus Weeps

11. Read John 11:28-32. (a) Who did Martha tell Mary was calling for her (verse 28)? (b) What did Mary believe wouldn't have happened if Jesus could have arrived much earlier (verse 32)?

Martha attempts to bring Mary out privately, but many mourners follow her. Like Martha, Mary is certain that Lazarus would not have died if Jesus had come earlier.

12. Read John 11:33-37. (a) What was Jesus's reaction to Mary's weeping (verse 33)? (b) What did Jesus do (verse 35)? (c) How did the people react (verses 36-37)?

Martha confesses her belief in Jesus. He is Lord. He is the Christ, the expected King who will rule forever. And he is the Son of God.

Jesus is *deeply moved in his spirit* (*angry in His spirit,* HCSB). The ESV gives an alternate translation of *indignant.* The underlying Greek word's root means "to snort with anger."[4]

Jesus is angry at how sin and death have afflicted the world. He may also be angry at the unbelief of some of the mourners.

And then…Jesus weeps.

Jesus Proves He Can Give Life

13. Read John 11:38-40. (a) Why didn't Martha want the stone removed as Jesus commanded (verse 39)? (b) What did Jesus tell her (verse 40)?

Martha protests because the body has begun to decompose. Jesus reminds her of his promise. Of course, she thinks he's speaking of the resurrection on the last day.

14. Read John 11:41-44. (a) Why did Jesus thank God for hearing him (verses 41-42)? (b) What happened when Jesus commanded Lazarus to come out (verses 43-44)? (c) Jump ahead to read verse 47. Then on the **8 Signs** chart, write "Raised Lazarus from the dead" on line 7.

Jesus wants the people to believe that God has sent him, so he prays aloud before calling forth the dead man. Lazarus's body recomposes, then he arises and comes out of the tomb.

Jesus has proven that he has life in himself and can give life to whomever he wishes.

Now it's plain what John meant when he said Jesus waited to come because he loved Martha, Mary, and Lazarus. He waited so they could participate in Jesus's greatest sign to date: raising a man four-days dead. They witnessed the evidence that Jesus was the giver of life. They and their faith would be remembered by all. He gave them better than they asked for.

Recall the words of the prologue: "In him was life, and the life was the light of men" (John 1:4). Now we can see this does not merely mean Jesus was alive. No, it means he *was* life and *gives* life.

The Astonished Crowd Reacts

15. Read John 11:45-48. (a) How did many people at the tomb react (verse 45)? (b) What did some do (verse 46)? (c) What were the Jewish leaders afraid would happen if they didn't find a way to stop Jesus from performing signs (verse 48)?

While some see the sign as evidence God sent Jesus, others report it to the Pharisees who believe Jesus can't be from God. The miracle merely hardens their resolve.

The Little Details
D.A. Carson: Grave Clothes

The corpse was customarily laid on a sheet of linen, wide enough to envelop the body completely and more than twice the length of the corpse. The body was so placed on the sheet that the feet were at one end, and then the sheet was drawn over the head and back down to the feet. The feet were bound at the ankles, and the arms were tied to the body with linen strips. The face was bound with another cloth (*soudarion,* a loan-word from the Latin *sudarium,* "sweat cloth," often worn in life around the neck). Jesus' body was apparently prepared for burial in the same way (*cf.* 19:40; 20:5,7). A person so bound could hop and shuffle, but scarcely walk. Therefore when Jesus commanded Lazarus to come forth, and the *dead man came out,* Jesus promptly gave the order, *take off the grave clothes and let him go.*[5]

The Little Details
The Dinner at Bethany

John places the dinner events in John 12:2-8 rather than relaying events in chronological order. This keeps it near the reason for the dinner: honoring Jesus for raising Lazarus from the dead.

The parallel accounts in Matthew 26:6-13 and Mark 14:3-9 give more details. They explain that this dinner was held on Tuesday, not the same day the weary travelers arrived. It was at the house of Simon the leper (perhaps the siblings' deceased father).

Matthew and Mark note that Mary poured some of the ointment on Jesus's head, emphasizing his anointing as King. Jesus says she has anointed his body, for the abundance surely flowed over his body. John mentions only her pouring the ointment on his feet, linking it to the foot washing he's about to narrate and emphasizing Jesus's attitude of servanthood.

Luke's narration of a sinful woman who anointed Jesus's feet at the house of a Pharisee is a different incident that occurred around the time of John the Baptist's death (Luke 7:36-38).

One Man Should Die for All

16. Read John 11:49-52 below. Underline what Caiaphas said was better. Circle the word *prophesied*. Underline what John says he prophesied.

> But one of them, Caiaphas, who was high priest that year, said to them, "You know nothing at all. Nor do you understand that it is better for you that one man should die for the people, not that the whole nation should perish." He did not say this of his own accord, but being high priest that year he prophesied that Jesus would die for the nation, and not for the nation only, but also to gather into one the children of God who are scattered abroad.

These Jewish leaders don't believe Jesus is the Messiah, but they know more and more people do. They fear the crowds will try to crown Jesus, thinking he could free them from Rome. But the leaders think that will result in Rome putting down the rebellion and taking away their leadership roles in Judea. Later, John will hear about Caiaphas's words and realize they're prophetic.

17. Read John 11:53-57. (a) What did the Jewish leaders plan (verse 53)? (b) What did Jesus no longer do (verse 54)? (c) What feast was at hand (verse 55)? (d) What orders had the Jewish leaders given (verse 57)?

Jesus gave life; as a result, the Jewish leaders resolved to take life.

18. ♥ Describe a time when God gave you better than what you prayed for.

Mary Anoints Jesus for Burial

It's no surprise that Lazarus, Martha, and Mary wish to honor Jesus for bringing Lazarus back from the dead.

19. Read John 12:1-3. (a) When did Jesus arrive in Bethany (verse 1)? (b) What did Mary do (verse 3)?

Jesus probably arrives in Bethany on Saturday after sunset.[6] A few days later, the siblings honor Jesus at a dinner. Mary shows extravagant love, pouring a pound of perfume on Jesus and filling the house with its scent.

20. Read John 12:4-8. (a) What was Judas Iscariot about to do (verse 4)? (b) Why did Judas complain about the perfume (verses 5-6)? (c) What did Jesus say the perfume was for (verse 7)?

Judas Iscariot rebukes Mary, but Jesus comes to her defense, telling him to leave her alone, for the anointing is for his burial. In ancient times, bodies were perfumed and covered with spices to mask the horrible odor that wafted a few days later.

In this lesson, we saw that sometimes bad things happen to bring about a greater good. In this case, Jesus proved he can give life to the dead. But John tells us that Caiaphas prophesied that Jesus should die for the nation, speaking better than he knew. In the next lesson, Jesus will fulfill still more prophecies.

Day 4

Israel's King

Another Passover is approaching.

People React to Jesus's Arrival

Those who hear that Jesus is at Bethany have mixed reactions.

The Chief Priests Plan Death

21. Read John 12:9-11. (a) When the crowd learned that Jesus had arrived in Bethany, what did they do (verse 9)? (b) What did the chief priests then do (verse 10)? (c) Why (verse 11)?

News of Jesus's arrival in Bethany raises a huge stir on Saturday, especially when they hear that Jesus will come to Jerusalem on Sunday.

Jesus Enters Jerusalem as King and Savior

On Sunday, Jesus makes his way to Jerusalem.

22. Read John 12:12-15. (a) What did the people shout when welcoming Jesus to Jerusalem (verse 13)? (b) How did Jesus arrive (verse 14)?

> News of Jesus's arrival in Bethany raises a huge stir on Saturday, especially when they hear that Jesus will come to Jerusalem on Sunday.

Hosanna means "save us." The people greet Jesus with shouts of Psalm 118:25-26, declaring him the *King of Israel*. Thus, they want Jesus to save them from Roman rule. But his disciples bring Jesus a donkey's colt, not a war horse, and he rides it into the city.[7] By doing

The Little Details
Why the Other Gospels Omit Lazarus's Resurrection

The other Gospels show Jesus raising others from the dead. For example, Mark records Jesus raising a child from the dead (Mark 5:35-42).

But John 12:10 tells us that "the chief priests made plans to put Lazarus to death as well." The other Gospel writers may have wished to protect Lazarus and his family. They tell of the dinner, but they don't give its purpose. John wrote his Gospel after the other three Gospels were in circulation, probably between 35 and 50 years after the resurrection. That's long enough that Lazarus was no longer endangered.

The disciples don't understand the significance of all that is happening.

---

so he fulfills Zechariah 9:9: "Behold, your king is coming to you; righteous and having salvation is he, humble and mounted on a donkey, on a colt, the foal of a donkey." While most of verse 15 comes from Zechariah 9:9, *fear not* likely comes from Isaiah 40:9: "Fear not; say to the cities of Judah, 'Behold your God!'"

Those Who Saw Lazarus Raised Bear Witness

> 23. Read John 12:16-19. (a) When did the disciples understand all that was happening to Jesus (verse 16)? (b) Who continued to testify that they had witnessed Jesus raise Lazarus from the dead (verse 17)? (c) How did the Pharisees react (verse 19)?

The disciples don't understand the significance of all that is happening. John explains that some things they will understand later, after Jesus is *glorified*.

> 24. ♥ Describe a time when you didn't recognize the significance of what was happening. How did you feel when you later realized the significance?

The Pharisees Are Not Doing Any Good

John 12:19 (NASB) reads, "So the Pharisees said to one another, 'You see that you are not doing any good; look, the world has gone after Him.'" By *you are not doing any good,* the Pharisees mean they're not succeeding in stopping people from following Jesus. But John writes it in a fashion that carries a double meaning: Their plans to kill Jesus are not good.

Jesus's Hour Comes

The Jews excited about the sign and the leaders dismayed by it aren't the only ones seeking Jesus in Jerusalem.

> 25. Read John 12:20-23. (a) Who besides Jews came to the feast (verse 20)? (b) What did they want (verse 21)? (c) When Jesus heard they sought him, what did he announce (verse 23)?

The Greeks probably seek Philip because his name is Greek. If they come from the Greek Decapolis, they may even know Philip since his hometown is close to the Decapolis border.

We're not told whether Jesus talks to them. But we are told that his immediate response is to announce, "The hour has come for the son of Man to be glorified" (John 12:23).

Jesus Is the Grain That Dies to Bear Fruit

26. Read John 12:24-26. (a) What happens when a grain of wheat falls to the earth and dies (verse 24)? (b) What will happen to those who love this life (verse 25)? (c) What about those who hate this life in this world (verse 25)? (d) What must Jesus's servants do (verse 26)? (e) What will the Father then do (verse 26)?

Jesus likens what he is about to do to what happens to a grain of wheat. The grain must fall to the earth and die to bear fruit. He does not love his life in this world so much that he would reject the Father's mission. And he wishes his followers to be the same. Then the Father will honor them.

Jesus Is Troubled by What Is About to Come

When the Word became flesh, he took on the ability to suffer.

27. Read John 12:27-30. (a) How does Jesus feel (verse 27)? (b) What is his resolve (verse 27)? (c) What does he ask the Father to do (verse 28)? (d) What did the Father answer (verse 28)? (e) For whose sake was the voice (verse 30)?

Jesus knows what is about to happen, and his soul is troubled. But he sets himself to fulfill his purpose for coming. The Father answers his prayer audibly to strengthen the faith of his followers.

Jesus Will Draw All People to Himself

28. Read John 12:31-33 below. Underline the two things that would happen now. Circle what Jesus says will happen to him. Box what Jesus was describing.

> Now is the judgment of this world; now will the ruler of this world be cast out. And I, when I am lifted up from the earth, will draw all people to myself." He said this to show by what kind of death he was going to die.

The ruler of this world is Satan. God made Adam and Eve the rulers of the world under him, but when they believed the Serpent and ate the forbidden fruit, the one to whom they submitted ruled instead.

Lifted up indicates *what kind of death* Jesus will suffer. But it also describes the exaltation of the suffering servant: "Behold, my servant shall act wisely; he shall be high and lifted up, and shall be exalted" (Isaiah 52:13).

The Little Details
Chronology of Jesus's Final Week

Here's a possible chronology for the events John gives during Passion Week.

Sunday

Triumphal entry (12:12-19)

Monday

Teaching (12:20-50)

Tuesday

Mary anoints Jesus (12:2-6)

Thursday afternoon

Passover sacrifice of lambs

Thursday evening

Jesus washes disciples' feet (13:1-20)

Last supper (Passover meal and start of Feast of Unleavened Bread; 13:21-30)

Teaching, prayer (13:31–17)

Thursday evening to Friday

Gethsemane (18:1)

Friday

Betrayal, arrest, crucifixion (18–19)[8]

God made Adam and Eve the rulers of the world under him, but when they believed the Serpent and ate the forbidden fruit, the one to whom they submitted ruled instead.

---

29. Read John 12:34 below. Circle how long the Christ should remain.

> So the crowd answered him, "We have heard from the Law that the Christ remains forever. How can you say that the Son of Man must be lifted up? Who is this Son of Man?"

The crowd connects the glorification of *the Son of Man* (verse 23) with *the Christ*. It also connects death with Jesus's statement, *when I am lifted up from the earth* (verse 32). They don't know how a Christ who rules forever can die.

Jesus declines to answer and instead tells them what they need to know now.

30. Read John 12:35-36. (a) What does Jesus tell the people to do while the light is with them (verse 35)? (b) What must they do to become sons of light (verse 36)?

Jesus hides himself to illustrate his words. He is the light who will soon be gone from their sight. Now is the time to believe.

In this lesson we've seen that Jesus raising Lazarus from the dead convinced more people that he is the Christ. But it also hardened some Jewish leaders' resolve to stop him. Still, Jesus rode into Jerusalem on a donkey colt, fulfilling prophecy. Moreover, the crowd shouted for him to save them. Then, when Greeks came to see him, Jesus announced his time had come and began talking about his impending death. In fact, he said he was like a grain that must fall and die to bear fruit. Further, he claimed he would draw all people to himself when he was lifted up. In the next lesson, we'll see how the brewing situation fulfills even more prophecy.

Day 5

Who Has Believed?

Jesus has come to Jerusalem amid shouts of "Save us!" But while his signs strengthen faith in many, they harden the resolve of others against him.

Some Don't Believe Jesus Is Who He Claims to Be

The people know Jesus has raised Lazarus from the dead. But what will they do with that knowledge?

31. Read John 12:37-38. What did unbelief fulfill?

John explains that the people's unbelief is in fulfillment of Isaiah 53:1, which is in the fourth servant song. *What he heard from us* is Jesus's teaching. *The arm of the Lord* is the power Jesus has shown in his miraculous signs. In Isaiah, the suffering righteous servant laments over people's unbelief.

32. Read John 12:39-40. Why else could the people not believe?

Jesus's message and miracles merely hardened the resolve of those who had set their hearts against him.

33. Read John 12:41. Why did Isaiah prophesy these passages?

His glory may mean the glory that Isaiah saw at his calling, for he "saw the Lord sitting upon a throne, high and lifted up" while heavenly creatures declared "the whole earth is full of his glory" (Isaiah 6:1,3). Or *his glory* may refer to the glory Isaiah saw as he prophesied about the Messiah, the suffering righteous servant, and the coming glorious kingdom. Either way, "the glory of God described in Isaiah 6:1-3 anticipates the glory of the incarnate Christ."[9]

Some Jewish Leaders Hide Their Faith in Jesus

34. Read John 12:42-43. Why did some of the Jewish leaders hide their belief in Jesus?

We seek the glory that comes from people over the glory that comes from God when

- we hide our belief in God to escape criticism;
- we follow the rules of people instead of the commands of God;
- we fill our hearts with envy and jealousy; and
- we practice acts of righteousness in public so others will praise us.

35. ♥ What is a way you can show you love the glory that comes from God more than the glory that comes from people?

Jesus Claims Belief in Him Is Belief in God and That Seeing Him Is Seeing God

Jesus hid himself to demonstrate that he would be among the people only a little while longer (John 12:36). Now he cries out.

36. Read John 12:44-45. (a) According to Jesus, belief in him is also belief in whom (verse 44)? (b) According to Jesus, seeing him is also seeing whom (verse 45)?

Jesus's message and miracles merely hardened the resolve of those who had set their hearts against him.

The Little Details
"Made Him Known" *(John 1:18)*

John 1:18 reads, "the only God, who is at the Father's side, he [Jesus] has made him known." The Greek word for *made known* is the word from which we get "exegesis." It means "to narrate." D.A. Carson writes, "the Word-made-flesh, 'narrated' or 'exegeted' God to man."[10]

From Jesus's words, we can now better understand John's prologue: "In the beginning was the Word, and the Word was with God, and the Word was God" (John 1:1); "And the Word became flesh and dwelt among us, and we have seen his glory, glory as of the only Son from the Father, full of grace and truth" (John 1:14); and "No one has ever seen God; the only God, who is at the Father's side, he has made him known" (John 1:18).

Jesus Says He Is the World's Light

> **37.** Read John 12:46. Why did Jesus come into the world?

John's prologue says, "In him was life, and the life was the light of men. The light shines in the darkness, and the darkness has not overcome it" (John 1:4-5). Now we've seen Jesus give life that shines in the darkness, light that dispels spiritual darkness.

> **38.** Read John 12:47-50. (a) What will happen to those who hear Jesus's words but reject him and his words (verses 47-48)? (b) Who does Jesus say commands him what to say (verses 49-50)?

Jesus claims that seeing him is seeing the Father and that everything he says is at his Father's command. Those who reject Jesus's words will be judged by those words on the last day because those words come from God.

The Good News

In John 11–12, Jesus makes incredible, polarizing claims. He asserts he is the resurrection and the life. Then he demonstrates that he has the power to give life by raising Lazarus from the dead. Later, Jesus enters Jerusalem on a donkey, fulfilling messianic prophecy. But when Mary anoints him with perfume, he says it is for his burial. Similarly, Jesus likens himself to a grain that must die to bear fruit. Yet he also says he will draw all people to himself when he is lifted up. Consequently, while some proclaim Jesus is King, others are hardened in their resolve against him and plot to kill him. They don't know it, but even this fulfills prophecy. Furthermore, Jesus claims that belief in him is belief in God and seeing him is seeing God. Moreover, he says he is the world's light and his words are the Father's words.

> **39.** ❤ Which of these items of good news means the most to you today? Why?

In our next chapter, Jesus ceases his public teaching to prepare his disciples for ministry and for living as his disciple when Jesus is no longer present in the same way.

> 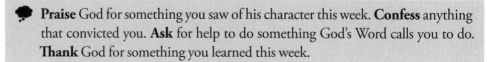 **Praise** God for something you saw of his character this week. **Confess** anything that convicted you. **Ask** for help to do something God's Word calls you to do. **Thank** God for something you learned this week.

Karla's Creative Connection

In this week's key verse, John 11:25, Jesus declares himself to be the resurrection and the life. He says those of us who believe in him, though we will die here on earth, will live eternally with him beyond the grave. Having recently lost my husband of 49 years, this verse brings comfort to my soul and fills me with hope for the day when I will see him once again.

As I was pondering ideas for this verse, I thought about how there is no resurrection without death. So the cross became the focal art element of the design. And as I visually "planted" flowers at the foot of the cross, I thought about how most flowers grow from a seed—a seed that appears dead and yet holds within it the beauty and bounty of new life, a flowery reminder of the new life that awaits us on the other side of this earthly life.

To celebrate this beauty and promise this week, I want to share a fun and easy way for you to create your own unique flower garden.

Simply start by drawing a circle with a pencil you can erase later and a smaller set of circles within it. To evenly space the petals around the center, draw the first four petals directly across from each other. Then add the next petals in between to fill in. To make a fuller flower, add a second layer of petals in between the petals of the first layer as shown. Finish by adding tiny strokes to the center just for fun.

In the above row of flowers, you can see that by simply changing the size of the center and the shape of the petals you can create an endless variety of flowers to add to your garden or bouquet.

And finally, if you add a few small details, your flowers will take on their own beautiful personalities.

Karla

Chapter 7

John 13:1–14:31
The Servant King

What evidence did Jesus offer that his imminent death was part of God's plan?

The Righteous Servant

Years ago, Pam's husband, Bill, and my husband, Clay, planned a ministry together. As we prayed over this and made tentative plans, we realized that one of the first things we had to do was start attending the church Bill pastored even though it was 50 miles south of us.

But that meant I would have to leave the women's ministry leadership team at our current church, where I oversaw the quarterly women's breakfasts, led a weekly small group within the women's Bible study meetings, served on the women's retreat team, and wrote our women's ministry newsletter.

As I prepared to leave, I met with everyone who would be taking over these roles. I gave them my documents, contact lists, and procedures (knowing they would change them!). I met one final time with my team and small group, turning over my roles to gifted servant leaders. I gave a farewell talk, and we said tearful goodbyes.

In our reading today, Jesus knows he's about to depart, so he meets with his team—his disciples—one last time to turn over to them many of his roles. He delivers a farewell talk often called the Upper Room Discourse.

God's Word to Us in the Old Testament

Our Bibles record the farewell speeches of a number of great servant leaders. Let's look at two speeches that are related to what we'll read in John today.

Two Servant Leaders' Speeches

Moses was called "Moses the servant of the LORD" (Deuteronomy 34:5). As **God's servant**, Moses led the Israelites to the promised land. But Moses knew he couldn't go in with them, so he **passed leadership** to Joshua. Then he **prepared the people for his departure** with a long speech in which he reminded them of how they should live in their new home. The speech fills most of the book of Deuteronomy. Moreover, Moses left behind five books and a psalm to guide people after his death.

Likewise, the Lord called King David "my servant David" (1 Kings 14:8). Though **he ruled as king, he remained the Lord's servant**. Like Moses, when David knew he would soon die, he passed on his leadership role to his son Solomon. They co-reigned until

The Little Details
Israel as a Type of Jesus

Israel was called God's servant and God's son. As such, the nation was a type of Jesus, the ultimate servant and the only begotten Son. As types, events in Israel's history foreshadowed events in Jesus's life. That's why the Gospel authors tell us Jesus fulfills certain prophecies about Israel.

For example, when wise men told King Herod that the king of the Jews had been born in Bethlehem, Herod killed all the young boys there. But an angel had told Joseph to flee to Egypt with Mary and the baby Jesus. Matthew 2:15 says that Jesus coming back out of Egypt fulfilled Hosea 11:1: "Out of Egypt I called my son."

But Hosea 11:1 speaks of God calling *Israel* out of Egypt in the exodus. Matthew means that this is a typological fulfillment: Just as the Israelites went to Egypt to escape death from famine, so Jesus went to Egypt to escape death from Herod's sword. Just as God called the Israelites out of Egypt to be his (collective) son, so God called Jesus out of Egypt as his only begotten Son.

David departed to the "house of the Lord" he'd sung about.[1] He **gathered the nation's leaders before him and spoke of what they should remember and what they should be certain to do** (1 Chronicles 28–29).

Also like Moses, David left behind many psalms that told the story of his struggles and joys amid the faithfulness of God. In one such psalm he wrote, "Even **my close friend** in whom I trusted, **who ate my bread, has lifted his heel against me**" (Psalm 41:9).

The Lord Promised Another Servant

But as we've read, the people eventually forgot the words from both Moses and David. Through Isaiah, God both warned of the coming exile and offered hope. He promised to fix Israel's unrighteousness by sending a righteous king and a **righteous, suffering servant**. Isaiah prophesied about the servant in four servant songs. We read parts of them in earlier chapters. Let's read the first two in their entirety now.

 Take a moment to pray for insight as you read God's Word.

1. Read Isaiah 42:1-9, keeping in mind that the Lord God is speaking directly to the servant. What is one way these verses relate to Jesus?

In the second servant song, the servant speaks. He tells of how the Lord God called him from the womb of his mother. Then he speaks of how God said to him, "You are my servant, Israel, in whom I will be glorified" (Isaiah 49:3). This means the nation of Israel was a type of this future servant. The future servant's task is to bring the people of Israel back to the Lord (verse 5).

2. Read Isaiah 49:1-12. In verses 1-6, the servant speaks and sometimes quotes what God has told him. In verses 7-12, the Lord answers the servant. What is one way these verses relate to Jesus?

Even though Isaiah speaks of both the Messiah and this servant as **righteous** (9:7; 42:6; 53:11) and **anointed by God's Spirit** (11:2; 42:1), people didn't connect the two because the fourth servant song tells of the servant's death.[2] After all, how could a dying servant be a Messiah who reigns forever?

The Lord Promised to Cleanse People When the New Servant King Reigned

A century after Isaiah, the Lord said that he would **cleanse** his people (Ezekiel 37:23). He declared that "**David my servant** shall be their prince **forever**" (verse 25). From this we know that King David's temporary reign foreshadowed the permanent reign of the future righteous king who would be known as God's **servant**.

God's Word to Us in John

In the Bible, Jewish days run sundown to sundown. In the year AD 30[3] (the year we'll read about today), the Passover sacrifices are on Thursday afternoon, and the Passover meal is that evening. John's Gospel has come to the events of that Thursday.

Jesus has finished his public ministry. There is but one more sign for him to give. But he must prepare his disciples for that one and communicate what it is he wants them to do afterward. So he begins his farewell speech to his disciples.

3. ♥ Read John 13:1–14:31. What stands out to you? Why?

Today we read how two servant leaders passed on their leadership to others so people would continue to walk with God and do his work. We read that the Messiah will be a servant leader who will rule at a time when God cleanses his people. We also saw that God promised to send a suffering righteous servant to his people. In the next lesson, we'll see how Jesus demonstrates he is that servant.

The Little Details

The Upper Room Discourse

The other Gospels explain that Jesus ate the Passover meal in an upper room of a large house. Jesus's teaching before, during, and after supper is sometimes called the Upper Room Discourse or the Farewell Discourse.

Professor Emeritus Gerald L. Borchert notes that John arranges his narrative in a chiasm, which is like an outline but with the main point in the center and with points equal distance from the center related:[4]

A   The foot washing
  B   Loneliness & anxiety
    C   The Paraclete
      D   The vine
    C'   The Paraclete
  B'   Anxiety & loneliness
A'   The prayer

Jesus has finished his public ministry. There is but one more sign for him to give.

Pam's Heart-to-Heart with the Great I Am—
"I Am the Way and the Truth and the Life"

Jesus answered, "I am the way and the truth and the life.
No one comes to the Father except through me."
John 14:6 NIV

The Way

Jesus states he is the path and journey to the presence of the Father in heaven. The good news is Jesus wants us to know the way of God even more than we want to know the will of God. People often ask, "How can I know God's will?" which is why, in *7 Simple Skills for Every Woman*, I included a series of tests and decision-making skills that help people discern God's will. A simple one, The Happiness Decision Cycle, is reflective of Jesus as the Way: "Whoever has my commands and keeps them is the one who loves me. The one who loves me will be loved by my Father, and I too will love them and show myself to them" (John 14:21 NIV). God shows his love by revealing more of who he is, and we show our love with obedience that draws us closer to the heartbeat of God, where it's easier to discern his will.[5]

The Truth

Jesus is not merely truth based on opinion, sincerity, emotion, ideas, polls, or presentations. Jesus is truth based on fact. God, the Creator, is the litmus test and plumb line of Truth. You can value Truth by layering the Word into your life:

- **Listen:** Take in the Word through an audio Bible, media and podcasts, internet Bible videos, worship music, or recording yourself reading the Bible.

- **Look:** Read the Bible, create and read Scripture-based memes, and read Christian books, commentaries, Bible studies, and blogs.

- **Link:** Using Scripture, create art, clothing, or practical items. When you do, God's truth is kept before you.

- **Lavish:** Share the Word with others. I do that by speaking, sharing in live and virtual conversations, and giving in Christ's name.

- **Live it!** Live out the Word. Obedience to Jesus is a powerful tool for good news in the plans of God. Often God tells *his* story using *our* life as the illustration.

The Life

My friend Rebecca Friedlander is a filmmaker who documented the early saints of Celtic heritage. In her movie *Thin Places*, she shares a phrase that has stuck with me as a beautiful way to do life with God: "Live your prayers and pray your life."[6]

When COVID-19 entered our world, most people experienced a whirlwind of emotions. Soon the news was reporting a steep uptick in anxiety, depression, and suicide. As I was packing my bags to shelter in place in an RV to be a full-time caregiver for my in-laws—one frail of mind, the other frail of body—I felt Jesus whisper, *Keep believing. All those verses are still true. I am God, and I am good.* I knew this was a watershed moment for my faith. And likely for most believers' faith worldwide. Would I—would we—keep believing and teaching that God is good when the world seemed so bad?

As the "Shelter at Home" orders locked in place for an uncertain duration, I was compelled to contemplate, *Who will I allow God to mold me into for life now and after the coronavirus crisis?* We are not the first generation to deal with such devastation. Pandemics like the Black Death plague, the decade-long Dust Bowl, and the 9/11 terrorists' attacks are just a few examples. Much of the New Testament was written in a society that fed Christians to the lions or used them as human torches for light—and their eyes were faithfully looking up to their eternal life.

Early in the lockdown, I was a speaker for a virtual conference, and in a prayer meeting, a woman from England mentioned that Shakespeare wrote several great plays during a quarantine (*Macbeth*, *King Lear*, *Antony and Cleopatra*). This got me thinking about other victories won and significant contributions forged in a lockdown.

In the bubonic plague, Isaac Newton was quarantined away from Cambridge and the theory of gravity was formed. During WWII, C.S. Lewis went on radio to bring calm during bombing, a message that turned into *Mere Christianity*, and Dietrich Bonhoeffer stood up to Hitler and the Holocaust, and his writings have inspired decades of pastors since. Look to the Bible and see that several of Paul's letters were written from prison; Jonah spent three days in a great fish and then became an evangelist turning a nation to God; and Joseph was unjustly locked away only to be released to rise in leadership, and in a famine God used him to save nations, God's people—and his own family.

We can choose to RISE rather than RETREAT when tough times hit. We have LIFE in us! *Zóé*, Greek for *life*, is "*life* (physical and spiritual). *All* life…, throughout the universe, is *derived*—i.e. it always (only) comes from and is sustained by *God's self-existent life.*"[7]

This life links back to Genesis 2:7 (NIV): "The LORD God formed a man from the dust of the ground and breathed into his nostrils the breath of life." The same God who breathed life into humankind is the Christ who is the *bread of LIFE, who is the light of LIFE, the resurrection and the LIFE, who gives eternal LIFE and the abundant LIFE.* Ask Jesus to breathe life into you and your circumstances today.

Pam

Experiencing Scripture Creatively

- Write an encouraging letter to someone about the coming resurrection. Or write a letter to God about your longing for the resurrection.

- Write a poem or song about the resurrection and share it with others.

- Choose a key word that stood out to you in your reading today, such as *love, way, truth,* or *life.* Follow Karla's instructions at the end of this chapter for writing that word in joined lettering in your Bible or a journal.

The Little Details

D.A. Carson: The Servant

We must picture the disciples reclining on thin mats around a low table. Each is leaning on his arm, usually the left; the feet radiate outward from the table. Jesus pushes himself up from his own mat. The details are revealing: Jesus *took off his outer clothing, and wrapped a towel round his waist*—thus adopting the dress of a menial slave, dress that was looked down upon in both Jewish and Gentile circles... Thus he *began to wash his disciples' feet,* thereby demonstrating his claim, "I am among you as one who serves" (Lk. 22:27; *cf.* Mk. 10:45 par.). The one who was "in very nature God... made himself nothing" and took "the very nature of a servant" (Phil. 2:6-7)...The matchless self-emptying of the eternal Son, the eternal Word, reaches its climax on the cross. This does not mean that the Word *exchanges* the form of God for the form of a servant; it means, rather, that he so dons our flesh and goes open-eyed to the cross that his deity is *revealed* in our flesh, supremely at the moment of greatest weakness, greatest service.[9]

The Servant Who Washes

Jesus and his disciples gather on Thursday for the Passover meal served after sundown. They recline on thin mats around a low table, leaning on one elbow while their "feet radiate outward from the table."[8]

> 4. Read John 13:1-2. (a) What had come (verse 1)? (b) What did Jesus do to the end (verse 1)? (c) What had the devil put into Judas's heart (verse 2)?

Jesus as Servant

Since people wear leather sandals, their feet get grimy as they walk on dusty roads and tread through puddles. In homes, the lowest servant's job is to wash feet.

> 5. Read John 13:3-5. (a) Where did Jesus know he was going (verse 3)? (b) What did he do for the disciples (verse 5)?

Jesus knows where he's from and where he's going. He knows *the Father* has *given all things into his hands,* so he begins *to wash the disciples' feet.*

Jesus Cleanses People

For the one who is their Lord and leader to take on the job of a lowly servant makes Peter (if not all the disciples) uncomfortable.

> 6. Read John 13:6-9. (a) When Peter protested, what did Jesus assure him would happen afterward (verse 7)? (b) When Peter protested again, what did Jesus tell him (verse 8)? (c) At that, what did Peter want (verse 9)?

Peter may call Jesus Lord, but he speaks up when he thinks Jesus isn't doing what Peter thinks he ought!

> 7. Read John 13:10-11. (a) Did Peter need a complete bath (verse 10)? (b) Are all of them clean except for their feet (verse 10)? (c) What is the one who is not clean going to do (verse 11)?

All the disciples are *completely clean* except for their *feet*. The one who is not clean will betray him. Moreover, even though Jesus knows who will betray him, he washes that disciple's feet.

Jesus has made it clear here that washing symbolizes something. In the Old Testament, animal sacrifices cleaned people spiritually so they could approach God. Thus, Jesus is saying all but one of them are spiritually clean except for their feet.

Remember when Jesus explained to Nicodemus that he must be "born of water and the Spirit" to enter the kingdom of God?[10] Jesus referred to Ezekiel 36:25-27:

> I will sprinkle clean water on you, and you shall be clean from all your uncleannesses, and from all your idols I will cleanse you. And I will give you a new heart, and a new spirit I will put within you. And I will remove the heart of stone from your flesh and give you a heart of flesh. And I will put my Spirit within you, and cause you to walk in my statutes and be careful to obey my rules.

Jesus is acting out the fulfillment of this passage. He tells Peter, *afterward you will understand*. Later, they will see that the foot washing foreshadows the mission Jesus is about to complete: Jesus takes the part of a lowly servant in order to cleanse his people from all defilements. (See the sidebar for the symbolism that will be clearer later.)

Jesus Commands His Disciples to Serve One Another

8. Read John 13:12-15. What does Jesus want his disciples to learn from what he has just done?

If Jesus as Teacher and Lord will take the form of a lowly servant, then so should all his followers.

9. Read John 13:16-17. (a) Who is not greater than who (verse 16)? (b) What will happen if Jesus's disciples are servants to one another (verse 17)?

Jesus sends his followers out into the world. His followers are not greater than he is. Therefore, they ought all to be willing to serve in lowly ways. If they do, they'll be *blessed*. Old Testament scholar Allen P. Ross says *blessed* is "the joyful spiritual condition of those who are right with God and the pleasure and satisfaction that is derived from that."[11]

10. ♥ (a) Is it wise to do the actions Jesus says God will bless? Explain. (b) What are some menial tasks today? (c) Describe how you could serve someone this week.

The Little Details
Completely Clean Except for Feet

Jesus's washing of the disciples' feet symbolizes three things. First, the foot washing symbolizes what Jesus will do on Friday: completely cleanse them from their sins by his atoning death.

Second, it symbolizes that when he does so, they will be clean. But as they walk through life, their feet will be soiled, so to speak. That is, they will sometimes sin, and they will need to confess the sin to cleanse what amounts to soiled feet. Thus, John writes in 1 John 1:9, "If we confess our sins, he is faithful and just to forgive us our sins and to cleanse us from all unrighteousness."

Third, it shows us that we are to imitate Jesus by serving our brothers and sisters in humility.

- - - - - - - - - - - - - - - -

If Jesus as Teacher and Lord will take the form of a lowly servant, then so should all his followers.

- - - - - - - - - - - - - - - -

When Jesus shared his bread with Judas, who then left to betray him, Jesus said this event fulfilled Psalm 41:9: "Even my close friend…who ate my bread, has lifted his heel against me." That's because King David was a type of the future Messiah. As such, events in his life sometimes foreshadowed events in Jesus's life. In this case, the betrayal David faced by a friend who ate with him foreshadowed the betrayal Jesus faced by Judas. (See chapter 1, Day 5 for an explanation of types.)

Not all of Psalm 41 applies to Jesus, however. In verse 4, David confesses sin, and that certainly doesn't apply to Jesus.

Jesus Foretells His Betrayal

One of the disciples is not spiritually clean.

> **11.** Read John 13:18-19. (a) What Scripture will the one who will betray him fulfill (verse 18)? (b) Why does Jesus tell his disciples that he knows one of them will betray him (verse 19)?

Jesus quotes Psalm 41:9. This is a psalm King David wrote about someone who betrayed him. Because David is a type of Jesus, many events in his life foreshadow events in Jesus's life. Jesus means the betrayal that David faced was a type of the betrayal that Jesus now faces.

Jesus makes it plain that he knows who will betray him so that when it happens, the disciples won't be so taken aback that they abandon their belief that *I am he*—that he is the one about whom Isaiah and the others prophesied. In the context of spiritual cleaning, he may allude particularly to Isaiah 43:25: "I, I am he who blots out your transgressions for my own sake, and I will not remember your sins."

> **12.** In John 13:20, when a person receives someone whom Jesus sends, what two other beings does that person receive?

Because they will believe Jesus's claims that "I am he," Jesus will send them to tell others the good news. Those who receive them also receive Jesus and the Father. That's good news!

In this lesson, we saw Jesus as a servant leader who cleanses people. Therefore, he commands his followers to likewise serve one another. Additionally, he foretells his betrayal so that his disciples will still believe "I am he" when it happens. Further, he tells them that people who receive them receive Jesus and the Father.

In the next lesson, Jesus gives his disciples another command and foretells more about what is about to happen.

Day 3

The New Standard of Love

I was so surprised the first time I read that Leonardo da Vinci's famous painting *The Last Supper* didn't accurately portray it! I should have guessed, since it showed everyone seated on just three sides of a table.

For supper, Jesus reclines with his disciples at a low table, something done only at special occasions.[12] Judas Iscariot is apparently "on his left, a place of honor."[13] John rests on Jesus's other side, then Peter next to John.

> Because David is a type of Jesus, many events in his life foreshadow events in Jesus's life.

Jesus Identifies His Betrayer

Jesus has just told them that "the Scripture will be fulfilled, 'He who ate my bread has lifted his heel against me'" (John 13:18).

> **13.** Read John 13:21-25. (a) How was Jesus feeling (verse 21)? (b) What was about to happen (verse 21)? (c) Did the disciples know to whom Jesus referred (verse 22)?

If Jesus and John are leaning on their left elbows (as was most common) and John is to Jesus's right, then John can easily lean back so that his head is next to Jesus's. He does so and quietly asks who the betrayer is.

> **14.** Read John 13:26-30. (a) Who would betray Jesus (verse 27)? (b) What happened to the betrayer (verse 27)? (c) Did the other disciples know what was going on (verses 28-29)? (d) What did the betrayer do (verse 30)?

Dipping bread into the common cup and handing it to someone is a sign of honor and friendship. It's as if Jesus gives Judas every chance to repent.[14] But Judas does not, and he who ate Jesus's bread becomes a vessel for Satan and leaves to betray the one who has shown him God's ways.

Some thought Judas is going to *buy what we need for the* weeklong *feast.* Others assumed Jesus told Judas *he should give something to the poor,* as was customary on Passover. *And it was night*—Judas exchanges the light of the world for the darkness of night.

Jesus Will Be Glorified

Jesus turns his attention to his remaining disciples.

> **15.** Read John 13:31-33. (a) Who is to be glorified (verses 31-32)? (b) What does Jesus call the Eleven (verse 33)? (c) How long will Jesus remain with them (verse 33)?

Now connects Jesus's glorification with the betrayal. He speaks tenderly to his disciples, calling them *little children.* He lets them know he is leaving them.

Jesus Commands Love for One Another

Jesus has important instructions for them to follow when he departs. Just as Moses explained the law to his followers when he knew he was about to die, so now Jesus explains his commands to his followers when he knows he is about to die.

16. Read John 13:34-35. (a) What command does Jesus give (verse 34)? (b) Whose example should they follow in obeying that command (verse 34)? (c) What will happen if his disciples obey this command (verse 35)?

Love one another. In a sense, this is not a new command, for the Old Testament taught that God's people should love others. But it's the *way* Jesus loves that's new: *Just as I have loved you, you also are to love one another.* He has shown them what he means by love in his daily interactions with them and by washing their feet. But he's about to show the greatness of his love in a way they can't imagine.

Jesus Foretells Peter's Denial

The disciples don't understand why they can't follow Jesus anymore.

17. Read John 13:36-38. (a) What does Peter ask (verse 36)? (b) When will Peter follow him (verse 36)? (c) What does Peter say he will do (verse 37)? (d) What does Jesus say will happen before the rooster crows in the morning (verse 38)?

Peter wants to follow. In his exuberance, he claims he will lay down his life for Jesus. But Jesus knows better. Indeed, Peter will deny him three times that night.

18. ♥ Think of three people: a close family member, a friend, and an acquaintance. How can you love each of them this week as Jesus has loved you? Be specific. Consider whether you need to forgive, share what you've learned about Jesus's good news, or give support in a special way.

- Family member:

- Friend:

- Acquaintance:

He has shown them what he means by love in his daily interactions with them and by washing their feet. But he's about to show the greatness of his love in a way they can't imagine.

In this lesson, we saw Jesus comfort his disciples. To prepare them for what's coming, he foretold who would betray him and Peter's denials. He connected the betrayal to his glorification. And he commanded his disciples to love one another as he loves them. In the next lesson, Jesus will make incredible claims.

Day 4

The Way, Truth, and Life

Jesus is preparing his disciples for his imminent departure. Despite the agony he faces, his concern is for his followers, the Eleven. They know he's leaving, but they don't know how or why.

Jesus Prepares a Place for His Disciples in His Father's House

19. Read John 14:1-3. (a) What doesn't Jesus want his disciples to do (verse 1)? (b) What should they do instead (verse 1)? (c) When Jesus goes, what will he do (verse 2)? (d) What else will he do (verse 3)?

The disciples are distraught that Jesus is leaving them. They had expected him to set up a kingdom on earth immediately. But Jesus tells them he's preparing a place for them in his *Father's house.*

Jesus Is the Way to the Father, the Truth, and the Life

20. Read John 14:4-5. (a) What does Jesus say the disciples know (verse 5)? (b) Why does Thomas say they actually don't know that (verse 6)?

Thomas expresses the disciples' confusion. He doesn't understand what Jesus means by *I will come again and will take you to myself.*

21. (a) In John 14:6 below, circle the three things Jesus says he is. (b) Underline the only way someone can come to the Father. (c) In the **7 "I Am" Statements** chart in the back of the book, on line 6 enter the three things Jesus says he is.

    Jesus said to him, "I am the way, and the truth, and the life. No one comes to the Father except through me."

Jesus answers Thomas by saying he himself is the way to where he is going, to his Father's house. He is the truth—the revelation of God, the Word who became flesh, "full of grace and truth" (John 1:14). He is the life—the one with life in him who therefore gives eternal life (John 1:4; 11:25).

Those Who See Jesus See the Father

The disciples are still confused.

In John 14:2, Jesus tells his disciples that he goes to prepare a place for them in his Father's house. Where he's going is to the cross and resurrection. It's the cross and resurrection that prepare the place for them.

Isaiah 53:8,10 says the suffering servant will be "cut off out of the land of the living" but "when his soul makes an offering for guilt, he shall see his offspring; he shall prolong his days." His death is an offering for guilt that gives those who receive him the "right to become children of God" (John 1:12). The promise in Isaiah 53:10—that after his death, the servant will prolong his days—points to the resurrection.

John 14:3 reads, "I will come again." That could refer to Jesus's appearances after his resurrection, the coming of the Holy Spirit, or his coming at the end of the age to bring those who belong to him into his eternal kingdom. Since he's taking them to the place he's prepared for them in his Father's house, the eternal kingdom fits the context best.

The Little Details
Greater Works

Jesus's public teaching was somewhat veiled. After the resurrection, his meaning will be clearer. The disciples will be filled with the Holy Spirit and will preach the gospel by the power of the Holy Spirit. They will fully understand Jesus's teaching about his suffering and resurrection. Because of that, many people will be born again and will enter the kingdom of heaven. Before Jesus's death and resurrection, this couldn't happen.

For an encouraging look at asking in Jesus's name, see *Fearless Prayer* by Dr. Craig Hazen.

22. Read John 14:7-9. If they know and see Jesus, whom else do they know and see (verses 7,9)?

That's quite a claim. But it explains why Jesus is the only way to the Father. For the Word who was God and who became flesh can reveal the way to the Father. This is very good news. There is a way to the Father, and it's through Jesus.

23. Read John 14:10-11. (a) What relationship does Jesus say he and the Father have (verse 10)? (b) What does Jesus want Philip to believe (verse 11)? (c) What evidence does Jesus give (verse 11)?

Jesus wants Philip to believe his words. If his words are difficult, then Philip should believe them on the evidence of the works Jesus has done.

Jesus's Followers Can Ask in Jesus's Name

24. Read John 14:12-14. (a) What will those who believe in Jesus do (verse 12)? (b) Why (verse 12)? (c) How should believers ask (verse 13)? (d) What will Jesus do (verse 14)?

Because Jesus is going to the Father, his followers will do even greater works. Asking in Jesus's name means asking in accordance with Jesus's character so *that the Father may be glorified in the Son*. That encourages us to pray boldly and often.

25. ♥ Describe a time when Jesus answered a prayer you asked for in his name in order to glorify God.

The Father Will Send Another Helper

Jesus will not leave his disciples alone.

26. Read John 14:15-17. (a) What will those who love Jesus do (verse 15)? (b) What will the Father give Jesus's disciples at Jesus's request (verse 16)? (c) Who is this helper (verse 17)? (d) What is his relationship to Jesus's disciples (verse 17)?

There is a way to the Father, and it's through Jesus.

The Father will give another *Helper* (NIV *advocate*; KJV *Comforter*). The Greek word *paraklētos* means "legal assistant, advocate."[16] Jesus has been their helper. When he leaves, he will ask the Father to send them another Helper, the Spirit of truth. Right now, the Spirit is with them, but later he *will be in you.*

The Old Testament spoke of a time when the Lord God would "sprinkle clean water" on his people so they "shall be clean from all...uncleannesses."[17] Once they were clean, God would do this: "I will put my Spirit within you, and cause you to walk in my statutes and be careful to obey my rules."[18] So God promised he will put his Spirit in cleansed people so they can obey him.

Because Jesus Lives, You Also Will Live

27. Read John 14:18-20. (a) What will Jesus do (verse 18)? (b) What will the disciples do that the world won't do (verse 19)? (c) When they see that Jesus lives, what will they know (verse 20)?

Any doubts and confusion the disciples still have will clear up when Jesus comes to them.

In this lesson, Jesus says he's leaving to prepare a place for his followers in his Father's house. He claims to be the way, the truth, and the life. Further, he claims to be the *only* way to the Father. Indeed, he says those who have seen him have seen the Father. Moreover, Jesus's disciples can ask what they want in Jesus's name so the Father is glorified in Jesus. Also, Jesus promises not to leave them alone, for he will send a Helper, the Holy Spirit, who will teach them and remind them of Jesus's words. Not only that, but because Jesus lives, so will his followers.

In the next lesson Jesus explains he's not leaving his followers alone.

Day 5

The Giver of Peace

Jesus is comforting and preparing his disciples for his departure.

The Father Loves Those Who Love Jesus

28. Read John 14:21. (a) Who loves Jesus? (b) Who will be loved by Jesus's Father? (c) What will Jesus do for that person?

Jesus repeats that those who keep his commandments are those who love him.

The Little Details
D.A. Carson: Paraclete

In John's usage, the legal overtones are sharpest in 16:7-11, but there the Paraclete serves rather more as a prosecuting attorney than as a counsel for the defence. NIV's "Counsellor" is not wrong, so long as "legal counsellor" is understood, not "camp counsellor" or "marriage counsellor"—and even so, the Paraclete's ministry extends beyond the legal sphere...

The one whom Jesus will ask the Father to send is called "another Paraclete"..."Another Paraclete" in the context of Jesus' departure implies that the disciples already have one, the one who is departing. Although Jesus is never in the Fourth Gospel explicitly referred to as a *paraklētos*, the title is applied to him in 1 John 2:1 (NIV "one who speaks...in our defence"). That means that Jesus' *present* advocacy is discharged in the courts of heaven; John 14 implies that *during his ministry* his role as Paraclete, strengthening and helping his disciples, was discharged on earth. "Another Paraclete" is given to perform this latter task.[19]

The Little Details

D.A. Carson: "The Father Is Greater Than I" (John 14:28)

The only interpretation that makes adequate sense of the context connects *for the Father is greater than I* with the main verb [*If you loved me*]...but understands the logic of the *for* or *because* rather differently: If Jesus' disciples truly loved him, they would be glad that he is returning to his Father, *for* he is returning to the sphere where he belongs, to the glory he had with the Father before the world began (17:5), to the place where the Father is undiminished in glory, unquestionably greater than the Son in his incarnate state. To this point the disciples have responded emotionally entirely according to their perception of *their own* gain or loss. If they had loved Jesus, they would have perceived that his departure to his own "home" was *his* gain and rejoiced with him at the prospect. As it is, their grief is an index of their self-centredness.[20]

The disciples will be able to teach what Jesus taught them because the Holy Spirit will help them.

The Father and Jesus Will Dwell with Those Who Love Jesus

29. Read John 14:22-24. (a) What will anyone who loves Jesus do (verse 23)? (b) What will happen to that person (verse 23)? (c) Who doesn't keep Jesus's words (verse 24)? (d) Whose word is Jesus giving them (verse 24)?

This disciple thinks Jesus will return and set up his kingdom in Jerusalem, and so he's confused over how the disciples will see Jesus but the world won't. He's distressed that Jesus is leaving. So Jesus assures him that he and the Father *will come to him and make our home with him*. Some scholars think this refers to the Holy Spirit's indwelling; others think it means the Father, Son, and Holy Spirit all indwell believers.

What Jesus wants them to remember, though, is this: All who love Jesus keep his word. Obeying him is a sign of loving him.

30. ♥ (a) Why is it foolish to say you love Jesus if you don't intend to obey him (John 14:23-24)? (b) Describe how obeying Jesus has blessed you.

The Holy Spirit Will Teach Jesus's Disciples

31. Read John 14:25-26. (a) When Jesus leaves, who will the Father send in Jesus's name (verses 25-26)? (b) What two things will he do (verse 26)?

These are ways the Holy Spirit helps. The disciples will be able to teach what Jesus taught them because the Holy Spirit will help them.

Jesus Gives Peace

32. Read John 14:27. (a) What does Jesus leave with his disciples? (b) What should they therefore not let happen?

In those days, Rome enforced peace with a brutal sword. That's not how Jesus will give peace. The Messiah, after all, is called the Prince of Peace (Isaiah 9:6).

Jesus Is Going to the Father

Jesus continues to comfort his disciples.

33. Read John 14:28-29. (a) Why should they rejoice that Jesus is going away and coming again (verse 28)? (b) Why did Jesus tell them he's leaving (verse 29)?

The disciples aren't rejoicing because they're thinking more about their loss than about how good it will be for Jesus to return to the Father and to glory.

Satan Has No Claim on Jesus

34. Read John 14:30-31. (a) Who was coming (verse 30)? (b) Why does Jesus do what the Father commands (verse 31)?

The ruler of this world—Satan—is on his way. Even though *He has no claim on* Jesus, Jesus obeys the Father's commands. Jesus has said if we love him, we'll obey him. Here, he demonstrates that he likewise obeys the Father's commands so that the world knows he loves the Father. *Rise, let us go from here* may mean they were to prepare to leave the room where they had supper.

The Good News

In John 13–14, we see Jesus as a servant leader who cleanses people. He commands his followers to serve and love one another. He explains that his disciples show their love for him by keeping his commands.

He foretells his betrayal and Peter's denials so that the disciples will still believe he is who he says he is when it all happens. He even connects his betrayal to his glorification.

Christ says he's leaving to prepare a place for his disciples in his Father's house. Jesus says he's the only way to the Father; more so, he is the way, the truth, and the life. He claims that those who have seen him have seen the Father.

Jesus promises blessings. For example, his disciples can ask what they want in Jesus's name so the Father is glorified in Jesus.

Although he's departing, Jesus promises not to leave them alone, for he will send them a Helper, the Holy Spirit, who will teach them and remind them of Jesus's words. Because Jesus lives, so will his disciples. He will manifest himself to those who love him. He and the Father will make their home with them. And he gives them his peace.

35. ♥ Which of these items of good news means the most to you today? Why?

In the next chapter, Jesus continues his farewell teaching with important words that all his followers need to know.

Praise God for something you saw of his character this week. **Confess** anything that convicted you. **Ask** for help to do something God's Word calls you to do. **Thank** God for something you learned this week.

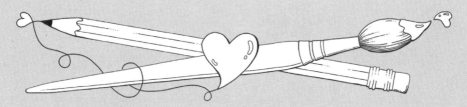

Karla's Creative Connection

Because I want you to focus on several key words in this week's verse as you're coloring, I chose to emphasize them with a joined lettering style. This allows you time as you color to dwell on the name of Jesus, to ponder who Jesus declares himself to be—the way, the truth, and the life—and to think about how God becomes our Father through our relationship with Jesus. Using this joined lettering style not only gives you time to meditate on these key words but brings a pleasing continuity to the design itself.

I started by using the block letter style you learned in chapter 4. However, for this creation, you'll make simple but thoughtful modifications, including closer spacing between the letters and changing angles or individual letter styles in order to create connecting points. Writing out your words with pencil first will enable you to visualize the changes you'll need to make.

And always remember: Practice makes progress! So to get you started, let me share some of the modifications I made in order to letter the words *way*, *truth*, and *life*. From here, you'll learn how to create your own.

① Here we have typical block letters. Notice there is no obvious place to connect the letters so we need to make some modifications.

② To give connecting points, traded the typical "a" for one that gives me greater freedom to manipulate and I added a small flourish to the top of the "y" to allow it to connect to the "a."

③ It's easy to create a playful look to your words by adding small flourishes like I did here to the "w" and adding loops to letters with "tails."

① Some letters, like the lowercase "t," are easy to connect as you can see here; but, if you were to try to connect the "r" to the "u" or the "u" to the "t," it would not be as easy to read.

② Here I've traded the lowercase "r" for an uppercase so I could life and extend its "leg" to connect with the "u." I also used an uppercase "u" so I could have more room to angle and extend its "leg" to connect to the "t."

① This is a good example of how challenging the "l" and the "i" can be because written as typical block letters they have no options for connecting points so you have to create them yourself.

② I chose to use an uppercase "L" to connect to the "i" but you could also use a handwritten "l" with a loop so it would naturally connect. This is also a good example for you to see that sometimes it's perfectly fine not to connect the letters at all.

As you can see, there are no rules when it comes to the art of joining block letters in this way. It's simply a matter of play until you get the look you like. As you can see in the word *Father* in this week's bookmark and coloring page, this style is perfect for script lettering. Just make sure to give yourself plenty of room between your letters and open up the loops to give them space.

Karla

Chapter 8

John 15:1–16:33
The Vine

What did Jesus say to keep his followers from falling away?

Day 1

Looking for Fruit

Our backyard has a wrought iron fence that was perfect for a grapevine, so we planted one near the corner of the yard. Initially, we lightly tied the fast-growing shoots to the fence to train them where to go. After that the new, green tendrils quickly wrapped around the fence top. Soon we had incredibly sweet, pale-pink grapes hanging at eye level.

Every fall, my husband pruned the branches. Come spring, most of the new shoots attached to the fence, but he had to watch for and prune branches that strayed into our fruit trees or across the path behind our yard. New shoots were malleable, and he often needed to guide them until they gripped onto the right spot and hardened there.

Unlike the bendy shoots, the vine's trunk was thick and strong—so strong that it eventually dislodged our fence!

Just as we planted the grapevine for it to bear grapes, so God plants his people in the world for them to bear fruit—the fruit of godly character and bringing others to know him. Just as we pruned any branches that grew in ways that wouldn't bring us fruit, so God prunes his people of ways that don't bring him fruit. And just as the powerful grapevine trunk nourished and strengthened its canes, so Jesus in power nourishes and strengthens his followers.

God's Word to Us in the Old Testament

The Bible uses *fruit* as a metaphor for what people produce, such as children, deeds, character, and bringing others to know the Lord.

For example, I shared what I learned about Jesus with my friend Linda. As I kept reading the Bible, she started asking me what it said about certain topics. But she didn't think anyone should necessarily follow all its commands. Eventually, she told me I had become "too" Christian. That hurt, but I kept praying for her. A couple of years later, she woke up crying, her heart telling her there was more to knowing God than what she knew. She says she knew I knew, though, so she came to my house and told me she was ready to accept Jesus as her Lord and Savior. She no longer believed she was good enough to enter heaven without Jesus. Linda's coming to faith in Jesus was fruit!

The Little Details
D.A. Carson: The True Vine

In the Old Testament the vine is a common symbol for Israel, the covenant people of God...Most remarkable is the fact that whenever historic Israel is referred to under this figure it is the vine's failure to produce good fruit that is emphasized, along with the corresponding threat of God's judgment on the nation. Now, in contrast to such failure, Jesus claims, "I am the *true* vine," *i.e.* the one to whom Israel pointed, the one that brings forth good fruit. Jesus has already in principle, superseded the temple, the Jewish feasts, Moses, various holy sites; here he supersedes Israel as the very locus of the people of God. (A similar contrast between Israel and Jesus is developed in various ways in the Synoptics: *e.g.* in the temptation narrative, Mt. 4:1-11 par.)[1]

Against that backdrop, Jesus now claims to be the true vine that will bear fruitful branches in the world.

Israel in Time Bore Bad Fruit

By Isaiah's time, both Israel and Judah were ignoring God's commands and even sacrificing children to idols. Through the prophets, the Lord God likened Israel to a **grapevine** he'd brought out of Egypt and carefully planted. But when he looked for the grapes of justice and righteousness, he found only the wild grapes of bloodshed and outcries (Isaiah 5:7). Israel did not produce the **fruit** for which it was planted. And so Isaiah prophesied the imminent exile of Israel and the later exile of Judah.

But as usual, God accompanied his warnings with a message of grace.

> Take a moment to pray for insight as you read God's Word.

> 1. In Isaiah 27:6 below, underline what would happen in the days to come. Circle what would be filled with fruit this time.
>
>   In days to come Jacob shall take root, Israel shall blossom and put forth shoots and fill the whole world with fruit.

Jacob was Abraham's grandson whom God renamed *Israel*. The Lord graciously and miraculously brought exiles back to the land, where they awaited the Messiah—the king who would establish a nation for them.

God's Word to Us in John

In Jesus's day Jews are again planted where Israel and Judah used to be in the regions of Galilee, Judea, and Perea ("beyond the Jordan" or Transjordan). Although non-Jews are hearing the Old Testament preached at synagogues, the whole world is not yet filled with fruit.

Where we left off in the last chapter, Jesus has withdrawn from public ministry and is preparing his disciples for what is coming.

> 2. ♥ Read John 15:1–16:33. What stands out to you? Why?

Summary

So far, we've read that the prophets likened God to a vinedresser who planted Israel as a vine. But instead of bearing the good fruit of justice and righteousness, Israel bore bloodshed and distress. So God exiled the people for a time. But he promised there would again be a vine that takes root and fills the world with fruit. Some exiles returned and appeared to be the promised replanting. In Jesus's day, however, they're not filling the world with the fruit God wants.

Against that backdrop, Jesus now claims to be the true vine that will bear fruitful branches in the world.

Pam's Heart-to-Heart with the Great I Am—"I Am the True Vine"

"I am the true vine, and my Father is the vinedresser."
John 15:1

A few years before I wrote this book, Bill and I downsized to move near to and help care for his then 88-year-old parents. To support our move, Bill's sister and brother-in-law offered to have us live at their vineyard while we looked for a live-aboard boat that would dock near the parents' home. I was thrilled that for nearly a year, I would train as a vinedresser of a working vineyard. On the last page, you noted what stood out to you in John 15. Let's look again at John 15:1-11,16 (emphasis added) with a focus on the interlinked relationship of the branches, vine, and vinedresser:

> "I am the **true vine**, and my **Father is the vinedresser**. Every branch in me [**the vine**] that does not bear fruit he [**the vinedresser**] takes away, and every branch that does bear fruit he [**the vinedresser**] prunes, that it may bear more fruit. Already you are clean because of the word that I [**the vine**] have spoken to you. Abide in me [**the vine**], and I in you. As the branch cannot bear fruit by itself, unless it abides in **the vine**, neither can you, unless you abide in me [**the vine**]. **I am the vine**; you are the branches. Whoever abides in me [**the vine**] and I in him, he it is that bears much fruit, for apart from me [**the vine**] you can do nothing. If anyone does not abide in me [**the vine**] he is thrown away [**by the vinedresser**] like a branch and withers; and the branches are gathered, thrown into the fire, and burned. If you abide in me [**the vine**], and my words abide in you, ask whatever you wish, and it will be done for you. By this my Father [**the vinedresser**] is glorified, that you bear much fruit and so prove to be my [**the vine's**] disciples. As the Father [**the vinedresser**] has loved me, so have I [**the vine**] loved you. Abide in my [**the vine's**] love. If you keep my [**the vine's**] commandments, you will abide in my [**the vine's**] love, just as I have kept my Father's [**the vinedresser's**] commandments and abide in his [**the vinedresser's**] love. These things I [**the vine**] have spoken to you, that my [**the vine's**] joy may be in you, and that your joy may be full...
>
> You did not choose me [**the vine**], but I [**the vine**] chose you and appointed you that you should go and bear fruit and that your fruit should abide, so that whatever you ask the Father [**the vinedresser**] in my [**the vine's**] name, he [**the vinedresser**] may give it to you.

In every season in my role as a vinedresser, I daily walked the vineyard to aid the vine in producing fruit by caring well for the branches. Right after the harvest, I walked through the vineyard looking for places to prune so the vine could produce more. When and where I removed a branch, we applied TECH-GRO B-Lock, a mix of nutrients and sealer, to bind up the wound to keep the good nutrients in and the bad elements out. In the winter, we burned the tossed branches, then cared for the soil to enhance fruit from the vine in the next season.

As the branches began to bud, my role was to watch over the tender, vulnerable buds by trying to keep the bugs and birds away. In addition, we took measures to prevent freezing if the temperature dropped. As the leaves grew thicker and grape clusters began to appear, keeping the vines well-watered was key. Then as the scorching sun beat down, I trimmed back sucker branches that had no fruit, so the fruitful branches could hydrate to increase the yield. I wired up the branches to shade the growing clusters and help support the branches as the fruit grew heavier.

Then, come harvest, as a vinedresser I hand cut the beautiful, sweet grapes. In addition, the vinedresser hosts a harvest celebration and leads others in rejoicing for the bounty of the harvest.

My relationship with God grew daily as I prayer-walked the vineyard. Stepping into the role of the vinedresser, I felt the attention our Father in heaven extends to us, caring for our every need, so we can become branches who bear more fruit. I also saw the vital importance of being a branch secured strong and stable into the vine—the source of life and fruit.

Plan a vineyard excursion: Visit a winery to walk through the vineyard. Pull up an internet video and take a virtual walk. Maybe purchase grapes, jelly, or a beverage made from grapes, then picnic as you enjoy reading the John 15 passage above. Underline your role and responsibility as a branch. Thank Jesus for being the vine, the source of all the fruitful blessings of your life, family, and ministry. In a journal (perhaps with a drawing of grapes or a vineyard on the cover), begin an ongoing list, thanking the vinedresser for the tender loving care he extends to you every day.

Experiencing Scripture Creatively

- Visit a vineyard with family or friends. Compare the strong trunk of the vine to the slender branches. Discuss John 15:1.

- Create fabric art using cross-stitch, embroidery, or appliqué to illustrate a grapevine bearing fruit. Add words from John 15. See www.DiscoveringTheBible Series.com for instructions on how to print a bookmark on fabric that you can then embroider.

- Illustrate John 15 in your Bible or journal by following Karla's instructions at the end of the chapter for drawing a grapevine.

Day 2

The True Vine

In the last lesson, we read that the Lord God likened Israel to a choice grapevine he planted, protected, and nourished only to have it produce wild fruit (bloodshed and outcries) instead of good grapes (justice and righteousness).

Jesus Is the True Vine

Judas Iscariot has left to betray Jesus, and Jesus continues to teach the Eleven.

> **3.** Read John 15:1-2. (a) In this metaphor, who is Jesus (verse 1)? (b) Who is the Father (verse 1)? (c) What happens to branches that don't bear fruit (verse 2)? (d) What happens to fruitful branches (verse 2)? (e) In the **7 "I Am" Statements** chart at the back of the book, write "The true vine" on line 7.

Israel became a vine that produced bad fruit, but Jesus is the *true vine*. In both metaphors, the Father is the vinedresser. A *branch...that does not bear fruit* is someone like Judas Iscariot who appears to be a follower but whose betrayal belies it.

The Father prunes *every branch*—that is, every weak cane that shoots out from the strong trunk—that does bear fruit so it will bear even more. Consequently, all true Christians will bear fruit.

> **4.** Read John 15:3-4 below. Circle what the disciples already are. Box the three instances of the verb *abide*. Underline what Jesus wants you to do.
>
> Already you are clean because of the word that I have spoken to you. Abide in me, and I in you. As the branch cannot bear fruit by itself, unless it abides in the vine, neither can you, unless you abide in me.

Dr. Craig Hazen explains *clean*:

> It is a bit cryptic for Jesus to say, "You are already clean" at this point in his discourse. It seems like a sudden diversion from the vineyard metaphor. But looking at the Greek words being translated gives us more information. The Greek word translated "clean" (or "cleansed") is the same Greek word for "pruned." So one could read it as Jesus saying to the eleven disciples, "You have already been pruned and hence [are] ready to bear fruit."
>
> But using "clean," as most translators do, makes sense on several levels. First, pruning a branch during peak growing season...is quick, barehanded work of snapping off soft extraneous shoots. In our modern parlance, this kind of pruning could easily be considered "clean-up" work. Second, just hours earlier Jesus had washed the disciples' feet and said to them, "Those who have had a bath need only to wash their feet; their whole body is clean. And you are clean, though not everyone of you" (John 13:10). By contrasting the disciples with

The Little Details
Craig Hazen: Pruning

Every branch that does bear fruit can expect to be pruned in order to bear more and better fruit. If we are bearing fruit, the expert gardener will prune us, shape us, and perfect us so that our yield will grow.

In viticulture, pruning is essential to healthy plants and abundant fruit production. In spring and summer, when fruit is actually growing on the plant, pruning is effective at getting better sun, airflow, and room for the grape clusters in the fast-growing canes and shoots. Pruning also focuses the plant's energies on fruit production rather than on tendrils, water sprouts, suckers, and foliage. Pruning helps keep disease from affecting the rest of the plant because bad leaves and shoots can be removed. And plant sickness is most likely to generate and spread in dense foliage that has not been pruned. (It's worth meditating on all these benefits of pruning. Vineyards, both ancient and new, are ripe with spiritual analogies.)[2]

The Little Details

D.A. Carson: "Cuts Off" (John 15:2 NIV)

Several popular writers... argue that *airō* does not here mean "cuts off" (NIV) but "lifts up [from the ground]"—*i.e.* the fruitless branches are "lifted up" so that they may gain the exposure to sun that has been denied them, and thereby become abundantly fruit-bearing. However, of its twenty-four occurrences in the Fourth Gospel *airō* might be rendered "take" or "lift up" eight times...and "take away" or "remove" sixteen times...More importantly... in the context of viticulture it is not the most natural way to take it. Despite arguments to the contrary, there is no good evidence of which I am aware to confirm that lower stalks of grapevines were seasonally "lifted up" from the ground. Moreover, the sharp contrast of v. 2, on the traditional interpretation, prepares the way for v. 6. This more recent interpretation sounds like an attempt to prevent embarrassment at the thought of branches "in me" being cut off, in contradiction (it is thought) to such passages as 6:37-40. But... these fears are unfounded.[4]

Judas during the foot washing, Jesus was emphasizing not physical cleanliness by water, but a spiritual purity. He is likely doing the same in 15:3.[3]

> 5. Read John 15:5-6. (a) What are Jesus's followers in this metaphor (verse 5)? (b) What can they do apart from Jesus (verse 5)? (c) What happens to branches that don't abide in the vine (verse 6)?

As Hazen puts it, "In the context of remaining or abiding in Jesus, he is saying we can do nothing to accomplish *things of an eternal, holy, and spiritually meaningful nature.*"[5] In other words, unattached branches can't bear the fruit God wants. The people represented here are those with superficial faith that can't endure. Jesus isn't speaking about true believers, for he said previously, "All that the Father gives me will come to me, and whoever comes to me I will never cast out" (John 6:37).

Jesus Explains the Vine Metaphor

Jesus now further explains his vine metaphor.

Jesus's Disciples Bear Fruit That Glorifies God

> 6. Read John 15:7-8. (a) What can you do if you abide in Jesus and his words abide in you (verse 7)? (b) What glorifies the Father (verse 8)?

Those who abide in Jesus and have his words abiding in them can ask for whatever they wish, for their desires fit Jesus's words in them. When we bear fruit, we prove that we're Jesus's disciples, and we glorify the Father.

Not only that, but since the vinedresser prunes fruitful branches so they'll bear more fruit, we can expect the Father to prune the parts of us that hinder fruitfulness. For example, he may put us in circumstances that make us aware of unloving habits, ungodly attitudes, and untrusting fears so that we'll seek his pruning activity.

Jesus's Disciples Abide by Keeping His Commandments

> 7. Read John 15:9-11. (a) How has Jesus loved his disciples (verse 9)? (b) How do we abide in Jesus's love (verses 9-10)? (c) Why did Jesus say these things (verse 11)?

Here Jesus explains that a branch that abides in the vine refers to a follower who abides in Jesus's love by keeping Jesus's *commandments*. And why not abide in his love when he loves us just as the Father loves him? Moreover, keeping his commandments results in Jesus's joy being in us.

> **8.** Read John 15:12-13. (a) What is Jesus's commandment (verse 12)? (b) What is the greatest love (verse 13)?

Jesus summarizes his commands in a single statement: *Love one another as I have loved you.* Leviticus 19:18 reads, "You shall not take vengeance or bear a grudge against the sons of your own people, but you shall love your neighbor as yourself: I am the LORD." So the idea of loving others was already known as God's command. But Jesus takes it further. Now his followers must love others as Jesus loves them. Jesus explains: The greatest love is *that someone lay down his life for his friends.* The love he wants to see is sacrificial love.

Jesus Calls Disciples Who Obey Him "Friends"

> **9.** Read John 15:14-15. If you do what Jesus commands, what are you?

Jesus is Lord. Servants simply obey their Lord without knowing the reasons why. But Jesus says those who obey him he calls friends, and he reveals what he's heard from the Father to his friends. That's another way obeying Jesus brings joy (verse 11).

This is similar to what Jesus told the Jews who professed belief earlier: "If you abide in my word, you are truly my disciples, and you will know the truth, and the truth will set you free" (John 8:31-32). There, Jesus said that abiding in his word—knowing it, thinking on it, obeying it—results in knowing truth that frees from slavery to sin.

The Father Grants Requests Made in Jesus's Name

> **10.** Read John 15:16-17. (a) Why does Jesus choose and appoint disciples (verse 16)? (b) If his disciples fulfill what they are chosen for, what can they do (verse 16)? (c) Why does Jesus command these things (verse 17)?

Jesus explains that the disciples did not choose him. Rather, he chose them. And he chose them for the purpose of bearing abiding fruit. As they go about fulfilling what he has appointed them for, they can make requests of the Father in Jesus's name; that is, they can make requests that are according to Jesus's will and character for the purpose of glorifying the Father. This is how they will bear abiding fruit.

Go and bear fruit suggests that the apostles' primary mission is to go out into the world and spread the good news, resulting in more people coming to believe Jesus is the Messiah. But it can also include other fruit: loving as Jesus loves, knowing truth, and being set free from sin. These all increase joy. Jesus's commands ensure that we love one another.

The Little Details
Friends of God
Both Abraham and Moses are called God's friend (2 Chronicles 20:7; Exodus 33:11). But nowhere in the Bible does a person call God or Jesus "my friend." He is Lord.

Jesus says those who obey him he calls friends, and he reveals what he's heard from the Father to his friends.

---

11. ♥ How can you better love others as Jesus loves you? In what specific areas would you like the Holy Spirit to help you love better?

We read some good news today. Jesus said he is the true vine, his Father is the vinedresser, and his followers are the branches. Thus, just as branches connected to a vine's trunk bear fruit, so Jesus's disciples connected to him will bear fruit. In this way, he overcame the shortcomings of the former kingdoms, which bore poisonous fruit.

Jesus's followers abide in Jesus by keeping his commands. That results in joy and fruit. Also, Jesus calls disciples who obey him his friends and says he reveals things of God to them. Moreover, the Father grants requests Jesus's followers make in Jesus's name.

In the next lesson, Jesus continues to prepare his disciples for his departure.

Day 3

The One the World Hates

Several women friends once told me they believed that if someone with whom a Christian shared the gospel didn't respond in faith, that Christian had stepped out of God's will. So not wanting to step out of God's will, they seldom shared Jesus's good news.

But we will discover today that this burdensome belief is false.

The World Will Persecute Jesus's Followers

12. Read John 15:18-19. (a) What should Jesus's followers know (verse 18)? (b) According to Jesus, why does the world hate his followers (verse 19)?

Earlier, Jesus told his siblings, "The world cannot hate you, but it hates me because I testify about it that its works are evil" (John 7:7). People can't receive Jesus's offer of eternal life without first accepting that their deeds are evil and that they therefore need his offer. That's the message Jesus gave to the upstanding religious leader Nicodemus, and it's the message everyone needs to hear.

But not everyone wants to hear that message. Most people want to believe they're good—good enough, in fact, to enter heaven on their own merits. They avoid examining thoughts, conscience, and motives by Jesus's standards: "People loved the darkness rather than the light because their works were evil. For everyone who does wicked things hates the light and does not come to the light, lest his works should be exposed" (John 3:19-20).

Just as branches connected to a vine's trunk bear fruit, so Jesus's disciples connected to him will bear fruit.

13. Read John 15:20-21. (a) Many persecuted Jesus; therefore, who else will they persecute (verse 20)? (b) Some kept Jesus's word; therefore, who else's word will they keep (verse 20)? (c) Why will people persecute Jesus's followers (verse 21)?

The Little Details
D.A. Carson: "They Would Not Be Guilty" (John 15:24)

Contrary to my girlfriends' expectations, Jesus said to expect negative responses, even persecution. Negative responses are a sign that someone does not know the Father yet. They are not necessarily a sign that the message giver's delivery is flawed.

14. Read John 15:22-23. (a) What do those who reject Jesus's words have no excuse for (verse 22)? (b) If someone hates Jesus, whom else do they hate (verse 23)?

The idea is not that if Jesus had not come the people would have continued in sinless perfection—as if the coming of Jesus introduced for the first time sin and its attendant guilt before God (the Greek behind "they would not be guilty of sin" is, more simply, "they would not have sin"). Rather, by coming and speaking to them Jesus incited the most central and controlling of sins: rejection of God's gracious revelation, rebellion against God, decisive preference for darkness rather than light…Jesus has *done among them what no one else did* (v. 24), yet despite so many signs "they still would not believe in him" (12:37). Religious interest that pursues signs may be suspicious (4:48), and faith based on sight is intrinsically inferior (20:29); even so, it is infinitely better than no faith, and the signs and works of Jesus make a legitimate claim on faith (4:34: 5:36; 9:32-33; 10:38). Rejection of Jesus' words (v. 22) and works (v. 24) is thus the rejection of the clearest light, the fullest revelation; and therefore it incurs the most central, deep-stained guilt.[6]

Jesus's words are the Father's words. Therefore, when people reject Jesus's words, they also reject the Father's words. When they hate Jesus, they hate the Father too.

Yet many who hate Jesus believe they love God. But what they love is a god created in their own image, a god whose judgments and beliefs parallel their own.

Jesus's Rejection Was Foretold

The disciples expected everyone to rally behind Jesus as so many had when he rode the donkey into Jerusalem. But Jesus explains that the coming rejection is foretold.

15. Read John 15:24-25. (a) If those who rejected Jesus hadn't seen his miraculous signs, what would their status be (verse 24)? (b) When they saw the signs, how did they react (verse 24)? (c) Whose Law did their hatred fulfill (verse 25)?

Those who hate Jesus saw the signs yet chose not to accept what they signified. But because they saw the signs, *they have no excuse for their sin* (verse 22).

Their own Scriptures (*Law* here is shorthand for what we now call the Old Testament) foretold Jesus's coming in various promises, prophecies, and portents, many of which we've already seen. Furthermore, the prophets called David a type of the future righteous king. That means events in David's life portended (or foreshadowed) events in Jesus's life. David wrote, "More in number than the hairs of my head are those who hate me without cause; mighty are those who would destroy me, those who attack me with lies" (Psalm 69:4). Thus, Jesus is telling his disciples that the event that occasioned the writing of this psalm foreshadowed the persecution Jesus now faces.

The Holy Spirit and the Disciples Will Bear Witness About Jesus

Some hate Jesus without cause and will therefore also hate his disciples. But that isn't a reason to stop spreading the good news.

16. Read John 15:26-27. (a) By what two names does Jesus call the one he would send them from the Father (verse 26)? (b) What will he do (verse 26)? (c) What must the disciples also do (verse 27)?

The Holy Spirit himself will bear witness about Jesus. The disciples who have been with him during his earthly ministry must tell all that they witnessed too. Why? Because people need to hear the good news.

17. Read John 16:1-2. (a) Why is Jesus telling them about the hardships they will face when they proclaim his message (verse 1)? (b) What's the first hardship they should expect (verse 2)? (c) What additional hardship will eventually come (verse 2)?

When the disciples first believed Jesus was the Messiah, they may have anticipated skirmishes with Rome. But now Jesus tells them to expect increasing persecution from Jewish brethren. That's shocking. Not that they haven't seen the Jewish leaders' animosity and threats, but Jesus is so powerful that they surely feel safe with him. Yet now he says he's leaving and that they will face death threats.

18. Read John 16:3-4. (a) Why will people persecute Jesus's followers (verse 3)? (b) Why is Jesus telling them about the persecution to come (verse 4)?

Jesus assures his disciples that they will face persecution and even death as they share what they witnessed Jesus do *because* the persecutors *have not known the Father*. He tells them now so that when persecution comes, they'll know it's not because they've done something wrong or because God is not with them. Rather, it's because their persecutors don't know the Father.

19. ♥ Share a time when you told someone about the good news but that person responded to it negatively. What comfort do you take in the fact that Jesus said his good news will not always be greeted favorably?

The disciples who have been with him during his earthly ministry must tell all that they witnessed too. Why? Because people need to hear the good news.

My friends, if you're sharing the good news of Jesus Christ, not all will respond with joy. Some may need time. Some may reject it. Some may treat you badly. How people respond is between them and God. We can rejoice that we've shared the good news as Jesus wants and leave the results in God's hands. The Holy Spirit will bear witness about Jesus too. That's good news.

In the next lesson, we'll discover more good news about the Holy Spirit.

Day 4

The Spirit of Truth

Two weeks ago as I write, my husband Clay's brother was diagnosed with a malignant, inoperable brain tumor. The family was shocked because he'd seemed to be in perfect health until a few days before. It took everyone time to wrap their heads around the news.

Likewise, the Eleven can't wrap their heads around Jesus saying he's leaving to return to the Father. They don't know what he means. As readers, we understand what Jesus means better because John has alerted us that Jesus knows he's going to die (John 12:33). But the disciples can't mesh their understanding of a Messiah who is supposed to restore God's kingdom with Jesus saying he's leaving.

Jesus Will Send the Spirit of Truth

> **20.** Read John 16:5-7. (a) Where is Jesus going (verse 5)? (b) What has filled the disciples' hearts (verse 6)? (c) Why is it to their advantage that Jesus leaves (verse 7)?

The disciples are deeply saddened. The glorious future they had imagined is disintegrating. Nonetheless, Jesus places great importance on his sending the Helper—the Holy Spirit—to them. Indeed, this is another claim to a divine prerogative.

The Holy Spirit Will Convict

> **21.** Read John 16:8-11. (a) What three things will the Holy Spirit convict the world about (verse 8)? (b) Why of sin (verse 9)? (c) Why of righteousness (verse 10)? (d) Why of judgment (verse 11)?

The Holy Spirit convicts people of their sin to help them realize they need a Savior so that they might turn and *believe in* Jesus. He convicts them of their false standards of righteousness that will never get them to the Father. He convicts them of false judgments about Jesus and righteousness, for the true judgment is coming and *the ruler of this world—* Satan—*is judged* and condemned.

The disciples can't mesh their understanding of a Messiah who is supposed to restore God's kingdom with Jesus saying he's leaving.

The Holy Spirit Will Guide into Truth

22. Read John 16:12-13 below. Box the reason Jesus will not tell them more now. Circle who will come. Underline the three things he will do.

> I still have many things to say to you, but you cannot bear them now. When the Spirit of truth comes, he will guide you into all the truth, for he will not speak on his own authority, but whatever he hears he will speak, and he will declare to you the things that are to come.

Confusion and sorrow leave the disciples unable to bear all that Jesus wants to say. But the Holy Spirit will take up where Jesus leaves off and guide them *into all truth*.

23. ♥ Choose one of the following: Describe a time when you were reading the Bible and the Holy Spirit showed you how the passage applied to your life. Or describe a time you were praying and the Holy Spirit caused you to remember a Bible passage that helped you.

The Holy Spirit Will Glorify Jesus, Who Has All the Father Has

24. Read John 16:14-15. (a) Whom will the Spirit of truth glorify (verse 14)? (b) What belongs to Jesus (verse 15)? (c) What will the Spirit of truth declare (verse 15)?

All that the Father has is mine. That's another claim to having that which only the Divine should have.

The Disciples Will See Jesus Again

Jesus has told them he will send the Holy Spirit to them so that the Holy Spirit will guide them into all truth. Next he prepares them for what is to come.

25. Read John 16:16-19. (a) What will happen in a little while (verse 16)? (b) What will happen in another little while (verse 16)? (c) Do the disciples understand Jesus (verses 17-18)?

The disciples are confused.

26. Read John 16:20. (a) How will the disciples initially respond to the coming events? (b) In contrast, how will the world respond? (c) But how will they later respond?

Their reaction will differ greatly from the world's reaction.

27. Read John 16:21-22. (a) How does a woman giving birth move from sorrow to joy (verse 21)? (b) When Jesus sees them again, what will happen (verse 22)?

Jesus alludes to Isaiah 26:16-19. There, the people are in great distress and writhe like a woman about to give birth. But they birth only wind, so they "accomplished no deliverance in the earth" (verse 18). Nonetheless, God promises, "Your dead shall live; their bodies shall rise. You who dwell in the dust, awake and sing for joy!" (verse 19).

28. Read John 16:23-24. (a) What promise is in these verses? (b) Why (verse 24)?

On the day the disciples see Jesus, they won't ask any more questions about all this, for they'll understand. Then they'll be able to make requests of the Father in Jesus's name. *In my name* means in alignment with what Jesus's name stands for.

Amid troubling news, Jesus gives his disciples good news. He will send the Spirit of truth, the Holy Spirit. Then the Spirit of truth will convict and guide as he glorifies Jesus. Furthermore, Jesus possesses all that the Father possesses (that's another claim to divinity). And even though he's leaving, the disciples will see him again and be filled with joy. Then they will ask of the Father in Jesus's name, and the Father will answer them, filling them with joy.

In the next lesson, we'll see Jesus offer more comforting news.

Day 5

Jesus Has Overcome the World

Have you ever prepared for something you expected to be one way, but it turned out to be entirely different? In my younger years, I accepted a job as a receptionist that would have lots of "phone work." What my new boss hadn't explained was that by phone work, he meant cold-call sales. If he had, I wouldn't have signed up.

As Jesus continues to prepare his disciples for his departure, they may be wondering just what they're signing up for. He continues to explain.

The Little Details
Craig Hazen: Petitionary Prayer

I won't dig deeply into why some teachers put petitionary prayer on the bottom shelf, but I will briefly mention three things I have noticed. First, it might be a reaction to our materialist age and how it has negatively affected the church. Prayer for things seems to play into this unhealthy materialistic appetite and hence muddies the pure water of prayer. Second, it might be a logical consequence of Reformed (Calvinist) theology that has difficulty with the idea that asking in prayer can actually change the outcome of a situation already ordained by God...Third, more people than you might expect think petitionary prayer is in some way bothering God with unimportant matters.

...The effect of this kind of thinking is that we are missing out on much that the Lord wants us to have. Asking is key. It actually helps to form the kind of relationship that God wants to have with us—one in which we are deeply dependent on him.[7]

Amid troubling news, Jesus gives his disciples good news. He will send the Spirit of truth, the Holy Spirit.

The Little Details
Craig Hazen: John's Recall of Jesus's Teaching

When we arrive at chapter 15…we are already near the end of the story. In his account, John lingers on the last hours of Jesus's life… It would be easy to imagine this because those hours would have been seared into John's mind in a special way for the rest of his life. Trauma can stamp vivid memories onto the psyche. Witnessing or being nearby the personal agony, painful prayers, the arrest, the trials, the violent scourging, the innocent Jesus dying slowly on a Roman cross—and then hiding in fear for your life—was maximally distressing. And it would have been more so for people like the disciples who had the most profound hope that Jesus would take the throne of Israel and replace both the Romans and the corrupt religious establishment.

So the final teaching times, those surrounding such deep pain and disappointment, were not something that John could or would forget. In addition…Jesus promised his disciples that the Holy Spirit would come to comfort them and remind them of everything Jesus had said to them (John 14:26).[8]

The Father Loves the Disciples

Jesus has expressed his great love for the disciples. Now he has additional good news.

> **29.** Read John 16:25-27. (a) What would Jesus no longer do in an hour that's coming (verse 25)? (b) Then, how will they be able to ask for things from the Father (verse 26)? (c) Why can they ask (first part of verse 27)? (d) Why is that (rest of verse 27)?

What an incredible message: "For the Father himself loves you, because you have loved me and have believed that I came from God" (John 16:27).

> **30.** Next to John 16:28 below, underline both instances of *Father*. Circle both instances of *world*. Box *now*. Then draw clouds to the right of the first line, representing where the Father is. Draw a circle representing the world below the clouds. Draw an arrow from the clouds to the left side of the world. Draw another arrow from the right side of the world to the clouds.
>
> I came from the Father
>   and have come into the world,
>   and now I am leaving the world
> and going to the Father.

Since the disciples believe Jesus came from God, Jesus summarizes what's happening.

> **31.** Read John 16:29-30. (a) What do the disciples think Jesus is now doing (verse 29)? (b) Why do they believe Jesus came from God (verse 30)?

Jesus had said the hour was coming when he'd *speak plainly*, and the disciples think the time is now and profess belief.

The Father Is with Jesus

> **32.** Read John 16:31-32. (a) What does Jesus reply to the disciples' profession (verse 31)? (b) What will happen to the disciples (verse 32)? (c) Although they will abandon him, what does Jesus know (verse 32)?

Jesus knows their faith is not yet strong and that they will abandon him. But he knows the Father is with him anyway.

Jesus Gives Peace and Overcame the World

33. Read John 16:33. (a) Why does Jesus tell the disciples they will abandon him? (b) What will they have in the world? (c) Why should they take heart?

The disciples don't yet realize what's coming. Jesus lets them know they will indeed scatter and leave him alone but that the Father is with him. He lets them know all this so they will have peace despite their failures and troubles.

34. ♥ How may verse 33 apply to your current troubles? How can you take heart?

The Good News

John 15–16 offers more good news. Jesus is the true vine, his Father is the vinedresser, and his followers are the branches. Thus, as disciples abide in Jesus like branches abide in a vine, they will bear fruit. Indeed, they abide by keeping Jesus's commands. Furthermore, Jesus calls disciples who obey him his friends and says he reveals things of God to them. Moreover, the Father grants requests that Jesus's followers make in Jesus's name. Still, Jesus's followers shouldn't be alarmed if they share the good news and some reject it.

Additionally, Jesus will send the Spirit of truth, the Holy Spirit, who will convict and guide as he glorifies Jesus. Also, Jesus possesses all that the Father possesses, which is another claim to divinity. And even though he's leaving, the disciples will see him again and be filled with joy. Moreover, the Father loves the disciples. Even though the disciples temporarily will abandon Jesus during the difficulties to come, the Father will be with Jesus. Although the world offers tribulation, Jesus has overcome the world and offers peace.

35. ♥ Which of these items of good news means the most to you today? Why?

In our next chapter, Jesus prays for his disciples before soldiers arrive to arrest him.

Praise God for something you saw of his character this week. **Confess** anything that convicted you. **Ask** for help to do something God's Word calls you to do. **Thank** God for something you learned this week.

Even though the disciples temporarily will abandon Jesus during the difficulties to come, the Father will be with Jesus. Although the world offers tribulation, Jesus has overcome the world and offers peace.

Karla's Creative Connection

Jesus is truly the master storyteller. As I read John 15:5, where he paints a picture of himself as the vine and us as the branches, I could easily visualize him as a strong, sturdy grapevine and myself as one of the branches. When you ponder the picture, you can see why it's so important that we remain in him, allowing his life to flow in us and through us to produce healthy leaves and spiritual fruit. As we abide in him and allow his words to abide in us, we are nourished, pruned, and protected from disease and destruction, enabling us to bear eternal fruit for God's glory and the blessing of others. It's such a beautiful picture of God's perfect plan for our lives and our fruitfulness!

In illustrating this verse, drawing clusters of grapes is relatively easy—lots of circles in somewhat of an upside-down pyramid. But because the leaves were a bit more of a challenge, I want to share a little visual trick so you can draw your own. And it all starts with a heart...so fitting.

1. Start by drawing a heart in pencil. 2. Add small circles as shown. 3. As you ink your leaf, wrap your line around the circles and add zig-zag lines where shown. 4. Add a stem, a tendril, and some veins. Erase your pencil lines, and you have yourself a nice grape leaf to attach to your fruit!

And just look at all the other leaf designs you can create by simply starting with a heart!

God's creation is our best source of inspiration! Take a neighborhood walk and observe all the different shapes and sizes leaves come in. You may even be surprised. And then use your God-given imagination to create a few of your own.

Karla

Chapter 9

John 17:1–19:27
Consecrated for a Mission

Why did Jesus go forward knowing he faced betrayal?

Day 1 ──────────────────────

Betrayed

"Y ou're a horrible person for saying bad things about your father!" I was five and had sought help from my mother after my father had tried to kill me. Or so I believed. It was many years before I understood he simply had a violent temper.

My father told me, "You had a choice to hurt me or protect me. You chose to hurt me." He added something about not forgiving me, but I didn't understand what he meant or how I'd hurt him.

His mother—my grandmother—told me I shouldn't be afraid because I was stronger than my father was. To prove it, she bounced me on his chest while he lay on the floor and pretended to be hurt. She said, "See? You're hurting him!" I thought that was what my father meant by hurting him, and I screamed. I knew she was lying about who was stronger, and I was terrified about what punishment might happen later. I was crushed that I was so bad that I hurt him when I didn't want to or mean to.

After that, the only adults I trusted were my maternal grandparents. They didn't call me a liar or tell me I was bad, and I felt safe with them. But soon my parents forbade me from talking to them or anyone about homelife anymore. Then something happened—I don't remember what—that made me believe my parents had fooled my maternal grandpa. I remember only my grandfather's kind, sad face as we parted. My father had told me no one would ever believe me, and now it seemed he was right.

Now I see that it was no wonder that, nearly a decade later, I interpreted the Gospels the way I did. After I prayed that night after reading through John 8, I realized I'd judged Jesus and the Father incorrectly, but I didn't know how I should now think of them. If they weren't like my deceitful dad and deceived (so I thought) maternal grandpa, what were they like? I tried to let the Bible tell me, but many things I just didn't understand.

The chapters we'll read today, however, gripped my attention. Because I knew betrayal, three facts astonished me. First, Jesus *allowed* himself to be betrayed to obtain something good for those he loved. Second, he had no doubt that the Father knew the truth and would later vindicate him. Third, Jesus trusted his Father even through horrific events. These chapters displayed God's incomprehensible love, a love I hadn't known existed.

The Little Details
Psalm 22

Psalm 22 remarkably portrays the crucifixion. In fact, Jesus linked the psalm to the cross by quoting its first verse: "My God, my God, why have you forsaken me?" (Matthew 27:46).

Psalm 22:6-7 describes how the Jewish leaders treated him: "I am...scorned by mankind and despised by the people. All who see me mock me." Matthew 27:43 gives the Jewish leaders' words: "He trusts in God; let God deliver him now, if he desires him." These words match the mockers' words in Psalm 22:8: "He trusts in the LORD; let him deliver him."

If you'd like to learn more about Psalm 22, see our book *Discovering Jesus in the Old Testament*.

God said that one of the ways he would fix Israel's sin problem was through a future righteous servant whom Isaiah described in four servant songs.

God's Word to Us in the Old Testament

John's early readers knew the Old Testament narratives told of many betrayals, some past and some prophesied for the future. Let's look at some that relate to the chapters we'll read in John today.

David's Psalm 22 Foreshadowed the Suffering Future King

As we've seen, the Old Testament paints King David as a type of the future righteous Messiah. That means that some events in David's life foreshadowed events in the Messiah's life.

When David was young, a **prophet announced that David would one day be king**. But when the current king heard that the people credited David with more military victories than they credited to him, jealousy drove him to try to kill David. Soon he feared that God had chosen David to be the next king. So he falsely accused David to his troops and sent them to pursue and kill the young man.

For years, David suffered as he fled attacks on his life. During those difficult times, he wrote Psalm 22. There, he writes of his strength diminishing and a **thirst** that cleaves his tongue to his jaws. He describes his enemies' actions: "**They have pierced my hands and feet—I can count all my bones—they stare and gloat over me; they divide my garments among them, and for my clothing they cast lots**" (Psalm 22:16-18).

Then suddenly the psalm turns to praise as it describes the Lord's rescue of David so that **all nations will worship before God**, "for kingship belongs to the LORD" (verse 28). Its final words declare that all posterity shall tell of the Lord "that **he has done it**" (verse 31).

Zechariah and David Prophesied About a Future Royal Priest

Under the law of Moses, priests descended from Moses's brother, Aaron. Their duties included **teaching God's commands**, **interceding in prayer** at the incense altar, and **offering sacrifices** for the people (Deuteronomy 33:10). When they entered the priesthood, they had to be **sanctified with blood** on their **extremities**.[1]

But after the exile came this prophecy: "There shall be a priest on his throne" (Zechariah 6:13). This prophecy was remarkable because the Messiah would descend from David, not Aaron.

The Psalms held a clue, though. There, David prophesied that a future king whom he called "my Lord" would be "a priest forever after the order of Melchizedek" (Psalm 110:1,4). Long before Moses's day, Melchizedek was the priest and king of Salem (later known as Jerusalem). His was a different priesthood.

Isaiah Prophesied About a Future Suffering Servant

God said that one of the ways he would fix Israel's sin problem was through a future righteous servant whom Isaiah described in four servant songs. We read the first two songs in chapter 7. Let's now read the third.

 Take a moment to pray for insight as you read God's Word.

1. Read Isaiah 50:4-9, which are the words of the righteous servant. (a) Who teaches the servant (verse 4)? (b) How is the servant treated (verse 6)? (c) Does mistreatment stop him from doing God's will (verses 5,7)? (d) Who helps the servant (verse 9)?

Zechariah Prophesied About a Pierced One

Psalm 22 isn't the only Old Testament mention of someone being pierced. During the days of the second temple, Zechariah prophesied about the day "the Lord will be king over all the earth" (Zechariah 14:9). Among his oracles is this in Zechariah 12:10:

> I will pour out on the house of David and the inhabitants of Jerusalem a spirit of grace and pleas for mercy, so that, when they **look on me, on him whom they have pierced**, they shall mourn for him, as one mourns for an only child, and weep bitterly over him, as one weeps over a firstborn.

Here the Lord identifies himself with the **one who is pierced**.

Zechariah also prophesied this: "'Awake, O **sword**, against **my shepherd**, against the man who stands next to me,' declares the Lord of hosts. '**Strike the shepherd**, and the **sheep will be scattered**'" (Zechariah 13:7).

2. ❤ Describe a time you were betrayed. How did you feel?

God's Word to Us in John

In the last chapter, we stopped reading amid the events of Passover in a year when the Passover meal falls on the **day of Preparation** (Thursday sundown to Friday sundown). On the day of Preparation, Jews prepare for the Sabbath by readying meals and doing any other work forbidden on the Sabbath. The **Sabbath** they prepare for is special, for it's also part of the **Feast of Unleavened Bread**.

Jesus has been preparing his disciples for his imminent departure. They are shocked, confused, and troubled. Now, he pauses to pray.

3. ❤ Read John 17:1–19:27. What stands out to you? Why?

We read Psalm 22, which described events in David's life that stunningly parallel the crucifixion. We read two other prophecies about the crucifixion as well. Against those Old Testament readings, we read about Jesus's prayer, arrest, crucifixion, and burial. The good news is that the Lord God foretold the events—no one defeated his plans. Next we'll look at what is often called the High Priestly Prayer.

> Jesus has been preparing his disciples for his imminent departure. They are shocked, confused, and troubled. Now, he pauses to pray.

Pam's Heart-to-Heart with the Great I Am—
"I Am the Light of the World"

Again Jesus spoke to them, saying, "I am the light of the world.
Whoever follows me will not walk in darkness, but will have the light of life."
John 8:12

Christ claims he *is* the light of the world. In HELPS Word-Studies, *light* (*phós*) is referred to as "the manifestation of God's self-existent life; divine illumination to reveal and impart life, through Christ."[2]

Jesus is the light that the darkness cannot overcome:

> The light shines in the darkness, and the darkness has not overcome it (John 1:5 NIV).

> This is the message we have heard from him and declare to you: God is light; in him there is no darkness at all (1 John 1:5 NIV).

Jesus, the light that conquers darkness, is good news! To gain this victory over darkness, we are to follow him—accompany Jesus and travel the same road his disciple did. The verse explains that when we maintain this intimate relationship with Jesus, we will not walk in darkness—"a brand of moral, spiritual *obscurity* (i.e., which blocks the light of God when faith is lacking)."[3]

Darkness Hates the Light

> Everyone who does evil hates the light, and will not come into the light for fear that their deeds will be exposed (John 3:20 NIV).

This Bible study is shining the light of Jesus—and the evil one hates this life-transforming illumination. Here's a snapshot of the roadblocks that hit my life as I wrote this study:

- Because of the COVID-19 pandemic, six months of live speaking was canceled or rescheduled in less than two days—the bulk of our income wiped away.

- We live on a live-aboard boat—or we *used* to. Our marina closed. My 91-year-old in-laws needed us as full-time caregivers to protect their health, so we "sheltered at home" in a tiny, 300-square-foot RV on their property.

- A hacker breached security of our webhost. (This violation made international headlines.) My husband's email and login information were stolen, and a hacker then used this to hijack Bill's Facebook page; used that page to steal and remove us as admins of our professional Facebook page; and—while we repeatedly reported this attack and frantically searched for a real person at Facebook to help us—sold our page to someone who filled the feed with violent and inappropriate images for six weeks! In addition, in the mess of all this, Facebook disabled my personal profile page, and the siege against us continued in cyberspace as the hacker tried to steal our personal money and tear down other areas of our online ministry.

The assault felt like we were experiencing 1 Peter 5:8: "Your adversary the devil prowls around like a roaring lion, seeking someone to devour."

How Can We Walk in the Light?

Years ago, our friends and authors Paul and Virginia Friesen invited us to speak on Catalina Island for a rustic family camp. Paul explained we would stay in the *deluxe* cabin, meaning "you have a lightbulb with a chain you can pull to turn on the light."

Pull the chain! Call out to the light of heaven. Then ask all those who walk in the light to link up with you!

Step into the Light:

You were formerly darkness, but now you are light in the Lord; **walk as children of light** (Ephesians 5:8 NASB).

Sing Light!

I will sing of your strength; I will sing aloud of your steadfast love in the morning. For you have been to me a fortress and a refuge in the day of my distress (Psalm 59:16).

Speak Light!

Personalize and pray out loud Ephesians 6:10-17 (NIV):

Be strong in the Lord and in his mighty power. Put on the full armor of God, so that you can take your stand against the devil's schemes. For our struggle is not against flesh and blood, but against the rulers, against the authorities, against the powers of this dark world and against the spiritual forces of evil in the heavenly realms. Therefore, put on the full armor of God, so that when the day of evil comes, you may be able to stand your ground, and after you have done everything, to stand. Stand firm then, with the belt of truth buckled around your waist, with the breastplate of righteousness in place, and with your feet fitted with the readiness that comes from the gospel of peace. In addition to all this, take up the shield of faith, with which you can extinguish all the flaming arrows of the evil one. Take the helmet of salvation and the sword of the Spirit, which is the word of God.

Shout Light!

You are a chosen race, a royal priesthood, a holy nation, a people for his own possession, that you may **proclaim the excellencies of him who called you out of darkness into his marvelous light** (1 Peter 2:9).

So I am shouting out the victory of light that we experienced in the above calamities: Satan lost, and God won! Turn your list of obstacles and darker times into a list of reasons to claim the Light and walk as light in the world.

Pam

Experiencing Scripture Creatively

- Select a favorite word or phrase from today's reading. Follow Karla's instructions at the end of this chapter for writing it in royal letters.

- Write a poem or song about John 18:36.

Jesus Prays

The Little Details

D.A. Carson: The Glory for Which Jesus Asks (John 17:5)

What is clear is that Jesus is asking to be returned to the glory that he shared with the Father before the world began…This does not mean that Jesus is asking for what might be called a "de-incarnation" in order to be returned to the glory he once enjoyed. When the Word became flesh (1:14), this new condition was not designed to be temporary. When Jesus is glorified, he does not leave his body behind in a grave, but rises with a transformed, glorified body…which returns to the Father…and thus to the glory the Son had with the Father "before the world began."[4]

I feared betrayal, and I feared false accusations. Even as an adult, my prayers when facing betrayal were always about bringing the truth out and vindicating me. But that's not how Jesus prayed when facing treacheries and lies.

Jesus Prays for Himself

After teaching his disciples for three years, Jesus's time with them is ending, and he's about to complete the mission for which he came into the world. He's also about to send his disciples out for the mission for which he has prepared them. He's prepared them for his departure in a speech similar to Moses's farewell speech, and he now turns to the Father in prayer.

Jesus Is the Christ and Has Authority to Give Eternal Life

Jesus begins by praying about his mission.

> 4. Read John 17:1-3. (a) What does Jesus ask the Father to do for him (verse 1)? (b) What authority does Jesus have (verse 2)? (c) To have eternal life is to know whom (verse 3)?

The hour has come to complete the work Jesus came to earth to do. He calls himself *Jesus Christ*, acknowledging that he is the Christ, the Messiah, the One anointed to rule forever.

Jesus Had Glory Before the World Existed

> 5. In John 17:4-5 below, circle the two actions Jesus completed. Underline the glory he asks to be glorified with.
>
> I glorified you on earth, having accomplished the work that you gave me to do. And now, Father, glorify me in your own presence with the glory that I had with you before the world existed.

Jesus has glorified the Father by accomplishing all that the Father sent him to do. Now he asks to be glorified with the same glory he had with the Father *before the world existed*. His prayer reflects the prologue's words: "In the beginning was the Word, and the Word was with God, and the Word was God. He was in the beginning with God" (John 1:1-2).

Jesus Prays for His Current Disciples

Jesus prays next for his current disciples. Just as Moses pronounced blessings over those he led when he knew his hour had come to die, so now Jesus prays blessings over those he leads because he knows his own hour has come to die. Just as Moses and the high priests interceded for the people, so Jesus intercedes for his own.

He calls himself *Jesus Christ*, acknowledging that he is the Christ, the Messiah, the One anointed to rule forever.

Jesus Manifests the Father

6. Read John 17:6-8. (a) What has Jesus manifested to those who belong to him (verse 6)? (b) What do the disciples know (verses 7-8)? (c) What words has Jesus given them (verse 8)?

Jesus said he *manifested your name* (ESV). The NIV translates this, "I have revealed you," which catches the thought behind the phrase. He revealed God's character, words, and plans. Seeing him was seeing the Father (John 14:9).

I have given them the words that you gave me. Even as Jesus faces the coming horrors, he fulfills the first two verses of the third servant song: "The Lord GOD has given me the tongue of those who are taught, that I may know how to sustain with a word him who is weary. Morning by morning he awakens; he awakens my ear to hear as those who are taught" (Isaiah 50:4). The Eleven *received* Jesus's words from the Father and *have come to know in truth* that the Father sent Jesus.

Jesus Desires His Disciples' Unity

7. Read John 17:9-11. (a) To whom did God give those who belonged to him (verse 9)? (b) To whom do they belong (verse 10)? (c) What does Jesus ask the Father to do for those who belong to them (verse 11)?

Jesus intercedes for his disciples, who will be left in the world when he leaves. He asks that they *be one, even as we are one.* In other words, Jesus asks the Father to bestow on the disciples the incredible unity he has with his Father.

Jesus Guards His Disciples

8. Read John 17:12-13. (a) Why was one of the 12 disciples lost (verse 12)? (b) Why has Jesus spoken all that he has on this evening (verse 13)?

Jesus's prayer confirms that Scripture foretold that one of his disciples must betray him. He probably refers to Psalm 41:9, a psalm of David: "My close friend...who ate my bread, has lifted his heel against me." *These things I speak* refers to either the prayer here in chapter 17 or to everything Jesus has said since Judas left. He is preparing them for what's coming—the way he's leaving the world—so they know it was part of his plan so that *they may have my joy.*

> Jesus asks the Father to bestow on the disciples the incredible unity he has with his Father.

The Little Details
Jay Sklar: Holiness

To be holy is to be set apart as distinct in some way. Normally, this takes place when a person or object is set apart as distinct by another person. In Exodus and Leviticus, the Lord himself frequently sets apart various people or objects as distinct. He does this with people either by entering into special relationship with them (Lev. 11:44-45; 20:7-8,24-26) or by having them go through various rituals that set them apart in a special way (Lev. 8:12,30). He usually sets objects apart as distinct, either by dedicating them to the Lord…or, in the case of the year of Jubilee, by treating it differently from other years…

The holiness of these people or objects may be called "dependent holiness," for the simple reason that it is completely dependent on another. All of these people or objects were at one point *not* holy; they became holy only because another person had set them apart as distinct.

The Lord's holiness, however, does not depend on anyone else. It is completely independent. The Lord is set apart as distinct because of his very nature.[5]

9. Read John 17:14-16. (a) Why has the world hated Jesus's disciples (verse 14)? (b) What does Jesus want the Father to do (verse 15)?

Jesus is *not of the world*. That's why he doesn't seek this world's glory. But we *are not of the world* either. That means we also should not pursue the world's glory but should seek the Father's glory. Jesus does not pray for his disciples to be taken out of the world that hates them; he prays instead for protection *from the evil one*—Satan.

Jesus Consecrates Himself to Sanctify His Disciples

Just as Moses told the Israelites they were chosen for a purpose and were to be holy, so now Jesus's prayer shows that his disciples were chosen for a purpose and are to be holy.

10. Read John 17:17-19 below. Underline Jesus's request (first five and last seven words). Circle what God's word is. Box what Jesus has done with his disciples. Double underline what Jesus has done to himself.

   Sanctify them in the truth; your word is truth. As you sent me into the world, so I have sent them into the world. And for their sake I consecrate myself, that they also may be sanctified in truth.

Sanctify means to make holy, to set apart for God's purposes. Jesus asks the Father to sanctify the disciples *in the truth; your word is truth*. Jesus is the Word who teaches truth (John 8:31-32), is himself the truth (14:6), and sends the Spirit of truth (14:16-17). The truth of God's word changes us. That's why we need it.

Jesus says *I consecrate myself* (in the NIV, *I sanctify myself*) so that the disciples can be sanctified—made holy. In other words, he commits himself to the holy work before him. He sets himself apart for the Father's purpose in sending him. Unlike priests under the law of Moses, the current high priest does not consecrate him. Rather, he consecrates himself.

Jesus Prays for Future Believers

Jesus prays next for you and me and all future believers.

11. Read John 17:20-22. (a) What does Jesus pray for us (verse 21)? (b) Why (verse 21)? (c) What does Jesus give us (verse 22)? (d) Why (verse 22)?

Jesus wants us to be in him, attached to the vine, and he wants us to be one in the same way that he and the Father are one. Unity among believers who abide in Jesus is what shows the world that the Father sent Jesus. That is our mission: showing the world that the Father sent Jesus. Jesus reveals to us his glory so that we can be one and fulfill our mission.

The Father Loves Jesus's Followers as He Loves Jesus

Next comes amazing news.

12. Read John 17:23-24 below. Underline what unity among believers shows the world. Circle how the Father loves us. Box where Jesus wants us to be. Double underline the reason.

> I in them and you in me, that they may become perfectly one, so that the world may know that you sent me and loved them even as you loved me. Father, I desire that they also, whom you have given me, may be with me where I am, to see my glory that you have given me because you loved me before the foundation of the world.

In that prayer resides incredibly good news: The Father loves us as he loves Jesus. And Jesus wants us to be with him where he will be glorified.

Jesus Continues to Reveal the Father

13. Read John 17:25-26. (a) What does Jesus call the Father (verse 25)? (b) What do those who believe in Jesus know (verse 25)? (c) What does Jesus make known to believers (verse 26)? (d) Why (verse 26)?

Jesus has revealed the Father and will continue to do so, even for future believers, so that the Father's love for Jesus may be in us.

14. ♥ What are some ways you fulfill your mission so that the world may believe that the Father sent Jesus to it?

Jesus's prayer consecrates him for completing the Father's mission. In that prayer resides good news. First, he is the Christ, and he can give eternal life. Second, he prays for his current disciples, whom he is sending out into a world that hates them so they can spread the word Jesus gave them. Third, he prays for future disciples (us!) to be one so that the world may believe that the Father sent Jesus. Fourth, he guards his disciples. In summary, this prayer, his final one while with his disciples, is for his own mission, his current disciples' mission, and our mission.

In the next lesson Jesus will face the betrayal he foretold.

Day 3

Jesus Faces Betrayal Without Turning Back

One of the things that astonishes me about Jesus's prayer is that he takes betrayal and lies as givens in this world. When he prayed, "Your word is truth" (John 17:17), he knew the

The Little Details
Jesus's Glory in Us

Jesus prays, "The glory that you have given me I have given to them, that they may be one even as we are one" (John 17:22). The apostle Paul tells us more about this: "We all, with unveiled face, beholding the glory of the Lord, are being transformed into the same image from one degree of glory to another. For this comes from the Lord who is the Spirit" (2 Corinthians 3:18). John himself tells us more in a letter: "When he appears we shall be like him, because we shall see him as he is" (1 John 3:2).

Jesus has revealed the Father and will continue to do so, even for future believers, so that the Father's love for Jesus may be in us.

The Little Details
The Servant's Ear

John tells us Peter cut off the high priest's servant's right ear and that the servant's name was Malchus (John 18:10). While Matthew and Luke tell us more details, only John gives the servant's name. John knew the man's name because he knew the high priest personally (John 18:15).

Matthew, writing for a Jewish audience interested in angels, records more of Jesus's rebuke: "Put your sword back into its place. For all who take the sword will perish by the sword. Do you think that I cannot appeal to my Father, and he will at once send me more than twelve legions of angels? But how then should the Scriptures be fulfilled, that it must be so?" (Matthew 26:52-54).

The physician Luke wrote for Gentiles and noted that not only did Jesus rebuke the disciple, but he healed the man's ear (Luke 22:51).

Father would never believe false accusations. He fully trusted the Father to shine light on truth and glorify him. How he could do this becomes clearer in his trials.

Jesus Protects His Disciples

John wrote for us how tenderly Jesus prayed for his mission and the mission of his disciples, including us. Now he shows us Jesus's courage.

> **15.** Read John 18:1-5. (a) How did Judas know where to find Jesus (verse 2)? (b) What did Jesus know (verse 4)? (c) What strikes you about Jesus's response (verses 4-5)?

Jesus left with his disciples means either he finished leaving the home where they supped or he left the city. Judas brings with him Roman *soldiers* to keep the peace in case of resistance or rioting. He also brings temple *officers* to arrest Jesus. They bring *lanterns and torches* because it is night.

> **16.** Read John 18:6-9. (a) What happened when Jesus identified himself (verse 6)? (b) How did Jesus protect his disciples (verse 8)? (c) Whose word did he fulfill (verse 9)?

The soldiers fell back, either in awe of this man about whom they had heard so much or because they were forced to by an encounter with the Divine.

> **17.** Read John 18:10-11. What reason did Jesus give for stopping Peter?

In this way, Jesus prevents Peter from getting into an altercation that would lead to his arrest. Clearly, Peter doesn't understand Jesus's mission. Note that Jesus's reply reflects the suffering servant's words: "I was not rebellious; I turned not backward" (Isaiah 50:5).

Jesus Faces a Trial Before Annas

> **18.** Read John 18:12-14. (a) What did the soldiers do to Jesus (verse 12)? (b) To whom did they lead him first (verse 13)?

The soldiers arrest Jesus but let his disciples go. Annas is a former high priest related to the current one, Caiaphas. John reminds us of Caiaphas's prophecy in John 11:50.

19. Read John 18:15-18. (a) Why could the other disciple enter with Jesus (verse 15)? (b) When the servant girl asked Peter if he was a disciple of Jesus, what did Peter answer (verse 17)?

Another disciple probably refers to John, for the details read like eyewitness testimony and he elsewhere speaks of himself similarly. While days are usually warm this time of year, the nights are cold. D.A. Carson notes, "Night proceedings in normal cases were doubtless viewed as illegal. Where the case was exceptional and the pressure of time extraordinary, doubtless legal loopholes could be found."[6]

Jesus Requests a Fair Trial
Sometimes those whose duty it is to protect betray their duty.

20. Read John 18:19-21. (a) What did Annas the former high priest ask about (verse 19)? (b) Whom does Jesus tell him to ask (verses 20-21)?

In formal hearings, the Jewish leaders must question witnesses before bringing charges. Indeed, they must question witnesses for the defendant first, then witnesses against him. But Annas questions Jesus instead of witnesses, perhaps excusing himself because the trial is informal. Nonetheless, Jesus directs him to obey the law by directing his questions to witnesses. It's an opportunity to repent and do what's right.

21. Read John 18:22-24. (a) How does Jesus correct the officer (verse 23)? (b) To whom did Annas send Jesus, still bound (verse 24)?

The officer slaps Jesus in the face, but Jesus does not back down. Instead, he asks the man to either bear witness himself as to what Jesus did wrong or explain why he slapped him for demanding his right to witnesses and a fair trial. Annas does not get the information he wants and sends Jesus to his son-in-law for the formal accusation.

22. ♥ Jesus allowed the officers and Jewish leaders to proceed, but he still spoke the truth about their actions. How can you follow Jesus's example? If possible, without using names, address a current situation.

Jesus's Prophecy About Peter Is Fulfilled
It's not only leaders who betray. At times, friends do too.

The Little Details
D.A. Carson: Timeline of Trials
There are several ways by which the diverse Gospel accounts of Jesus' passion, especially his arrest and trials, can be brought into a single story-line. There were two trials, one Jewish and one Roman. The former began with informal examination by Annas (18:12-14,19-23), possibly while members of the Sanhedrin were being hurriedly summoned. A session of the Sanhedrin (Mt. 26:57-68; Mk. 14:53-65) with frank consensus was followed by a formal decision at dawn and dispatch to Pilate (Mt. 27:1-2; Lk. 22:66-71). The Roman trial began with a first examination before Pilate (Mt. 27:11-14; Jn. 18:28-38a), which was followed by Herod's interrogation (Lk. 23:6-12) and Jesus' final appearance before Pilate (Mt. 27:15-31; Jn. 18:38b–19:16). Other reconstructions are possible, but this one usefully co-ordinates the biblical data.[7]

The Little Details
Pilate

Pontius Pilate was governor (or prefect) of Judea from AD 26 to 37. Historical documents describe him "as a morally weak and vacillating man who, like many of the same breed, tried to hide his flaws under shows of stubbornness and brutality."[8] When Jews protested his dealings, he responded fiercely, as when he mingled the blood of certain Galileans with their sacrifices (Luke 13:1).

23. Read John 18:25-27. (a) How many more times does Peter deny being Jesus's disciple (verses 25-27)? (b) What happened after the last denial (verse 27)?

Peter, once so sure that he would lay down his life for Jesus, now knows his limits. He has betrayed the Lord he loves. The rooster crows, just as Jesus foretold (John 13:38).

In this lesson, we see Jesus protect his followers even as he resolutely sets himself to fulfill his Father's mission. He thus demonstrates he has consecrated his life to obeying his Father. He also demonstrates he is the suffering servant who does not turn back from obeying the Lord God. Moreover, when the former high priest questions him in an unlawful way, Jesus asks him why and instructs him to obey the law. Further, Jesus's prophecy about Peter denying him three times before the rooster crows comes to pass, which should tell the disciples that, yes, Jesus knows the future and this is part of the Father's plan. Next both the high priest and the governor try Jesus.

Day 4

Jesus Stands Before His Adversaries

After my grandparents' deaths, my aunt told me they had always believed me. In fact, I wasn't the only one of my siblings who had talked to them. But no one knew what they could do that wouldn't make things worse for us.

Because of this, I relate to what happens when the military governor, Pilate, tries Jesus. Pilate believes Jesus is innocent, but finding a way to release Jesus eludes him.

Jesus Faces Pilate

After questioning Jesus, Annas sends him to Caiaphas, who as the current high priest must present the charges against Jesus to the governor. During Jewish festivals, great crowds come to Jerusalem. Because of this, Pilate comes to his local headquarters with soldiers so he can quickly quell riots. That Roman soldiers accompanied the temple officers when they arrested Jesus means that the Jewish leaders have already presented at least a partial case to Pilate.

24. Read John 18:28-30. (a) Why didn't the Jewish leaders enter the governor's headquarters (verse 28)? (b) When Pilate asks for the charges against Jesus, what do they answer (verse 30)?

Pilate believes Jesus is innocent, but finding a way to release Jesus eludes him.

The Jewish leaders wouldn't enter a Gentile's house because that would have made them ritually unclean and therefore unable to participate in festivals. *Passover* here refers to the entire eight-day celebration that begins with Passover and includes the Feast of Unleavened Bread.[9] The Jews are concerned about participating in the rest of the feasts, but John wants us to connect the current events to the Passover.

Jesus Will Be Lifted Up as He Foretold

Pilate's question annoys the Jewish leaders because they expected him to accept their judgment, not start another trial.

> **25.** Read John 18:31-32. (a) Why do the Jewish leaders want Pilate to judge Jesus (verse 31)? (b) What does John say this was to fulfill (verse 32)?

Pilate doesn't want to be involved in a religious spat, and he tells them to handle the matter on their own. But that won't do because the Jewish leaders want the death penalty and only the governor can arrange that.

John says the Jews turning Jesus over to Rome for crucifixion *was to fulfill the word Jesus had spoken to show by what kind of death he was going to die.* He refers to this, starting with Jesus's words: "'And I, when I am lifted up from the earth, will draw all people to myself.' He said this to show by what kind of death he was going to die" (John 12:32-33). Being *lifted up from the earth* means he will be lifted from the earth on a cross.

Jesus's Kingdom Is Not of This World

Pilate brings Jesus into his headquarters to interrogate him.

> **26.** Read John 18:33-35. (a) What did Pilate ask Jesus (verse 33)? (b) What does Pilate want to know (verse 35)?

The only charge against Jesus Rome cares about is whether he claims to be a *king* who will lead a revolt against Rome. But when Pilate asks Jesus if he is the *King of the Jews*, Jesus wants to know if he decided that on his own and is truly interested or is merely repeating the Jewish leaders' charge. Jesus's concern is for Pilate rather than for himself. Nevertheless, Pilate's reply shows he has no personal interest. Still, he wants to know what Jesus did to infuriate the Jewish leaders.

> **27.** Read John 18:36. (a) What does Jesus say about his kingdom? (b) What evidence for this does Jesus give?

Jesus's disciples are not fighting to protect Jesus. In fact, Jesus stopped Peter for attempting that very thing. To Pilate, it's obvious that Jesus is not a threat to Rome. Even so, he's intrigued by Jesus's claim.

To Pilate, it's obvious that Jesus is not a threat to Rome. Even so, he's intrigued by Jesus's claim.

The Little Details
Barabbas

The name *Barabbas* means "son of a father" or "son of a rabbi."[11] In Matthew 27:16, some ancient manuscripts give his name as "Jesus Barabbas," as the NIV shows. In the ESV, that passage calls him "a notorious prisoner." Thus, Pilate asks which Jesus the people want him to release (Matthew 27:17).

The ESV translates the last part of John 18:40 as "Barabbas was a robber" and adds a text note that *robber* could also be translated "insurrectionist." The NIV translates it, "Now Barabbas had taken part in an uprising."

Mark 15:7 tells us more: "Among the rebels in prison, who had committed murder in the insurrection, there was a man called Barabbas." Acts 3:14 calls him a murderer, confirming he was more than just a thief. He was either in a gang of robbers or part of a revolt. Either way, murder resulted.

Jesus Bears Witness to Truth

> **28.** Read John 18:37. (a) What is Jesus's purpose? (b) Who listens to Jesus?

Jesus uses Pilate's question as another opportunity to reach him, explaining that his purpose for coming into this world is *to bear witness to the truth*. Jesus knows the truth, for he came from the Father and is himself the truth.

> **29.** ♥ In John 18:37, Jesus said, "Everyone who is of the truth listens to my voice." (a) According to Jesus's standard, are you of the truth? (b) How do you make time to listen to Jesus's words?

Pilate Declares Jesus Not Guilty

Pilate has heard enough to reach his verdict.

> **30.** Read John 18:38-40. (a) How does Pilate respond to Jesus's statement about bearing witness to the truth (verse 38)? (b) What verdict about Jesus does Pilate tell the Jews (verse 38)? (c) What happens when Pilate offers to release Jesus as part of his Passover custom (verses 39-40)?

Pilate cynically asks, *What is truth?* He's not interested in knowing more. Instead, he returns to the Jewish leaders and gives them his verdict: *I find no guilt in him*. He offers to release *the King of the Jews*. But the Jews will have none of it and want a criminal freed instead.

Jesus's Punishment Fulfills More Scripture

> **31.** Read John 19:1-3. (a) How did Pilate punish Jesus (verse 1)? (b) What did the Roman soldiers do (verses 2-3)?

Pilate has Jesus flogged, here likely the least severe form of flogging. He means to appease the Jews and warn Jesus against further inciting them. The soldiers mock him, finding the idea of his being a king ludicrous. But in this, Jesus fulfills more of the third servant song: "I gave my back to those who strike, and my cheeks to those who pull out the beard; I hid not my face from disgrace and spitting" (Isaiah 50:6).

32. Read John 19:4-6. (a) Why did Pilate bring Jesus out before the Jewish leaders again (verse 4)? (b) What did the Jewish leaders shout (verse 6)? (c) Why did Pilate tell the Jewish leaders to do it themselves (verse 6)?

The Little Details
Flogging

Pilate brings Jesus out so they can see him punished and mocked. He hopes they will see that this beaten man is no contender for a crown and that they'll be satisfied that this punishment and mockery are enough. But they won't be appeased. When they shout *Crucify him!* he sarcastically tells them to do it themselves.

In this lesson, we saw that when Jesus prophesied that he would be lifted up in his death, he meant crucifixion. We learned, too, that Jesus's kingdom is not of this world, which is good news considering the corruption here. Moreover, he bears witness to the truth. Furthermore, we saw prophecies about the suffering servant fulfilled when Pilate declares Jesus not guilty but has him flogged to appease the Jews. Still, the Jews are not satisfied with Pilate's continued attempts to free Jesus. In the next lesson we'll see what they try next.

The Romans delivered three types of flogging.[12] They administered the *fustigatio*, the least severe, for light offences. Afterward, they released the victim, often with a warning. That's likely what John 19:1 describes: "Then Pilate took Jesus and flogged him." He declared Jesus innocent and offered to release him.

Next Rome used the harsh *flagellatio* for criminals who had committed more serious crimes.

Day 5

Jesus Is Lifted Up

Human betrayal doesn't shake Jesus's trust in his Father. After all, he knew the Father's love before the foundation of the world (John 17:24). And he knows his kingdom is not of this world (John 18:36). Thus, he fully trusts that the betrayals will be exposed and the Father will glorify him. His hope isn't in this world because he isn't of this world, and neither are those who belong to him (John 17:16). That means we can trust through betrayals, too, and we can have Jesus's joy in us (John 17:13).

Finally, the horrible *verberatio* accompanied other punishments, such as crucifixion. They tied the naked victim to a post. Torturers beat him repeatedly with a whip of leather thongs embedded with bone or metal, at times exposing bones and sometimes killing him. As the first step in crucifixion, this is what Mark 15:15 describes: "So Pilate, wishing to satisfy the crowd, released for them Barabbas, and having scourged Jesus, he delivered him to be crucified."

33. ♥ How can you imitate Jesus's response to a betrayal you've experienced?

Blood loss from two beatings left Jesus too weak to carry his cross the entire way to the site of the crucifixion (Matthew 27:32).

Jesus Submits to the Mission Before Him

The Jewish leaders tried Jesus in the middle of the night in their own courts. Early the next morning, they delivered Jesus to Pilate. Pilate found no guilt in him and tried to free Jesus, but the Jews shouted, "Crucify him!"

Here, Pilate continues to try to release Jesus, whom he has judged innocent.

The Jewish Leaders Charge Jesus with Claiming to Be the Son of God

The Jewish leaders know "son of God" is a title all the kings descended from David use, but they (correctly) charge Jesus with using the title in a divine way.

The Little Details
To What Passover Refers

Passover can refer to different times and events. First, it can mean the sacrifice of a lamb on the afternoon of Nisan 14 (the first month of the Jewish year). Leviticus 23:5 reads, "In the first month, on the fourteenth day of the month at twilight, is the LORD's Passover." What's translated "at twilight" means about 3:00 p.m. (halfway between noon and sundown).[13]

Second, *Passover* can refer to the meal eaten that night, which included the sacrificed lamb.[14] Since Jewish days started at sundown, it was eaten on Nisan 15 in remembrance of the destroyer passing over homes the night of the meal.

Third, since the seven-day Feast of Unleavened Bread immediately followed the Passover sacrifice,[15] people sometimes referred to all three collectively as Passover or the Feast of the Passover.[16]

Since the temple's destruction in AD 70, no Passover lambs have been sacrificed. So Jews today consider Nisan 14 a minor holiday and refer to Nisan 15 to 21 as the Feast of the Passover or Passover.[17]

34. Read John 19:6-11. (a) Why did the Jews claim Jesus should die (verse 7)? (b) How did Pilate react (verse 8)? (c) When Jesus wouldn't tell Pilate where he was from, what authority did Pilate claim to have (verse 10)? (d) Who had the greater sin, according to Jesus (verse 11)?

In that day, Romans are superstitious and believe divine men exist. Pilate no doubt has heard much about this miracle worker, and this claim that he is the Son of God frightens him, especially since he has just had Jesus flogged. Jesus tells him the one who *has the greater sin* is Caiaphas.

The Jewish Leaders Charge Jesus with Claiming to Be King

35. Read John 19:12-13. (a) What did Pilate try to do (verse 12)? (b) How did the Jews threaten Pilate (verse 12)? (c) On what did Pilate sit (verse 13)?

The Jews threaten to report Pilate to Caesar if he releases Jesus. Pilate sits on his judgment seat on a raised stone pavement.

36. Read John 19:14-15. (a) What day was it (verse 14)? (b) What did Pilate say to the Jews (verse 14)? (c) How did the Jews respond (start of verse 15)? (d) How did they respond when Pilate asked, "Shall I crucify your King?" (verse 15)?

The *day of Preparation* is sundown Thursday to sundown Friday, "the day before the Sabbath" (Mark 15:42). *Of the Passover* means it's the day of Preparation that occurred during the eight-day festival that began with Passover (the entire festival was sometimes called Passover). It is approximately noon.

Shall I crucify your King? asks Pilate. The answer tells more than they realize: *The chief priests answered, "We have no king but Caesar."* Just as their forefathers did before them, they reject God as King and offer allegiance solely to a human.

And in so doing, they reject the King that God sent to deliver them—the King they claim to eagerly await.

Jesus Is Lifted Up

Pilate has a choice: Shall he condemn an innocent man or save his own skin?

37. Read John 19:16-18. (a) What did Pilate finally do (verse 16)? (b) To where did they take Jesus (verse 17)?

Delivered him over...to be crucified means that Pilate sent him to first be scourged, the severest form of flogging. Then Jesus carried the crossbar on his bloodied shoulders as he stumbled down the road leading outside the city. Either hung around his neck or carried by a soldier in front of him was a placard with his name and crime. Finally, when he reached Golgotha, Roman soldiers hammered nails through his wrists into the crossbar, lifted the beam to the already standing stake, and nailed his feet to the cross. They lifted him between two criminals, the guiltless among the guilty, alike condemned.

While priests descended from Aaron were consecrated with animal blood on their extremities, this Priest was consecrated with his own.

Jesus, the King of the Jews

But what is the charge inscribed on the placard?

38. Read John 19:19-22. (a) What inscription did Pilate put on the placard that stated the crime for which Jesus was crucified (verse 19)? (b) What change did the chief priests request (verse 21)? (c) Did Pilate give in to them (verse 22)?

Above the crucified Son of God hangs the charge in three languages: *Jesus of Nazareth, the King of the Jews.*

Jesus's Death Fulfills More Prophecy

As Jesus hangs crucified, others' actions continue to fulfill Scripture.

39. Read John 19:23-24. (a) What did the soldiers do with Jesus's garments (verses 23-24)? (b) What does John say these actions fulfilled (verse 24)?

John quotes Psalm 22:18, the psalm of David that spoke of pierced hands and feet.

Jesus Cares for His Mother

Even dying in excruciating pain, Jesus's concern for others does not abate.

40. Read John 19:25-27. (a) Which disciple was at the cross witnessing all (verse 26)? (b) What did he do at Jesus's request (verse 27)?

Jesus delivers his mother to John's care, not leaving her with his unbelieving brothers but instead entrusting her to one whom he has prepared for this moment.

How can we not trust someone who even amid excruciating suffering still looks to others' needs?

The Good News

We saw Jesus enter the final stages of his mission with prayer. First, he consecrated himself for his mission. Second, he revealed the Father to his disciples, guarded them, and sanctified them for their mission. Third, he revealed that the Father loves Jesus's followers as he loves Jesus. Then we read how Jesus faced betrayal and a sham trial without turning back. We discovered how his prophecies about Peter's failures and the method of his death were fulfilled. We learned that Jesus's kingdom is not of this world. We witnessed how in his sufferings and death, he still looked out for others.

> 41. ♥ Which of these items of good news means the most to you today? Why?

In Psalm 22, the Lord God's rescue seems sudden and unexpected when David's words turn abruptly from lament to praise. It mirrors what the disciples experience in our next chapter's mighty rescue.

> **Praise** God for something you saw of his character this week. **Confess** anything that convicted you. **Ask** for help to do something God's Word calls you to do. **Thank** God for something you learned this week.

Jesus faced betrayal and a sham trial without turning back.

Karla's Creative Connection

In this week's key verse, Jesus declares that his kingdom is not of this world, which means neither is ours. It made me think about how Jesus sits on the throne of our hearts, as King of kings, and we are his ambassadors of this heavenly kingdom here on earth, being the heart, hands, and voice of Christ in this fallen world.

As I illustrated this verse, I thought about kingdoms and kings and royalty. Several years ago, I came across a letter style I saw as "royal," only to later learn it was inspired by circus signage. But I still love it, and I believe it has a royal flair fitting a king, so I want to share it with you this week.

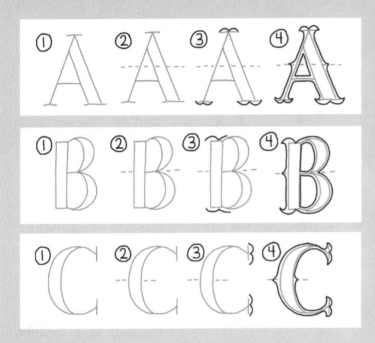

This letter style is a combination of thick and thin lines that you first hand draw in pencil. The key is adding "wings" or "fishtails" to the ends of the letters, as shown in step 3, before you trace it with ink.

To add a little more detail, draw a mark at half the height of your letters, as shown in step 2, and add a small spike off the side of your letter at the mark.

This letter style is perfect for adding side shading, and you can be more creative by adding pattern to the interior spaces of each letter.

I'm including the entire "royal" alphabet below for you to use as a visual guide for creating your own letters. As you examine each letter, you'll see that they each use the basic principles I've shared with you in creating the *A*, the *B*, and the *C*. With a little practice, you'll be including this letter style in your own Bible art in no time.

Karla

JESUS answered, "my kingdom is not of this WORLD"

John 18:36

Chapter 10

John 19:28–21:25
Jesus Is the Messiah

What evidence does John give that Jesus is the Messiah?

The Hope for Sinners

After facing betrayal and false accusations as a child, I insisted, "I don't lie." And as far as I know, I didn't. Until junior high.

My mother asked if I was the one who did something. I had, but I denied it. My brother laughed and said he saw me do it. I'd been caught in a blatant lie. They both laughed that I, the one who always insisted I didn't lie, had indeed lied.

That same year, I lied about a girlfriend who'd hurt me. Then I blamed someone else for something that was partly my fault, and I ended up getting the full blame.

Like Peter, I had believed I was better than I was until I faced a test. And just as Peter discovered he wasn't more courageous than the other disciples, so I discovered I wasn't more honest than my parents.

However, that revelation drove me to search out how to reach God, a quest that ultimately drove me to the Gospel of John. There I found not only the Way to the Father, but Jesus's response to sinners like my father, Peter, and me. In other words, God used truth to begin his sanctifying process in my life, just as Jesus prayed. As D. Martyn Lloyd-Jones writes, "No man would come to that point of repentance and belief and faith in Christ were it not that God had been dealing with him."[1]

For some, the process takes longer. In his later years, my father came to believe in Jesus as Messiah too. Hallelujah!

God's Word to Us in the Old Testament

As we've seen, God commanded people to celebrate annual festivals so that parents could teach their children about the festivals' significance. That way children could know God's mighty acts in history and follow him when they grew older.

But God also commanded these festivals for another reason. He made his plan to send Jesus into the world before its creation. To help people understand the significance of events in Jesus's life, he linked those events to the festivals.

John 19:14 informs us that the crucifixion took place on the "day of Preparation of the Passover"; that is, the Friday of an eight-day group of three celebrations often collectively called Passover.

The Little Details
The Feast of Firstfruits

Leviticus 23:11 reads, "On the day after the Sabbath the priest shall wave" the sheaf of barley as part of the Feast of Firstfruits. There's a little ambiguity as to when the Feast of Firstfruits was celebrated. The "more natural interpretation of the word *Sabbath* is that it refers to the actual Sabbath, meaning that the first sheaf was waved on Sunday."[4] But some argued that since the first day of the Feast of Unleavened Bread was a day of rest, then the waving should take place on the second day of the Feast, Nisan 16.

In the year of Jesus's crucifixion (either AD 30 or 33), however, Nisan 16 fell on Sunday, making it the Feast of Firstfruits under both calculations.

Paul connects the Feast of Firstfruits to the day Jesus was resurrected in 1 Corinthians 15:20-23: "Christ has been raised from the dead, the firstfruits of those who have fallen asleep... For...in Christ shall all be made alive. But each in his own order: Christ the firstfruits, then at his coming those who belong to Christ."

Three Celebrations

Passover

The Jews' first holy day of the year was **Passover**.[2] On it, they **sacrificed a perfect lamb**, obeying this command: "**You shall not break any of its bones.**"[3] That night they celebrated delivery from the land of slavery by feasting on the lamb.

Feast of Unleavened Bread

The seven days following Passover were the **Feast of Unleavened Bread**, a festival with sacrifices and shared meals. The first and last days were holidays spent at the temple. During this week, they ate no yeast as they remembered that their ancestors fled Pharaoh in haste with no time to let bread rise. In this way they continued to celebrate God's **redemption** from the land of slavery.

Feast of Firstfruits

A third feast connected to Passover was the **Feast of Firstfruits**. On the **day after the Sabbath after Passover**, Jews brought a sheaf of the first ripe barley stalks to the priest. They offered it to the Lord along with other sacrifices. They could not eat any of the new barley crop until they made this offering. This showed their gratitude for the new harvest and their **expectation of a greater harvest to come**.

The Fourth Servant Song

So far, we've read the first three of Isaiah's servant songs. Now let's read the final one.

> Take a moment to pray for insight as you read God's Word.

> 1. ♥ Read Isaiah 52:13–53:12. Record one way you've seen Jesus fulfill this prophecy and explain why it's meaningful to you.

God's Word to Us in John

In our reading, we paused on the day of Preparation (Thursday sundown to Friday sundown). Thursday evening, Jesus ate the Passover meal with his disciples. Then he was tried and crucified on Friday, the same Jewish day as the Passover meal.

The next day was an important Sabbath for two reasons. First, it was part of the Feast of Unleavened Bread. Second, it was the Sabbath that was followed by the Feast of Firstfruits.

> 2. ♥ Read John 19:28–21:25. What stands out to you? Why?

Today we read about three festivals tied to the events in the final chapters of John: Passover, the weeklong Feast of Unleavened Bread, and the Feast of Firstfruits. Our next lesson will show how the Passover lambs were a type of Jesus.

Pam's Heart-to-Heart with the Great I Am—Jesus Is Love

For God so loved the world, that he gave his only Son, that whoever
believes in him should not perish but have eternal life.
John 3:16

Christ didn't call himself love, but he showed himself to be love:

God's love was revealed among us in this way: God sent His One and Only Son into the world so that we might live through Him (1 John 4:9 HCSB).

I no longer live, but Christ lives in me. The life I now live in the body, I live by faith in the Son of God, who loved me and gave Himself for me (Galatians 2:20 HCSB).

This is how we have come to know love: He laid down His life for us. We should also lay down our lives for our brothers (1 John 3:16 HCSB).

Walk in love, as the Messiah also loved us and gave Himself for us, a sacrificial and fragrant offering to God (Ephesians 5:2 HCSB).

Christ Calls Us to Love

You might wonder, *What can I do to bring hope, help, and healing? I'm just one person; we are just one family.* Jesus gives us a clear place to begin. Receive God's love and become a conduit of love to others:

A new commandment I give to you, that you love one another: just as I have loved you, you also are to love one another (John 13:34).

Love one another with brotherly affection. Outdo one another in showing honor (Romans 12:10).

Beloved, if God so loved us, we also ought to love one another (1 John 4:11).

In the NIV, love is mentioned 551 times, so obviously love is vital.[5]

First John 4:7 says, "Love is from God," and 1 John 4:16 proclaims, "God is love."

What Does Love Look Like?

Love is patient, love is kind. It does not envy, it does not boast, it is not proud. It does not dishonor others, it is not self-seeking, it is not easily angered, it keeps no record of wrongs. Love does not delight in evil but rejoices with the truth. It always protects, always trusts, always hopes, always perseveres. Love never fails (1 Corinthians 13:4-8 NIV).

In the *Men Are Like Waffles—Women Are Like Spaghetti Devotional Study Guide*, we explain:

The way to a more loving relationship is to *be* more loving! Let's look at what goes into love:

Patience: Long passion and is willing to wait.

Kindness: Gentle in behavior.

No envy: Does not boil over in relationships.

No boastfulness: Does not play the part of a bragger.

No pridefulness: Does not puff oneself up like a bellows.

No rudeness: Not indecent.

No self-seeking: Does not seek own interests.

No angering easily: Is not easily irritated and avoids sharpness of spirit.

No keeping track of wrongs: Does not record in a ledger book a list of offenses.

No rejoicing in evil: Finds no joy in the triumph of evil.

Rejoicing in the truth: Finds joy in all things truthful.

Protection: Covers like a roof.

Trust: Has faith in people without being gullible.

Hope: Sees the bright side of things, does not despair.

Perseverance: Carries on like a stout-hearted soldier.

Endurance: Love survives.[6]

Wouldn't the world be a much better place if each of us loved more like this?

What Does Toxic Anti-Love Look Like?

Choosing to love can feel like an uphill climb. But if we don't deliberately choose to take the high road of love, we can slip into toxic behaviors in relationships. When writing *7 Simple Skills for Every Woman*, I thought about how Satan loves to twist God's Word (like the half-truths he fed Adam and Eve in the garden and the trickery he used to tempt Jesus in the desert). I paraphrased 1 Corinthians 13 to identify toxic behaviors:

A toxic relationship is impatient and unkind. It is always envious and jealous. It boasts and is self-glorifying. It is arrogant and proud, self-centered, and rude. It easily loses its temper and keeps track of all offenses and holds a grudge. It is thrilled when people look and feel stupid. It loves a mistake because the error can be replayed over and over. It runs to evil, never protects others, and gives up on people and life easily.

Toxic relationships poison the Golden Rule and turn it into, *Do unto others before they do it to you. Exploit others before they exploit you.* And toxic people would scoff at Jesus's example of sacrificing for others. Instead, they tend to sacrifice others for their own benefit or entertainment.[7]

Will You Love Like Jesus?

Since you can't control circumstances or others but you *can* control your thoughts, choices, and behaviors, which traits of love from 1 Corinthians 13 do you want to ask God to strengthen in you?

Experiencing Scripture Creatively

- Follow Karla's instructions at the end of the chapter to create doves on place cards. Write "Peace be with you—John 20:21" below the doves. Place a card next to each family member's table setting.

- Illustrate John 20:31 in your Bible or journal.

Day 2

The Passover Lamb

So far, Peter has denied knowing Jesus three times. Pilate has crucified Jesus, recording his crime as "the King of the Jews." John, Jesus's mother, and several other women stood by Jesus's cross. Then Jesus told John to take Mary to John's home.

Jesus Fulfills More Scripture About Passover

John wrote that his purpose for writing is "so that you may believe that Jesus is the Christ" (John 20:31). Thus, he describes events that show Jesus fulfilling prophecies.

Jesus's Crucifixion Fulfills More Prophecies

On Day 1, we read the fourth servant song. From what we've read in John already, Jesus fulfilled these verses in Isaiah 52:13–53:12:

- When soldiers lifted Jesus on the cross, they fulfilled the first part of Isaiah 52:13: "Behold, my servant shall act wisely; he shall be high and lifted up."

- His torso ripped by floggings, his head bloodied from thorns, and his extremities pierced by nails fulfilled 52:14: "His appearance was so marred, beyond human semblance, and his form beyond that of the children of mankind."

- The unbelief Jesus encountered fulfilled 53:1: "Who has believed what he has heard from us?"

- The rejection he faced fulfilled 53:3: "He was despised and rejected by men; a man of sorrows, and acquainted with grief; and as one from whom men hide their faces he was despised, and we esteemed him not."

- His refusal to fight his arrest and conviction fulfilled 53:7: "He was oppressed, and he was afflicted, yet he opened not his mouth; like a lamb that is led to the slaughter, and like a sheep that before its shearers is silent, so he opened not his mouth."

- The sham religious trial and rejection of Pilate's verdict of innocence fulfilled 53:8: "By oppression and judgment he was taken away; and as for his generation, who considered that he was cut off out of the land of the living, stricken for the transgression of my people?"

- His crucifixion between two criminals fulfilled this part of 53:12: "He poured out his soul to death and was numbered with the transgressors."

King David's Sufferings Are a Type of Jesus's Sufferings

John has still more evidence that Jesus is the Messiah.

> 3. In John 19:28-30 below, circle the word describing what was finished. Box what the bystanders gave Jesus to drink. Box the type of branch they used. Underline what happened after he received the drink.
>
> After this, Jesus, knowing that all was now finished, said (to fulfill the Scripture), "I thirst." A jar full of sour wine stood there, so they put a sponge full of the sour wine on a hyssop branch and held it to his mouth. When Jesus had received the sour wine, he said, "It is finished," and he bowed his head and gave up his spirit.

John wrote that his purpose for writing is "so that you may believe that Jesus is the Christ" (John 20:31). Thus, he describes events that show Jesus fulfilling prophecies.

The Little Details
Joseph of Arimathea

Joseph of Arimathea "was a disciple of Jesus, but secretly for fear of the Jews" (John 19:38). At the crucifixion, Joseph "took courage and went to Pilate and asked for the body of Jesus" (Mark 15:43).

Joseph was "a respected member of the council, who was also himself looking for the kingdom of God" (Mark 15:43). He was rich (Matthew 27:57). Though part of the council, he was "a good and righteous man, who had not consented to their decision and action" (Luke 23:50-51).

Crucified bodies were normally left hanging for vultures. If Jews took a body down, they buried it outside the city in a gravesite for criminals, not in a family tomb where they thought it would desecrate the other bodies in the tomb. But Joseph put Jesus's body in his own new tomb (Matthew 27:60).

Pilate would not have allowed Jesus's family to take down his body. That he gave Joseph permission speaks to both Joseph's rank and Pilate's belief that Jesus was innocent.[9]

Parched from blood loss, Jesus says, "I thirst," fulfilling Psalm 22:15: "My strength is dried up like a potsherd, and my tongue sticks to my jaws; you lay me in the dust of death." The sour wine fulfills Psalm 69:21, another psalm about David's sufferings: "For my thirst they gave me sour wine to drink." Jesus's final words *It is finished* echo the final words of Psalm 22: "He has done it." The mission the Father gave him, his suffering, and his obedience—all that is now finished.

The Passover Lambs Are a Type of Jesus

The bystanders lift sour wine on a branch of hyssop, the plant used to paint the Passover lambs' blood on doorposts so long ago.[8] Just as blood dripped from the top and sides of Hebrew doorways then, so now blood drips from the top and sides of the cross.

> 4. Read John 19:31-33. (a) What did the Jews want done to the three crucified men (verse 31)? (b) Why did the soldiers not do this to Jesus (verse 33)?

The Sabbath begins at sundown. This *Sabbath is a high day* because it's during the Feast of Unleavened Bread. It's also the Sabbath that determines on which Sunday they will celebrate the Feast of Firstfruits.

Breaking the legs of the two men leaves them unable to push themselves up to breathe, guaranteeing they'll die quickly. The soldiers know Jesus is dead because he's no longer pushing himself up to breathe.[10]

> 5. Read John 19:34-37. (a) What happened when the soldier pierced Jesus's side (verse 34)? (b) Why does John say he witnessed this himself (verse 35)? (c) Why did these things take place (verses 36-37)?

John witnesses the gush of blood and water[11] and testifies about it *that you also may believe*. The gush of water and blood is proof that Jesus has died and that Jesus is fully human.[12] It also reminds readers that Jesus said people must "drink his blood" to have life (John 6:54).

Further, John says that Jesus's legs not being broken fulfills the command not to break a Passover lamb's bones (Exodus 12:46). In other words, Jesus is the Passover Lamb to which all other Passover lambs pointed.

Jesus's Death and Burial Fulfill More Prophecies

John 19:37 says the soldier who pierced Jesus's side as others watched did so in fulfillment of Zechariah 12:10: "They look on me, on him whom they have pierced." God is pierced when his Shepherd is pierced.

Jesus's followers are stunned. They had expected this teacher and miracle worker to free them from Rome's rule and take David's throne on earth immediately.

6. Read John 19:38-42. (a) What did Joseph and Nicodemus do (verse 40)? (b) What did they do next (verse 42)?

And there, in a rich man's tomb, Jesus's body lay bound in linen cloths with 75 pounds of spices, fulfilling yet another prophecy in the fourth servant song: "They made his grave with the wicked and with a rich man in his death, although he had done no violence, and there was no deceit in his mouth" (Isaiah 53:9).

The Feast of Firstfruits Is a Type of the Resurrection

On Saturday, most Jews celebrate the Feast of Unleavened Bread. It's usually a joyous occasion, but Jesus's followers grieve.

On Sunday, everyone will bring bundles of barley stalks to the temple for the Feast of Firstfruits. The stalks are the first to ripen. The priest will wave the bundles before the Lord in gratitude because the seed planted in the ground will burst forth in a harvest of life. The bundles herald the full harvest yet to come.

But the feast is not topmost on the minds of Jesus's followers.

Jesus's Tomb Is Empty

Mary Magdalene was present at the crucifixion (John 19:25).

7. Read John 20:1-2. (a) What did Mary tell the two disciples (verse 2)? (b) How do you imagine she felt?

The *first day of the week* is Sunday. *The one whom Jesus loved* is John's way of referring to himself so that we know he gives eyewitness testimony.

8. Read John 20:3-7. (a) How did Peter and John react to Mary's news (verses 3)? (b) How do you think Peter felt when he saw what was and wasn't in the tomb (verses 6-7)?

The cloths used by Joseph and Nicodemus to bind Jesus's body are now lying in the tomb with no body enfolded in them.

9. Read John 20:8-10 below. Circle John's reaction to what he saw. Underline what they didn't yet understand.

    Then the other disciple, who had reached the tomb first, also went in, and he saw and believed; for as yet they did not understand the Scripture, that he must rise from the dead. Then the disciples went back to their homes.

John enters the tomb, sees how the cloths are lying, and believes! Thieves would have taken the expensive linen and spices. Unwrapping the body would have scattered the spices, and

The Little Details
Verses on Jesus Fulfilling Feasts

Paul says that not only is Jesus our Passover lamb, but we should rid ourselves of malice and evil to celebrate a continual Feast of Unleavened bread: "Cleanse out the old leaven that you may be a new lump, as you really are unleavened. For Christ, our Passover lamb, has been sacrificed. Let us therefore celebrate the festival, not with the old leaven, the leaven of malice and evil, but with the unleavened bread of sincerity and truth" (1 Corinthians 5:7-8).

Thieves would have taken the expensive linen and spices. Unwrapping the body would have scattered the spices, and carrying an unwrapped body would have attracted attention.

---

carrying an unwrapped body would have attracted attention. Whereas Lazarus came out of the tomb still wearing the graveclothes, John sees that Jesus's resurrection body passed through them.

John explains that the disciples *did not understand the Scripture, that he must rise from the dead*. We'll look at those verses next.

---

10. ♥ Describe an event that confused you before you better understood Scripture.

Jesus's Resurrection Fulfills Scripture

Even though Jesus presented himself as a servant, the disciples don't recognize that he is Isaiah's suffering servant. Why? Because the suffering servant had to die, whereas the Messiah must rule forever.

Certainly, the fourth servant song tells of the servant's death. But it tells us more—much more! Isaiah 53:10 prophesies that after the servant's death, the servant "shall see his offspring; he shall prolong his days." Yes, after his death he shall prolong his days. Isaiah 53:11 says of the servant who has died, "Out of the anguish of his soul he shall see and be satisfied."

Not only that, but the Lord God declares, "Therefore I will divide him a portion with the many, and he shall divide the spoil with the strong, because he poured out his soul to death and was numbered with the transgressors" (Isaiah 53:12). How can the Lord give portions and spoil to someone dead?

Additionally, David's psalms typologically foreshadow the Messiah's resurrection. Psalm 22, which so clearly speaks of the crucifixion, suddenly turns to praise at God's rescue, a rescue that brings a blessing of hearts that "live forever" (22:26). Psalm 16:10 reads, "For you will not abandon my soul to Sheol, or let your holy one see corruption."

And, of course, there are all those passages about the Messiah ruling forever, such as Ezekiel 37:25: "David my servant shall be their prince forever." And Isaiah 9:7: "Of the increase of his government and of peace there will be no end, on the throne of David and over his kingdom, to establish it and to uphold it with justice and with righteousness from this time forth and forevermore." These all speak of a time when death is conquered.

The Resurrection of the Righteous Foretold

The Old Testament doesn't foretell only the resurrection of the suffering servant and Messiah. Isaiah 25:8 promises that God "will swallow up death forever; and the Lord God will wipe away tears from all faces, and the reproach of his people he will take away from all the earth." Daniel 12:2 prophesies, "Many of those who sleep in the dust of the earth shall awake, some to everlasting life, and some to shame and everlasting contempt."

Moreover, in John 4:35-36, Jesus likened those ready to come to him to a harvest:

> Do you not say, "There are yet four months, then comes the harvest"? Look, I tell you, lift up your eyes, and see that the fields are white for harvest. Already the one who reaps is receiving wages and gathering fruit for eternal life, so that sower and reaper may rejoice together.

Now it's clearer why. Just as seed lay in the ground until life raised it up, so Jesus lay in the tomb until life raised him up. Just as the Jews raised the firstfruits of their harvest on Sunday before the Lord, so Jesus raised himself as the Firstfruits of the harvest of God's children on Sunday.

That Sunday in the temple, Jews offered the firstfruits of barley that had risen to life in their fields, while Jesus became the firstfruits of people to rise to life from this earth. As the firstfruits of barley anticipated the greater harvest to come, so the resurrection of Jesus anticipates the greater resurrection to come, for "Christ has been raised from the dead, the firstfruits of those who have fallen asleep" (1 Corinthians 15:20).

In this lesson, we saw that Jesus's crucifixion, death, and burial fulfilled many prophecies. Scripture even prophesied his resurrection, though the disciples didn't understand that until later. We saw that Passover pointed to Jesus because the Passover lambs were a type of Jesus. Likewise, the Feast of Firstfruits pointed to Jesus's resurrection, for his resurrection was but the first of a harvest of resurrections to come. In the next lesson, we'll see what happens when Jesus appears to his followers.

Day 3

Jesus Is Risen!

Now Jesus's followers are about to discover very good news.

Mary Magdalene Discovers the Good News That Jesus Is Risen

Weeping, Mary Magdalene follows the disciples back to the tomb. After Peter and John leave, she stoops to look into the tomb.

> 11. Read John 20:11-13. (a) What did Mary have to do to look inside the tomb (verse 11)? (b) What did Mary see (verse 12)? (c) Why was she weeping (verse 13)?

The angels' words should make Mary ponder the significance of the empty tomb, but even the presence of angels doesn't comfort her. Still not understanding, she starts to turn from the tomb and glimpses the figure of a man through her tears.

> 12. Read John 20:14-16. (a) Who stood behind her (verse 14)? (b) Who does she think he is (verse 15)? (c) What does she realize when he speaks her name (verse 16)?

Mary partially turns and sees someone. Jesus asks her whom she seeks, encouraging her to think of who Jesus said he was. When he calls her by name, she turns fully toward him. Mary Magdalene sees the risen Lord before even his eleven disciples.

The Little Details
Clay Jones: The Criterion of Embarrassment

All four Gospels report that it was women who first discovered that the tomb was empty. [Skeptic Bart D.] Ehrman agrees that we "have solid traditions to indicate that women found this tomb empty three days later." This is significant because in first-century Palestine, a woman's testimony wasn't considered trustworthy. I could give many examples, but I'll just quote one. Josephus writes, "But let not the testimony of women be admitted, on account of the levity and boldness of their sex." Therefore, that the Gospels record women as being the first to discover the empty tomb makes it likely because of what is called the "criterion of embarrassment." The criterion of embarrassment is a type of critical analysis where authors are presumed to be telling the truth if they record something that might be embarrassing to them or their cause. In short, no one in first-century Palestine would concoct a story with women taking the lead in the most vital discovery of Christianity![13]

The Little Details
Andreas J. Köstenberger and Scott R. Swain: "Receive the Holy Spirit"

The reference to Jesus breathing on his disciples while saying, "Receive the Holy Spirit" (20:22), probably represents a symbolic promise of the soon-to-be-given gift of the Spirit, not the actual giving of him fifty days later at Pentecost…The present pericope does not constitute the Johannine equivalent to Pentecost, nor is the proposal satisfactory that at 20:22 the disciples "were only sprinkled with His grace and not [as at Pentecost] saturated with full power." The present event does not mark the actual fulfillment of these promises other than by way of anticipatory sign…

The Greek verb *enephysēsen* means "breathed *on*" (NIV) rather than "breathed *into*" (TNIV). The theological antecedent is plainly Genesis 2:7, where exactly the same form is used. There God breathes his Spirit into Adam at creation, which constitutes him as a "living being." Here… Jesus constitutes them as the new messianic community, in anticipation of the outpouring of the Spirit subsequent to his ascension.[14]

13. Read John 20:17-18. (a) How does Mary respond when she realizes the person behind her is Jesus (verse 17)? (b) What message does Jesus want her to give the disciples (verse 17)?

Mary does not need to cling, for Jesus isn't going to the Father immediately. It's time for her to share the good news. Jesus is ascending to *my Father and your Father*. Because of his death and resurrection, his followers are now children of God and inheritors of the eternal life Jesus promised (John 3:16; 5:24).

Mary came looking for a lifeless body and instead finds Jesus whole and alive, standing on feet so recently impaled. It isn't possible, and yet, here he is!

Jesus's Disciples Discover the Good News That Jesus Is Risen

14. Read John 20:19-20. (a) Why were the disciples in a locked room (verse 19)? (b) What does Jesus's ability to enter a locked room tell us about his resurrection body (verse 19)? (c) What did he show them (verse 20)? (d) To what did their sorrow turn (verse 20)?

Jesus enters a locked room. How startled the disciples must be! No wonder his first words to them are *Peace be with you*. Now what happened to the graveclothes is apparent—he can pass through cloth and walls.

15. Read John 20:21-23. (a) What mission does Jesus give the disciples (verse 21)? (b) Whom did they receive from Jesus (verse 22)?

Jesus sends the disciples into the world just as the Father sent him. Then, just as God breathed life into Adam in Genesis 2:7, so Jesus breathes the Holy Spirit among his followers. Jesus sends them to tell the world about the good news that God offers forgiveness of sins through Jesus Christ. When people hear the gospel and repent, *they are forgiven*. If they reject the message, forgiveness *is withheld*.

Jesus Appears to Thomas
Those present now believe.

16. Read John 20:24-25. (a) Which disciple was missing when Jesus appeared in the locked room (verse 24)? (b) What did he refuse to believe (verse 25)?

What the disciples claim is indeed incredible. Plus, Thomas had his hopes crushed on Friday, and he's not willing to raise them again. No, he wants solid evidence.

17. Read John 20:26-27. (a) How were the doors (verse 26)? (b) What did Jesus do (verse 26)? (c) What evidence did Jesus give Thomas (verse 27)?

Again, Jesus appears among the disciples in a locked room. His words to Thomas show he hears his disciples even when he's not present. He gives Thomas the evidence he desires and tells him, *Do not disbelieve, but believe.*

18. Read John 20:28-29. (a) What does Thomas call Jesus (verse 28)? (b) Who does Jesus say will be blessed (verse 29)?

If these titles are not true, Jesus would have rebuked Thomas. Instead, he accepts them. Thomas has moved from skeptic to believer. Jesus says those who believe without seeing will be blessed. After all, they believe with less evidence.

19. ♥ (a) Jesus said, "Blessed are those who have not seen and yet have believed" (John 20:29). Are you among those blessed in this way? (b) If so, what enabled you to believe?

Belief is one of the key themes of the Gospel of John. *Do not disbelieve, but believe.*

The Purpose of the Gospel of John
John next explains why he wrote this Gospel.

20. Read John 20:30-31. (a) What did Jesus do that John did not write about (verse 30)? (b) Why did he write the Gospel (verse 31)? (c) Turn to the **8 Signs** chart and write "The resurrection" on line 8.

The Little Details
Clay Jones: The Hallucination Theory
So here is the most popular skeptical explanation: the disciples only hallucinated what they believed were actual appearances of the resurrected Jesus!

This hallucination theory, however, is plagued. First, many of the appearance testimonies involved more than one individual, but hallucinations are individual, subjective experiences that cannot be shared...As clinical psychologist Gary A. Sibcy reports, "I have surveyed the professional literature...and have yet to find a single documented case of a group hallucination"...That's no surprise, right? How could one share a hallucination?

Second, the disciples would have had to have interlocking hallucinations...Third, as theologian and lawyer John Warwick Montgomery points out, "Had anything, even a deluded state of mind, caused the disciples to distort Jesus' biography, the hostile witnesses would surely have used that against them." Fourth, the hallucination theory cannot explain the empty tomb or missing body...Finally, hallucinations rarely transform lives.[15]

The Little Details
The Word *agapaō* Versus *phileō*

Jesus's first two questions use the Greek word for love, *agapaō*. Peter's replies use the Greek word for love *phileō*, as does Jesus's third question. Many think Jesus is using a stronger word for love that a humbled Peter cannot bring himself to claim.

New Testament scholar D.A. Carson, however, says this is not the case. He gives eight arguments, including these four:[16]

1. John's Gospel uses the two verbs interchangeably (for example, 3:35 and 5:20).

2. The Greek Old Testament common then (LXX) uses the verbs interchangeably. For example, both are used of a rapist's "love" in 2 Samuel 13. Also, the Hebrew uses one word for love in Proverbs 8:17, but the LXX translates one as *agapaō* and the other as *phileō*.

3. At the time, *agapaō* was being used more because *phileō* had taken on an additional meaning of "to kiss."

4. The New Testament uses *agapaō* to describe love for the present age (2 Timothy 4:10), certainly not a form of higher love.

John wrote to Jews and those Gentiles who worshiped God, all of whom expected God to send the Christ, the Messiah. He wrote so that they would believe that Jesus is the Christ, because *by believing you may have life in his name.* In other words, the question John answers is not *Who is Jesus?* but *Who is the Christ?*

In this lesson, Mary Magdalene and Jesus's disciples discover the good news: Jesus is risen from the dead! And this is our guarantee that he can make good on his promise to raise us to eternal life with him. In the next lesson we'll see Jesus restore Peter.

Day 4

Jesus Restores Peter

At the Passover feast, Peter claimed greater faithfulness than the other disciples. But that same night, warming himself in front of a charcoal fire, Peter denied being Jesus's disciple three times. Jesus is about to address Peter's failure.

Jesus Reveals Himself Again

Jesus has some things left to say, but he again starts by caring for others' needs.

> 21. Read John 21:1-3. What did the seven disciples unsuccessfully try to do (verse 3)?

Nathanael comes from *Cana*, where Jesus turned water to wine, healed an official's son, and first *revealed* his glory (John 2:11; 4:46). *The sons of Zebedee* are John and his brother James.

> 22. Read John 21:4-6. (a) When did Jesus appear (verse 4)? (b) What miracle did he provide (verse 6)?

Once again, John plays on the light-dark theme. The disciples toil in darkness, but Jesus, the light of the world, appears just as the sun's first rays break the darkness.

> 23. Read John 21:7-8. (a) What does John tell Peter (verse 7)? (b) What did Peter do (verse 7)? (c) What did the other disciples then do (verse 8)?

Simon Peter rushes to Jesus even though Peter knows Jesus remembers his failure.[17]

> 24. Read John 21:9-14. How did Jesus serve the disciples?

Again Jesus shows himself to be a servant king. This is the *third* resurrection appearance to the disciples that John records.

Jesus Restores Peter

At Jesus's trial, Peter denied knowing Jesus three times. Jesus doesn't ignore Peter's failure but shows Peter he forgives him and wants his ministry to continue.

> **25.** Read John 21:15. (a) What does Jesus ask? (b) When Peter replies, what does Jesus tell him to do?

More than these likely means more than the other disciples love Jesus since Peter claimed to be more loyal than they were (John 13:37; Matthew 26:33-35). Here, Peter doesn't claim more love than they have; he merely claims to love Jesus. He knew the truth about himself, and that truth is sanctifying him, just as Jesus prayed.

> **26.** Read John 21:16. (a) What is Jesus's second question? (b) When Peter replies, what does Jesus tell him to do?

Jesus repeats his question but without qualifying it with *more than these*.

> **27.** Read John 21:17-19. (a) How did Peter feel about being asked if he loves Jesus a third time (verse 17)? (b) What will happen when Peter is old (verse 18)? (c) What was Jesus talking about (verse 19)? (d) What else did he say to Peter (verse 19)?

Jesus guides Peter into confessing his love three times, revoking the three denials he made before that other fire.

He gives Peter the task of caring for his disciples, letting him know he not only forgives him but still values him and has tasks for him to do. Jesus also tells Peter he'll one day get a re-do. He'll get another chance to prove his love by dying for Christ and glorifying God. This time he'll have the courage he needs. Jesus tells Peter, *Follow me*, showing that their relationship is fully restored.

> **28.** ♥ What does Jesus's response to Peter teach you about God's willingness to use our strengths despite our weaknesses?

The Little Details
Andreas J. Köstenberger and Scott R. Swain: Jesus's Divinity

John's claim that Jesus is "Christ" and "Son of God" amounts to more than asserting that Jesus is Israel's rightful king. Rather, these designations express the belief that Jesus was also divine and of heavenly origin...In John's Gospel Jesus is charged with blasphemy throughout his ministry...John's adaptation of the Isaianic "I am" formula and of the "glory" and "lifted up" motifs also intimately associate Jesus with God...Remarkably, Jesus is given "glory" by God...despite the fact that God does not share his glory with another (Isa. 42:8; 48:11).

In Isaiah, John found warrant for seeing Jesus as a figure properly identified with the "I am" of Isaiah and the exodus...and sharing the glory of God as the one who bore the transgressions of many and who was "lifted up" and exalted by God. Indeed, the Gospel's portrayal of Jesus as the Word sent by God, which, once it has accomplished its purpose, returns to the one who sent it, derives directly from Isaiah 55:11.[18]

The Little Details
Peter's Martyrdom

John's early readers knew Christians were dying for refusing to recant their testimony that they saw Jesus alive after the crucifixion. The disciples transformed from hiding frightened in a locked room to boldly proclaiming that Jesus had risen from the dead.

In fact, just weeks after denying Christ, Peter fearlessly proclaimed Jesus's resurrection before a crowd. Moreover, for years to come, Peter proclaimed he was a disciple of the risen Jesus. One day he received another opportunity to choose between life and acknowledging his relationship to Jesus. Just as Jesus foretold, this time Peter chose crucifixion rather than denying Christ.[19]

But there's more. The early church father Clement testifies that Rome martyred Peter's wife before they murdered him.[20] So Peter went from denying Christ to not only dying for Christ but seeing his beloved wife tortured and killed before he died.

Jesus Speaks of John

Jesus tells Peter, *Follow me.* That is what he needs to do.

> 29. Read John 21:20-23. (a) When Peter saw John following them, what did he ask (verse 21)? (b) Where did Jesus want Peter's focus to be (verse 22)? (c) How did some misunderstand Jesus's words to Peter (verse 23)?

John's story was not Peter's concern. Whether he would have to suffer as Peter would suffer wasn't Peter's to know. Jesus wanted Peter to focus on following Jesus.

> 30. Are you sometimes distracted by what the Lord may be doing in someone else's life? How can you apply Jesus's words to Peter to your situation?

In this lesson, we saw Jesus reveal himself again to his disciples. We also saw Jesus tenderly restore Peter, giving him a chance to revoke his denials and showing him Jesus still valued him. This is good news. It means Jesus is tender with our weaknesses as he works to strengthen us. It also shows he forgives sin. In the next lesson we'll tie together the Old Testament fulfillments John shows us.

Day 5

The Good News Revisited

John's Witness

John is about to close his book, but he has just a little more he wants you to know.

> 31. Read John 21:24-25. (a) What does John say he is doing in this Gospel (verse 24)? (b) Has John recorded everything Jesus did (verse 25)? (c) Does he even think that's possible (verse 25)?

In writing his Gospel, John bore witness to what he saw and experienced. He could not tell all, but he chose the narratives he thought would best testify to who Jesus is and why he came to the world. He is the Christ, and he came to give life. The shift to "we" may indicate "a shift from the narrative to a coda, a kind of afterword that gives the imprimatur of the group."[21]

In each chapter we read good news. But we didn't have the full picture yet. Now we can see more clearly the greatness of the good news.

More Fulfillments Mean More Good News

Messiah and God

The Old Testament prophesies that God will send a righteous Messiah descended from David who will rule forever. Now we know how he can rule forever: He conquered death to bring eternal life to all who believe in him.

David and the kings descended from him all held the title "son of God," a title that foreshadowed the identity of the Messiah who would rule forever: God's one and only Son, Jesus. That's why the prophet John the Baptist claimed he was the fulfillment of Isaiah's prophecy of one who would prepare people for God to visit earth (John 1:23 *cf.* Isaiah 40:3).

Isaiah 35:4-6 prophesies that when God arrives to save people, they will see blind eyes opened and the lame healed. Jesus did both. But when he claimed God's name—I AM—for himself and said he existed before Abraham, many missed that God had actually arrived. Jesus said belief in him is belief in God, and seeing him is seeing God.

Jesus is the Word of God who was God and who became flesh and tabernacled on earth. Jesus's identity reveals why the Messiah's "name shall be called...Mighty God" (Isaiah 9:6). These were mysteries in the Old Testament now revealed in Jesus.

The Lamb of God

John the Baptist identified Jesus as the Lamb of God who takes away the sin of the world. The Old Testament sacrificial system showed that people need purity to approach God. But sin defiled and brought the penalty of death. The sacrificial system showed that a perfect sacrifice could substitute for the sinner's life and cleanse sin. Thus, the entire Old Testament sacrificial system foreshadowed Jesus's sacrifice on the cross. His sacrifice finally and forever atoned for sin and purified believers. Now Jesus can baptize them with the Holy Spirit. Now they can live eternally in God's presence.

High Priest

Only a high priest could offer the sacrifices and perform the various rites on the Day of Atonement. Additionally, the high priest consecrated other priests for service in teaching God's ways, interceding for others in prayer, and offering sacrifices.

But Jesus consecrated himself for service. He taught God's ways and interceded for his followers. Then he offered himself as a sacrifice, functioning as both high priest and sacrifice. Thus, he fulfilled the prophecy that the Messiah would be "a priest forever" found in Psalm 110:4. Further, he sympathizes with our weaknesses as he strengthens us. Moreover, he continues to forgive sin, having offered the perfect sacrifice for it.

God's Temple

The Old Testament prophesied that the Messiah would build a temple for God's presence. Jesus identified the temple he's building as his own body, which he raised from the dead. After his resurrection, Jesus sent the Holy Spirit to indwell believers.[22] Just as God's Spirit filled the first temple, so now he fills believers (John 14:17).

The Little Details
Jay Sklar: Jesus as Both Priest and Sacrifice

When it comes to atonement, Leviticus teaches the following four points. First, atonement is made by priests who present sacrifices on behalf of the people (4:26,31; 5:6) and on behalf of themselves (16:11). Second, those sacrifices both ransom the sinner from judgment and cleanse his or her sin...Third, these atoning sacrifices must be continually repeated, whether for individuals throughout the year each time they sin (4:22-35; 5:1-6), or for the community once a year on the Day of Atonement (Lev. 16). Fourth, atonement is not earned by the Israelites; it is granted to them as a gracious gift from the Lord...

With Jesus, how much more. First, he is a perfect priest, who makes atonement for the people, but has no need to make atonement for himself (Heb. 7:26-27). Indeed, because of his perfection, he was able to present himself as the atoning sacrifice for the sins of others (Heb. 9:12,14,28; 10:19-22; cf. Isa. 53:11-12).

(continued on next page)

The Little Details
Jay Sklar: Jesus as Both Priest and Sacrifice
(continued from previous page)

Second, his sacrifice served both to ransom sinners from due punishment (Mark 10:45) and to cleanse them of their sin (1 John 1:9). Third, his one sacrifice has made full and final atonement for sin and does not need to be repeated at all (Heb. 7:26-27; 9:25–10:10). It was the ultimate Day of Atonement, in which he entered into the heavenly throne room itself to atone for sin, and atoned for it fully (Heb. 9:24-26). Indeed, his followers are described as being able to do that which Old Testament believers would never dare to do: enter into the Most Holy Place itself to enjoy fellowship with God, a sign that Jesus' sacrifice has cleansed them fully from sin and his priestly work has made a way of full access to God (Heb. 10:19-22). Finally, Jesus' sacrifice is the ultimate expression of the Lord's grace, for it is no longer guilty sinners presenting a sacrifice on behalf of themselves, but the offended King who is presenting the atoning sacrifice for the guilty sinner.[23]

The Light and Savior of the World

Isaiah prophesied of a suffering servant who would be the light of the world, not just of Jews. Jesus on earth was a light showing the way to God. But he was also a light that exposed deeds as true or evil. He taught that even the people who considered themselves most moral needed to be born again to enter the kingdom of God. Yet even those with false beliefs and immoral lives could come to him for eternal life. That's because God loves the world and gave his Son as a sacrifice so that all who believe on him may have eternal life. In fact, to all who receive him he gives the right to be children of God. Though as a light he exposed evil, he did not come to condemn the world. Rather, he came to the world to save people through his sacrifice.

The Prophet Like Moses

Moses prophesied that one day a prophet like him would arise and said that the people must listen to him. Until Jesus came, no prophet had ever done the works Moses did. But Jesus performed greater signs and wonders than Moses did, demonstrating that the Father sent him just as he'd sent Moses. Jesus turned water to wine, healed the sick, prophesied, and showed control over a sea. He raised the dead, something Moses did not do. Like Moses, he claimed authority to interpret how to apply the law and said the Father gave him all judgment. Jesus fulfilled the sacrificial system God set up through Moses.

The Bread of Life

Through Moses, God gave manna, the bread from heaven. Jesus multiplied bread and fed crowds. But unlike Moses, he claimed to be the bread from heaven that manna foreshadowed. He said that just as manna sustained life in the desert, so he is the living bread from heaven who gives eternal life to those who believe on and abide in him. He will do so by raising them to life.

The Good Shepherd

Isaiah 40:9-11 announced the good news that God himself would shepherd his people. Ezekiel 34 promises the same but adds that God will place his servant David over them as shepherd and prince. Thus, David as shepherd king foreshadowed the Messiah in this way as well. Jesus said he was the good shepherd who lays down his life for the sheep. He is also the gate through which his sheep pass to pasture.

The Resurrection and the Life

The Old Testament prophets proclaimed that God would one day raise the dead. Jesus demonstrated the ability to give life by first raising Lazarus from the dead, but more importantly, by raising himself from the dead. He offers secure, eternal life to those who believe in him. Not only that, but he's the only way to the Father. Indeed, he's prepared a place for us in his Father's house, for his kingdom is not of this world.

The Suffering Servant

The nation of Israel failed as God's servant. But Isaiah prophesied that Israel was a type of a future righteous servant who would perfectly serve God's purpose. In four servant songs, Isaiah prophesied that this servant will be the light to bring salvation to all nations. He will also open blind eyes. When Jesus claimed to be the light of the world, opened blind eyes, and washed his disciples' feet, he showed himself to be the suffering servant.

Isaiah foretold the righteous servant's suffering, including beating, mocking, and disfigurement by those who would despise him. He said the servant would be lifted up and pierced. Jesus's trial and crucifixion fulfilled all these prophecies.

But Isaiah also prophesied that, after the suffering servant's death, the suffering servant would prolong his days. When Jesus took his life up again, he fulfilled this too.

The four servant songs explain the reason for the righteous servant's suffering. Though innocent, he suffers in order to bear the sins of others, carrying their iniquities and justifying them.

The Seven Celebrations

For Jews, the first gathering of the year was for the **Passover** sacrifice and the **Feast of Unleavened Bread**. It declared and celebrated God's deliverance from the land of slavery and his provision on the journey to the promised land. Jesus's sacrifice on Nisan 15, the day of the Passover feast, delivers his followers from slavery to sin and provides for us as we journey to the new promised land. This promised land is in the new heaven and earth where we will dwell with God for eternity.

The **Feast of Firstfruits** celebrated the first of the barley harvest and pointed to Jesus's resurrection as the first among many.

The next celebration, the **Feast of Weeks** (also known as **Pentecost**), celebrated the wheat harvest. On Pentecost after Jesus's resurrection, he baptized his harvest of followers with the Holy Spirit (Acts 2:1-4).

But the seventh month of the year had three more celebrations, and their final fulfillments are yet to come. For Jesus said, "And if I go and prepare a place for you, I will come again and will take you to myself, that where I am you may be also" (John 14:3).

On the **Feast of Trumpets**, a trumpet sounded to call people to the temple after the harvest was over. Likewise, when the earthly harvest of souls is complete, another trumpet will sound to call for the ingathering of souls, as 1 Thessalonians 4:16-17 describes:

> The Lord himself will descend from heaven with a cry of command, with the voice of an archangel, and with the sound of the trumpet of God. And the dead in Christ will rise first. Then we who are alive, who are left, will be caught up together with them in the clouds to meet the Lord in the air, and so we will always be with the Lord.

The Feast of Trumpets was followed by the **Day of Atonement**, when the people's sins were taken away. In Jesus's first coming, he atoned for sin on the cross, but in his final coming he removes all sin and causes of sin (Matthew 13:41; Revelation 20:10-15). What the Day of Atonement pointed to will be fully and finally complete.

The final feast of the year was the **Feast of Booths**. It celebrated the Lord's good care on the journey to the promised land, its final day celebrating arrival. After sin is gone, the Lord God will bring the new heaven and new earth. He and his Lamb will dwell in our midst (Revelation 21:1-3). There will be no more death or mourning or crying. Our journey ends. We will arrive.

The Little Details
The Jewish New Year
Today, the Feast of Trumpets (Rosh Hashanah) extends over two days and includes a celebration of the civil new year. This change may have happened around the third century AD. Exodus 12:1-2 commands that the Jewish year begin on Nisan 1, so that remains the new year on the Hebrew religious calendar.

The Good News

The Gospel of John is filled with good news.

32. ♥ Which item of good news means the most to you today? Why? Look back at the chapter summaries if you'd like.

33. ♥ Review your **8 Signs** chart and list of **7 "I Am" Statements**. Which is most meaningful to you today? Why?

Praise God for something you saw of his character this week. **Confess** anything that convicted you. **Ask** for help to do something God's Word calls you to do. **Thank** God for something you learned this week.

The Gospel of John is filled with good news.

Karla's Creative Connection

In John 20:21, Jesus said, "Peace be with you. As the Father has sent me, even so I am sending you." What a perfect and beautiful verse with which to end our study of John! Just like for the disciples, sometimes we want to lock ourselves away behind closed doors, feeling fearful, weak, or inadequate. But just as we're living from a place of fear, in walks Jesus. He doesn't judge us or rebuke us because we're afraid; instead, he meets us right where we are and speaks peace to our heart. It's a peace that comes from his resurrected presence, his overwhelming grace, and the knowledge that our sins are forgiven.

The dove is known as a Christian symbol of peace. A dove carrying an olive branch in its beak brought peace to Noah, letting him know that he and his family had been saved, the floodwaters had receded, and a new life awaited them. In Luke 3:22, we're told that the Spirit of God "descended on" Jesus "like a dove." And the Bible says as we put our faith in Jesus, we, too, are saved into a new and everlasting life.

So with Jesus as our Prince of Peace and our hearts filled with the peace that comes from knowing him, I would love to share how to draw this wonderful symbol of peace.

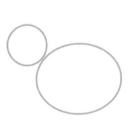

Start by drawing a small circle for the head and an oval for the body, in pencil, as shown.

Add lines to join the head to the body and add the tail. The dotted lines will help you keep the curve.

Add the wings, using the dotted lines to help you keep a nice curve as you scallop the edges.

Outline the body and wings with ink. Add his eye, the beak, and the olive branch.

Erase pencil lines and using a smaller pen size, if possible, add the details in the wings, tail, and leaves. You now have a lovely symbol of God's peace and presence in your life!

I hope you've been encouraged and challenged to creatively connect with God's Word and his heart for you during this Bible study. And I pray you'll continue to express your faith creatively. God bless you and keep you in his love and for his glory.

Karla

As you go through this workbook, you'll fill in these charts. The first answer of each is filled in for you.

8 Signs That Jesus Is the Messiah in John

	Sign	Verses
1.	Changed water into wine	2:1-11
2.		4:43-54
3.		5:1-15; 6:2
4.		6:1-14; 6:26
5.		6:16-21
6.		9:1-12, 16
7.		11:1-44, 47
8.		20:1-31

7 "I Am" Statements of Jesus

	Statement		Verses
1.	I am	the bread of life	6:35
2.	I am		8:12
3.	I am		10:7
4.	I am		10:11
5.	I am		11:25
6.	I am		14:6
7.	I am		15:1

Appendix

Creative Ideas

Engage with Scripture through the arts! Visit www.DiscoveringTheBibleSeries.com for info on items marked 🖥.

Visual Arts Options

- Find techniques for expressing Scripture with art in the Karla's Creative Connection offerings.
- Color the bookmarks at the start of each chapter, the full-page illustrations at the end of each chapter, and the bookmarks at the back of the book.
- Write a Scripture verse in calligraphy.
- Create an art journal: sketch, paint, and affix photos and words from magazines.
- 🖥 Overlay a Scripture verse on top of a photograph.
- Create a diorama or sculpture or piece of jewelry.
- Create fabric art using cross-stitch, embroidery, or appliqué.
- 🖥 Scan the bookmark, use photo editing software to color it, and print it on printable fabric to use as is or to embroider.
- Create greeting cards or T-shirts to encourage others.
- 🖥 In a journaling Bible, choose one verse to illuminate in the wide margin.

Performing Arts Options

- 🖥 Find a musical version of a Bible passage to play or sing.
- Act out a Bible passage as you read or recite it aloud to music (spoken Word poetry).
- Write music and lyrics based on a Bible passage.

Literary Arts Options

- Form a Bible passage's message into a poem of any type you like.
- Write an encouraging letter to someone based on a Bible verse.

Culinary Arts Options

- Celebrate a Christian holiday with a feast and talk about the meaning of the holiday.
- Celebrate answered prayer with a meal where you publicly give thanks.

Sharing Options

- Share your creations with your small group.
- 🖥 Post recordings, writings, and pictures in the Facebook group "Discovering Good News in John."
- Also share on Facebook, Instagram, and Twitter with #DiscoveringGoodNewsInJohn.

Notes

Chapter 1—John 1:1–2:25: The Word Was God

1. Greg D. Gilbert, "The Gospel," D.A. Carson, ed., 2015. *NIV Zondervan Study Bible* (now *NIV Biblical Theology Study Bible,* Grand Rapids: Zondervan, 2015), 2,686.

2. Adapted from Pam Farrel, *Becoming a Brave New Woman: Step into God's Adventure for You* (originally *Woman of Confidence*) (Eugene, OR: Harvest House, 2009), 172–73.

3. D.A. Carson, *The Gospel According to John* (Grand Rapids: Wm. B. Eerdmans, 1991), 116.

4. Craig S. Keener, *The Gospel of John: A Commentary* (Grand Rapids: Baker Academic, 2003), 1:364–65.

5. Carson, *John*, 122.

6. Carson, *John*, 125–26.

7. Carson, *John*, 127.

8. Jay Sklar, *Leviticus: An Introduction and Commentary,* ed. David G. Firth, Tyndale Old Testament Commentaries (Downers Grove: InterVarsity, 2014), 74, Kindle.

9. Carson, *John*, 128.

10. Carson, *John*, 129.

11. Exodus 33:20.

12. Matthew 3:2.

13. Matthew 3:5-6.

14. Malachi 4:5-6.

15. Deuteronomy 18:15-19.

16. Carson, *John,* 145.

17. Carson, *John,* 145.

18. Gerald L. Borchert, *John 1–11: An Exegetical and Theological Exposition of Holy Scripture,* ed. E. Ray Clendenen, New American Commentary (Nashville: Broadman & Holman, 1996), 132, WORD*search* CROSS e-book.

19. Sklar, *Leviticus*, 42.

20. Isaiah 42:1.

21. "While it sounds somewhat strange to modern ears for the author of a book to speak of himself in the third person as an actor in the events of his own book, it was a regular convention in the ancient world." Lydia McGrew, *The Eye of the Beholder: The Gospel of John as Historical Reportage* (Tampa: DeWard, 2021), 131.

22. Craig L. Blomberg, *Matthew: An Exegetical and Theological Exposition of Holy Scripture,* The New American Commentary (Nashville: Broadman & Holman, 1992), 167, WORD*search* CROSS e-book.

23. Keener, *John,* 1:489.

24. Amos 9:11-14.

25. Keener, *John,* 1:517.

26. Keener, *John,* 1:519.

27. McGrew, *Eye*, 291n47.

28. Ezekiel 37:24.

29. McGrew, *Eye,* 70.

Chapter 2—John 3:1–4:54: The Good News

1. Genesis 1:26-28.

2. Romans 5:12-14; 1 Corinthians 15:21-22,42; 2 Peter 1:4.

3. Of course, God knew Adam and Eve would not fulfill their commission as originally given.

4. Genesis 3:24.

5. Exodus 19:5-6.

6. Deuteronomy 5:22-27.

7. Leviticus 17:11.

8. Sklar, *Leviticus*, 53. Cf. Leviticus 17:11; Matthew 20:28; 1 Timothy 2:6; 1 Peter 1:18; Revelation 5:9.

9. Leviticus 16:30; John 15:3; 1 Corinthians 6:11; Titus 3:5; Hebrews 10:22; 2 Peter 1:9; 1 John 1:7,9.

10. Sklar, *Leviticus*, 50.

11. Leviticus 7:19-20; Romans 3:23.

12. Numbers 19:2-6,9,11-12.

13. Deuteronomy 12:4,8,31; 16:21-22.

14. Leviticus 19:4,31; Deuteronomy 18:10-11; 32:17.

15. Numbers 21:8.

16. Numbers 1:51; 3:38.

17. Leviticus 16.

18. 1 Chronicles 28:2; Psalm 99:5; 132:7; Isaiah 66:1.

19. Genesis 3:24; Exodus 26:31,33.

20. 2 Samuel 23:1; Acts 2:29-30.

21. Psalm 53:2-3.

22. Jeremiah 7:9-11; Romans 6:1-2,15.

23. The law of Moses offered assurance of forgiveness for unintentional sin and sins that might be intentional, but for which reparations could be made that showed repentance (such as stealing). It did not offer assurance that God would forgive intentional ("high handed") sin (Numbers 15:30-31). The truly repentant might consult a prophet, as David did (2 Samuel 12:13).

24. Carson, *John,* 189.

25. John 2:23.

26. Carson, *John,* 155.

27. "The eternal life begun by the new birth is nothing less than the eternal life of the eternal Word." Carson, *John,* 203.

28. In particular, the Essenes and Pharisees condemned each other's baptisms. Keener, *John,* 1:577.

29. Carson, *John,* 217.

30. Carson, *John,* 219.

31. *Taheb* means either "the Restorer" or "he who returns." Carson, *NIV Study Bible,* 220,226.

32. John 2:23.

Chapter 3—John 5:1–6:46: Expectations Meet Reality

1. Verses in the order referenced are Exodus 4:1-9; Numbers 12:13; Exodus 18:13-27; Exodus 19; Numbers 12:6-8; Exodus 14:21-22; Exodus 16:4,31.

2. Numbers 11:6; Exodus 16:35.

3. Exodus 20:8-10.

4. D.A. Hagner, "PHARISEES," ed. Merrill C. Tenney, *The Zondervan Pictorial Encyclopedia of the Bible,* 2nd printing (Grand Rapids: Zondervan, 1977), 4:745–52.

5. D.A. Hagner, "SADDUCEES." In Tenney, *Zondervan Encyclopedia,* 5:211–16.

6. J.H. Bratt, "ZEALOT." In Tenney, *Zondervan Encyclopedia*, 5:1036–37.

7. "740. artos," HELPS Word-studies (Helps Ministries, Inc., 2011), accessed 6/9/2021, https://biblehub.com/greek/740.htm.

8. Jennifer Kennedy Dean, *Prized: Experience the Tender Love of the Savior* (Birmingham, AL: New Hope Publishers, 2019), 57.

9. Dean, *Prized*, 56.

10. Adapted from Bill and Pam Farrel, *A Couple's Journey with God* (Eugene, OR: Harvest House, 2012), 120–21.

11. Carson, *NIV Study Bible*, 82–84.

12. Carson, *John*, 246.

13. Carson, *John*, 247.

14. Exodus 4:10.

15. Carson, *NIV Study Bible*, 244–45.

16. Carson, *NIV Study Bible*, 254.

17. Carson, *NIV Study Bible*, 265.

18. Carson, *John*, 206.

19. Lydia McGrew, *Hidden in Plain View: Undesigned Coincidences in the Gospels and Acts* (Chillicothe: DeWard, 2017), 27.

20. Carson, *John*, 268.

21. Numbers 1:46.

22. Carson, *John*, 288.

Chapter 4—John 6:47–8:36: Finding Truth

1. Genesis 17:9-12.

2. Leviticus 12:3.

3. Jeremiah 9:25-26.

4. Borchert, *John 1–11*, 287.

5. Borchert, *John 1–11*, 287.

6. Exodus 13:21.

7. Exodus 16:4,31.

8. Exodus 17:6.

9. Leviticus 23:33-43.

10. Mishna, *Sukkah* 5:2-4.

11. John 6:41.

12. Carson, *John*, 304.

13. John 5:18.

14. Matthew 4:13.

15. Deuteronomy 5:17.

16. The view that no one would know where the Messiah came from is not from the Old Testament. Carson, *John*, 317.

17. Carson, *John*, 329-30.

18. 2 Kings 14:25.

19. Emphasis added. Carson, *John*, 333.

20. Carson, *John*, 334.

21. Deuteronomy 13:9; 17:7.

22. John 6:38; 7:33.

23. Carson, *John*, 348.

24. Isaiah 50:5.

25. Carson, *John*, 349.

Chapter 5—John 8:37–10:42: The Good Shepherd

1. Louis Matthews Sweet, "SATAN," *The International Standard Bible Encyclopedia*, ed. James Orr (Chicago: Howard-Severance Co., 1915), s.v. "SATAN," WORD*search* CROSS e-book.

2. John 5:18.

3. Isaiah 50:7.

4. Keener, *John*, 1:771.

5. Carson, *John*, 357.

6. Keener, *John*, 1:769.

7. C.S. Lewis, *Mere Christianity* (New York: MacMillan, 1958), 40–41.

8. Numbers 12:9-11; 1 Corinthians 11:29-30.

9. McGrew, *Eye*, 368-69.

10. Isaiah 42:20.

11. Carson, *John*, 385, quoting Roy Clements, *Introducing Jesus* (Kingsway, 1986), 103.

12. Psalm 95:7.

Chapter 6—John 11:1–12:50: The Resurrection and the Life

1. Andreas J. Köstenberger and Scott R. Swain, *Father, Son and Spirit: The Trinity and John's Gospel*, ed. D.A. Carson (Downers Grove: InterVarsity, 2008), 100.

2. Carson, *John*, 411.

3. Carson, *John*, 415.

4. James Strong, *Strong's Talking Greek & Hebrew Dictionary*, (Austin, TX: WORD*search* Corp., 2007), s.v. "G1690," WORD*search* CROSS e-book.

5. Carson, *John*, 418-19.

6. Gerald L. Borchert, *John 12–21: An Exegetical and Theological Exposition of Holy Scripture*, ed. E. Ray Clendenen, New American Commentary (Nashville: Broadman & Holman, 2002), 34, WORD*search* CROSS e-book.

7. Matthew 21:1-8.

8. Adapted from "Harmony of the Gospels," Carson, *NIV Study Bible*, 2204-6.

9. Vern S. Poythress, *Theophany: A Biblical Theology of God's Appearing* (Wheaton: Crossway, 2018), 310.

10. Carson, *John*, 135,137.

Chapter 7—John 13:1–14:31: The Servant King

1. Psalm 23:6.

2. Isaiah 53:12.

3. The majority of scholars place the crucifixion in AD 30 (Carson, *John*, 607). Some place it in AD 33, which had Passover on the same day of the week as AD 30; for example, Harold W. Hoehner, *Chronological Aspects of the Life of Christ* (Grand Rapids: Zondervan Academic, 1978), chap. 5, Kindle.

4. Borchert, *John 12–21*, 74, WORD*search* CROSS e-book.

5. Adapted from Pam Farrel, *7 Simple Skills for Every Woman* (Eugene: OR: Harvest House, 2015), 29.

6. *Thin Places*, directed by Rebecca Friedlander (2019), 74 min, https://www.rebeccafriedlander.com/thin-places.html.

7. "2222. zóé," HELPS Word-studies (Helps Ministries, Inc., 2011), accessed 6/9/2021, https://biblehub.com/greek/2222.htm.

8. Carson, *John*, 463.

9. Carson, *John*, 463.

10. John 3:5.

11. Allen P. Ross, *A Commentary on the Psalms*, 3 vols. (Grand Rapids: Kregel, 2011–2016), 1:185.

12. Carson, *John*, 473.

13. Carson, *John*, 474.

14. Carson, *John*, 474.

15. Carson, *NIV Study Bible*, 482-83.

16. Carson, *John*, 499.

17. Ezekiel 36:25.

18. Ezekiel 36:27.

19. Carson, *John*, 499–500.

20. Carson, *John*, 508.

Chapter 8—John 15:1–16:33: The Vine

1. Carson, *John*, 513.

2. Craig Hazen, *Fearless Prayer* (Eugene, OR: Harvest House, 2018), 73.

3. Hazen, *Fearless Prayer*, 77–78.

4. Carson, *John*, 518.

5. Emphasis original. Hazen, *Prayer*, 82.

6. Carson, *John*, 526.

7. Hazen, *Prayer*, 104-5.

8. Hazen, *Prayer*, 62-63.

Chapter 9—John 17:1–19:27: Consecrated for a Mission

1. Leviticus 8:23-24.

2. "5457. phós," HELPS Word-Studies (Helps Ministries, Inc., 2011), accessed 6/9/2021, https://biblehub.com/greek/5457.htm.

3. "4653. skotia," HELPS Word-Studies (Helps Ministries, Inc., 2011), accessed 6/9/2021, https://biblehub.com/greek/4653.htm.

4. Carson, *John*, 557.

5. Sklar, *Leviticus*, 39.

6. Carson, *John*, 583.

7. Carson, *John*, 575-76.

8. Carson, *John*, 590.

9. Leviticus 23:5-6.

10. Carson, *John*, 591-92.

11. James A. Brooks, *Mark: An Exegetical and Theological Exposition of Holy Scripture*, ed. David S. Dockery, New American Commentary (Nashville: Broadman & Holman, 1991), 23:250, WORDsearch CROSS e-book.

12. Carson, *John*, 597.

13. Allen P. Ross, *Holiness to the Lord: A Guide to the Exposition of the Book of Leviticus* (Grand Rapids: Baker Academic, 2002), 412.

14. Exodus 12:11.

15. Leviticus 23:6.

16. Deuteronomy 16:1-3; Ezekiel 45:21.

17. Dovid Rosenfeld, "Passover—14th or 15th?," Aish HaTorah, accessed June 25, 2020, https://www.aish.com/atr/Passover-14th-or-15th.html.

Chapter 10—John 19:28–21:25: Jesus Is the Messiah

1. David Martyn Lloyd-Jones, *Sanctified Through the Truth: The Assurance of Our Salvation* (Westchester, NY: Crossway, 1989), 49.

2. Leviticus 23:5. God commanded that the new year begin in spring. However, modern Jews celebrate the civil new year in fall and the religious new year in spring.

3. Exodus 12:46.

4. Ross, *Holiness*, 417.

5. "How Many Times Is Love in the Bible?," Reference.com, last updated 3/23/2020, https://www.reference.com/world-view/many-times-love-mentioned-bible-f8eb228f4fe0a4.

6. Adapted from Bill and Pam Farrel, *Men Are Like Waffles—Women Are Like Spaghetti Devotional Study Guide* (Eugene, OR: Harvest House 2002), 57–58.

7. Adapted from Farrel, *7 Skills*, 128–29.

8. Exodus 12:22.

9. Carson, *John*, 629.

10. Exhaling required victims to push up on their wounded feet and pull with their shoulders. Breathing caused excruciating pain to their nailed feet and wrists and to their scourged backs. Crucifixion was designed to cause a slow, torturous, and humiliating death. See William D. Edwards, Wesley J. Gabel, and Floyd E. Hosmer, "On the Physical Death of Jesus Christ," *JAMA: The Journal of the American Medical Association*, 1986, 255:1455-63.

11. The "water" John describes was likely the fluid that surrounds the lungs and heart (serous pleural and pericardial fluid). Jesus's sudden death likely came from a heart rupture or cardiac arrest. Edwards, Gabel, and Hosmer, *JAMA*, 255:1455-63.

12. At the time of John's writing, a heresy arose that Jesus is fully God but not fully human.

13. Clay Jones, *Immortal: How the Fear of Death Drives Us and What We Can Do About It* (Eugene, OR: Harvest House, 2020), 178.

14. Köstenberger and Swain, *Father, Son and Spirit*, 101-2.

15. Jones, *Immortal*, 182-83.

16. Carson, *John*, 676-77.

17. The Lord appeared to Peter privately before appearing to the Eleven (1 Corinthians 15:5).

18. Köstenberger and Swain, *Father, Son and Spirit*, 41-42.

19. Sean McDowell, *The Fate of the Apostles: Examining the Martyrdom Accounts of the Closest Followers of Jesus* (Burlington: Ashgate, 2015), 91.

20. Clement, *Miscellanies* 7.11.63–64, quoted in Eusebius, *Eusebius—The Church History: A New Translation with Commentary*, trans. Paul L. Maier (Grand Rapids: Kregel, 1999), 118-19.

21. McGrew, *Eye*, 130.

22. Believers are the temple of the Holy Spirit and Christ's body on earth (1 Corinthians 6:19).

23. Sklar, *Leviticus*, 73-74.

Acknowledgments

All of Us

To our *Discovering Jesus in the Old Testament*, *Discovering Hope in the Psalms*, and *Discovering Joy in Philippians* readers, thank you for being our traveling companions on this creative devotional study journey. Without you, this project wouldn't have come to fruition. To Hope Lyda, our editor, we are grateful for your patience, insights, and encouragement. To Bob Hawkins, Kathleen Kerr, Kari Duffy, and the rest of the Harvest House team, thank you for taking on this project and embracing the vision. To Jean Kavich Bloom, our copy editor, we're blessed by your keen eye and fine attention to detail. Janelle Coury, thank you for the gorgeous interior. To our endorsers, VIP influencers, and launch team, thanks for investing in these Bible studies your gift of time.

Pam Farrel

A heart-felt thank you to my amazing husband, Bill, for balancing caregiving your parents, coaching people, and codirecting Love-Wise ministry, AND for being my sounding board, resident theologian, and in-house tech wonder! To Robin and Penny, thanks for being my Aaron and Hur. Your prayers carry me. To Jan, thank you for being a wonderful mix of creative wonder, techie whiz, fabulous assistant, and gracious friend. To our *Love-Wise Membership Community*, thanks for being the wind beneath our wings. To all of the precious women who have been in my *Discovering the Bible* Zoom face-to-face Bible studies—you are life-givers to me! To Jean, your rich Bible teaching helps me become a better believer. To Karla, your art inspires my soul and is a sanity-saver in these post-pandemic days. To Jesus, thank you for being the great "I am." All that I ever need is met in who you are.

Jean E. Jones

To Clay, thank you for reading the manuscript, offering insights, taking over chores so I can write, and being a wonderful and amazing husband. To Angie Wright, Jean Strand, Virginia Thompson, and Kerrie Parlett, you timed the lessons and gave valuable feedback—thank you! To Pam Farrel, thank you for your inspiring devotionals, marketing enthusiasm, and lasting friendship—your smile warms my heart. To Karla Dornacher, your art continues to inspire and amaze me, and I am grateful you are part of this team. To our Lord Jesus Christ, thank you for revealing yourself to me in the pages of John's Gospel. Thank you for dying and rising that we might have eternal life with you.

Karla Dornacher

Thank you to Michael, though you didn't get to see me finish the art and writing for this book, you were still my best cheerleader through it all! To my art group—Michelle, Gwen, Tammy, and Madeline—for your creative inspiration and encouragement. To my Bible study group—Sandi, Pat, and Joan—you are my solid rocks in this crazy world! To my online community, you are the best! To my co-authors Jean and Pam, your passion for the truth of God's Word inspires me to dig deeper—thank you! And the most thanks to the Lord! You comforted my heart and held my hand as I finished this book during the most painful days of my life. All the glory goes to you!

About the Authors

Pam Farrel

Pam Farrel is an international speaker, author of over 50 books, including *7 Simple Skills for Every Woman* and the bestselling *Men Are Like Waffles—Women Are Like Spaghetti*. Pam has loved studying and teaching the Bible for over 40 years. She is wife to Bill Farrel, and together they enrich relationships through their ministry, Love-Wise. She and her husband enjoy the beach near their home and a live-aboard boat, often making family memories with their three sons, three daughters-in-laws and five grandchildren.

www.Love-Wise.com | Twitter: @PamFarrel |Facebook: BillAndPamFarrel

Jean E. Jones

Jean E. Jones started teaching the Bible in high school and has served on women's ministry leadership teams for 20 years. She enjoys writing Bible study guides that help people put God's words into actions. With Pam and Karla, she wrote *Discovering Hope in the Psalms*, *Discovering Joy in Philippians*, and *Discovering Jesus in the Old Testament*. Jean has written for Crosswalk.com, *Today's Christian Woman*, and *Home Life*. She is a member of Women in Apologetics. Her husband, Dr. Clay Jones, is a visiting scholar at Talbot School of Theology.

www.JeanEJones.net | Twitter: @JeanEstherJones | Facebook: JeanEJonesAuthor

Karla Dornacher

Karla Dornacher is a storyteller at heart with a passion to inspire and encourage other women through her art and creativity. She has written and illustrated more than 20 books, licensed her art for use on numerous gift and home decor products, and self-published several Christian coloring books for adults. Karla offers a variety of Scripture art prints and digital ministry resources through her website and Etsy shop. Recently widowed, Karla now lives part-time in her van named Missy Grace and travels with her Schnoodle puppy named Tilly, sharing the love of Jesus and encouraging hearts with hope wherever God leads.

www.KarlaDornacher.com | Facebook: KarlaDornacher

I AM the good Shepherd

The good Shepherd lays down His Life for the sheep.

John 10:11

If you ABIDE in my WORD, you are truly MY DISCIPLES, and you will KNOW the TRUTH, and THE TRUTH WILL SET YOU FREE

John 8:31-32

Everyone who LOOKS to the SON and believes in Him shall have Eternal Life and I WILL raise them up at the last day

John 6:40 NIV

For God so loved the World that HE gave his only SON that WHOEVER believes in HIM should not perish but have Eternal Life

John 3:16

BUT TO ALL who did receive him who believed in His Name he gave THE RIGHT to become children of GOD

John 1:12

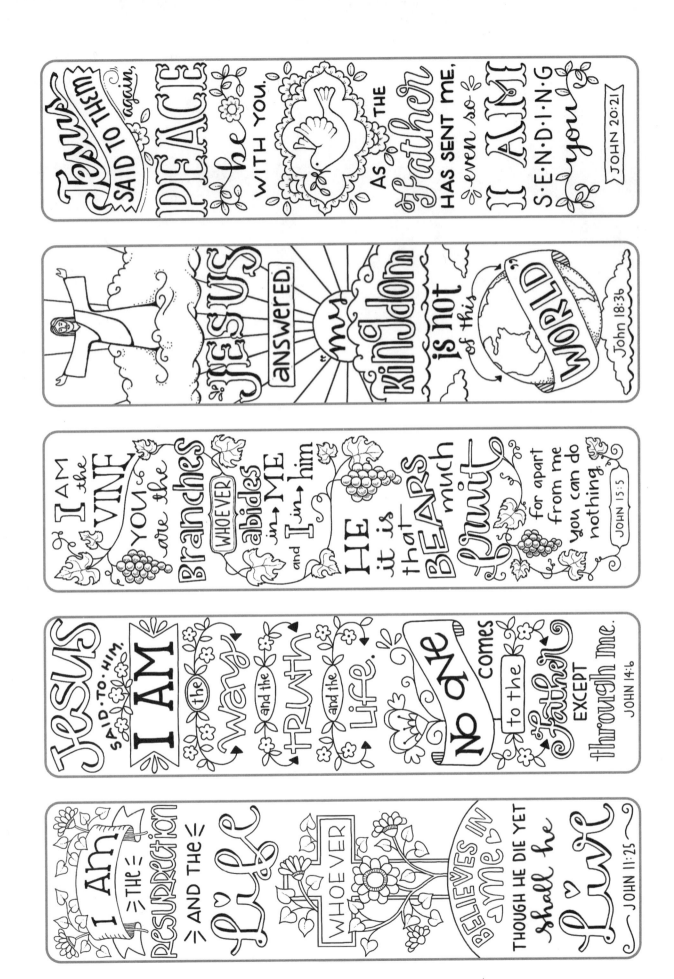

Jesus said to them again, PEACE be with you. As the Father has sent me, even so I AM S·E·N·D·I·N·G you. — JOHN 20:21

Jesus answered, "My kingdom is not of this WORLD." — John 18:36b

I AM the VINE, you are the Branches. WHOEVER abides in ME and I in him, HE it is that BEARS much fruit, for apart from me you can do nothing. — JOHN 15:5

Jesus said to him, I AM the way, and the TRUTH, and the Life. No one comes to the Father except through me. — JOHN 14:6

I Am the resurrection and the Life. WHOEVER believes in me, though he die yet shall he Live. — JOHN 11:25

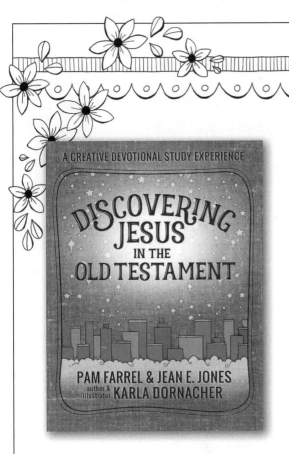

A CREATIVE DEVOTIONAL STUDY EXPERIENCE

DISCOVERING JESUS IN THE OLD TESTAMENT

PAM FARREL & JEAN E. JONES
author & illustrator KARLA DORNACHER

Experience the Old Testament as Never Before

Take a journey to discover all God has planned since before the foundation of the earth. You'll never grow tired of studying Scripture with this innovative and immersive Bible study experience. Through compelling instruction and motivational devotions, it reveals God's redemptive plan from the beginning of creation. Explore...

- timeline icons to help you track God's plan through the Old Testament

- key questions at the beginning of each section to guide your focus

- opportunities for creative expression, including full-page graphics and bookmarks to color

- sidebars that offer fascinating historical insights

- practical application questions to guide and deepen your walk with Christ

- online opportunities for connection and interactive community

As you discover new ways to engage with God's Word through this in-depth approach to studying Scripture, you will gain wisdom and understanding about his incredible, unchanging love for you.

Designed to be used for group study or for individual reflection.

To find out more about the complete series, explore many creative resources, and connect with the authors and other readers, visit DiscoveringTheBibleSeries.com.

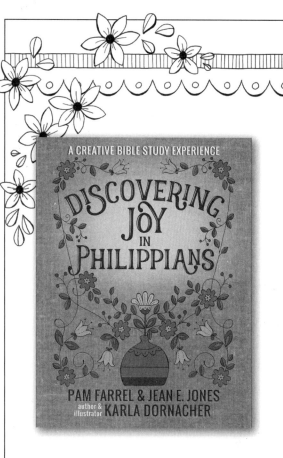

A CREATIVE BIBLE STUDY EXPERIENCE

DISCOVERING JOY IN PHILIPPIANS

PAM FARREL & JEAN E. JONES
author & illustrator KARLA DORNACHER

Share the Joy

If difficult days have ever left you discouraged, this interactive 11-week journey will help you engage creatively with God's Word and establish habits that lead to greater joy and peace. Refresh your delight in the Lord through:

Daily Lessons with an introduction and key questions for each chapter to help you dive deeper into the heart of Scripture and incorporate it into your life with *joy builder* activities

Choosing Joy Devotions and inspirational quotes to stir hope even in difficult times as you learn to trust God's faithfulness and rest in his strength no matter what circumstance you find yourself in

Creative Connections including bookmarks and coloring pages that provide an outlet to knit your heart to God and explore your faith through artistic expression

"…that your joy may be full." John 15:11

This unique discovery book includes ideas for group studies, verse-inspired artwork to color, fascinating details about the Bible, and online connections and communities so you can build up your joy and build up others!

To find out more about the complete series, explore many creative resources, and connect with the authors and other readers, visit DiscoveringTheBibleSeries.com.